Relativistic Naturalism

RELATIVISTIC NATURALISM

---

*A Cross-Cultural Approach
to Human Science*

QUIN McLOUGHLIN

New York
Westport, Connecticut
London

Library of Congress Cataloging-in-Publication Data

McLoughlin, Quin.
    Relativistic naturalism : a cross-cultural approach to human
science / Quin McLoughlin.
        p.   cm.
    Includes bibliographical references and index.
    ISBN 0-275-93870-0 (alk. paper)
    1. Social sciences—Philosophy.   2. Social psychology.   I. Title.
H61.M416   1991
300'.1—dc20   91-430

British Library Cataloguing in Publication Data is available.

Library of Congress Catalog Card Number: 91-430
ISBN: 0-275-93870-0

First published in 1991

Praeger Publishers, One Madison Avenue, New York, NY 10010
An imprint of Greenwood Publishing Group, Inc.

Printed in the United States of America

The paper used in this book complies with the
Permanent Paper Standard issued by the National
Information Standards Organization (Z39.48–1984).

10 9 8 7 6 5 4 3 2 1

To
Cynthia and Bruce
with my hope that
it will contribute to
greater human understanding
in their time

Contents

Figures

Preface

It may seem odd for a psychologist to attempt a work of this scope. Although my doctoral training is in psychology, I do not regard myself primarily as a psychologist. Psychology has been a means to an end for me. I started my undergraduate studies concerned with social justice, particularly in my own society. I wanted to understand why societies develop the way they do and how they can change. In those days at Columbia University, it was not necessary to have a major field of study, so I took whatever courses interested me beyond those required—mostly in philosophy and political science. Because they seemed to involve endless debate with no criteria for resolution, they were not very satisfying. I was, however, deeply impressed by some courses in anthropology revealing the great diversity of ways of life which humans could devise. I knew that being able to account for this was one of the keys to my quest.

When it came time for graduate school, sociology seemed the logical choice. However, prestigious though they were, my professors always seemed to be struggling with their underlying assumptions about human nature. It became clear to me that sociology rested on a foundation of a psychology of human nature. So, after getting an M.A. in sociology, I transferred into psychology.

I did not, of course, get the answer I sought to what is human nature. Rather, I got a whole range of answers, an introduction to the presumed components of it and a familiarity with a host of issues in every aspect of the discipline. It was disappointing to see the apparently unresolvable schism between the clinicians, who needed a general theory in order to deal with the whole person, and the experimentalists, who emphasized learning principles and regarded the general theories as unproven or unprovable speculation. Within the clinical/personality realm there was a variety of theories, each defended by its disciples and severely criticized by adherents to other theories. The most constructive result of my psychological studies was the recognition, contributed by psychoanalytic theory, of the fundamental importance of the developmental approach to understanding behavior. I was convinced that the child is father to the adult. There was also considerable antagonism between psychology and socioanthropology. The latter placed a lot of emphasis on culture, social system, and role structure, often seeming to give these concepts the quality of highly ordered forces acting on members of the group. Psychologists, on the other hand, focused on individual differences and paid little, if any, attention to normative aspects of behavior.

A constant problem was the fragmentation of the study of human behavior. Not only was there the gulf between psychology and socioanthropology, but there were also the disciplines of economics and political science in the social sciences and another set of disciplines in the humanities which were regarded as outside the scope of science, even though much of their content had to do with important aspects of human behavior. It was disillusioning to realize that among the faculty across and within all disciplines there was little spirit of pulling together toward a common goal.

Throughout the later years of this quest, I was plagued by the dominance of the view that scientific research was the only sure path to valid knowledge. The literature in all the social sciences was accumulating at a geometric rate. Periodically, my anxiety forced me to try to catch up with the research, each time resulting in disappointment and frustration. It was always so limited in the range of variables considered that it was easy to think of others that would likely alter the findings.

Upon completing my doctoral work, I found myself professionally a psychologist without clear answers to my basic questions but with a general sense of the size and shape of the task. I eschewed the mainstream career line of research and specialization, opting instead for a teaching-oriented university and gravitating to the developmental courses. Adult development emerged as a field, and I soon had a regular course load that covered the human life span. The students at my small urban university were of all ages and walks of life, including a smattering of foreign students. Their central interest in themselves, their children, and their parents combined with my special interest to direct the material toward development in this society. It was heavily biased toward the middle class, but both social stratification and cultural differences had to be borne in mind. I could not be comfortable teaching the disjointed, often trivial, material of the standard texts. I therefore attempted to provide a general framework that they could use in everyday life. Consequently, I was something like a psychological anthropologist with a specialization in American culture masquerading as a developmental psychologist. I lack the credentials of an anthropologist, but I believe that in many ways I think like one.

Looking back on this intellectual odyssey, it appears that the social sciences have not changed fundamentally despite many new developments and frequent appeals for integration and more interdisciplinary efforts. All of them still present a dual personality to the larger society. On the one hand, they each offer several schools of thought around which there is no general agreement and for each of which there are sound and serious criticisms. On the other hand, each discipline has its empirical wing that takes the position that valid knowledge of human affairs can only result from the application of the scientific method in a gradual, progressive process lasting into the indefinite future. Despite these two main positions, each in its applied form attempts to provide some guidance to policymakers and the general public via research findings for specific problems. Such attempts appear oblivious to the fact that these fragments of research have to be assimilated by the policymakers or the public into some larger framework of their own, and this framework constitutes the very common-sense sort of knowledge that scientists regard balefully as unproven speculation. I began to realize what a strange situation my society was in with respect to its knowledge of human behavior. While recognizing the social sciences as the authoritative source of such knowledge, it was being told by these scientists that they had, as young sciences, very little to contribute and that a sound understanding of human beings would not be available for a long time.

At the height of this dilemma, I became aware of developments in the philosophy of science which were throwing into question the assumptions behind the natural sciences. It was clear that the issues raised applied equally to the social sciences because the latter had modeled themselves on the natural sciences and aspired to its status. I began to realize that the social scientist has a general theoretical orientation before he engages in research. Yet, this contradicts the view that science is a method for the gradual, progressive development of general theory.

The issue of realism versus relativism of knowledge provided the keys to the resolution of this dilemma. It pulled together a number of strands of my thinking. To begin with, by raising the issue of the possibility of valid knowledge of reality, it focused attention on the assumptions behind the scientific method. Inevitably, it pointed to assumptions behind the fragmentation of study into the many disciplines of the social sciences and the humanities. This, in turn, gave credence to my conviction that the concept of worldview was central to the understanding of human affairs and also helped me to assimilate religion into my theory. It followed directly that the historical dimension, conceived in terms of changing world views, provided the perspective from which the state of the social sciences could be understood. It was a logical step to cultural differences in world-views and their development.

This book presents the results of my quest. It is a very broad theoretical effort, not a conventional academic review and analysis of relevant literature. Scholars in the social sciences are familiar with the difficulty of keeping up with the literature in their own and closely related fields. There was no way in which I could be familiar with all the literature in the many disciplines covered by my subject. Fortunately, it is not necessary to have such familiarity to appreciate the basic nature and approach of any discipline. I searched only for the key ideas that would help me with my quest. There are innumerable places at which references to similar ideas or credit could be given. Inevitably others equally worthy would be omitted. I have tried to limit my references to those which seemed to me to strengthen or clarify a point or provide a source the reader might find useful. I can only pay my debt to all those who have helped me with their work by adding to the literature the results of my own.

My aim has been to present a new general orientation to the enterprise of human science. It is a skeletal theory. My hope is that some of my colleagues will find it useful enough to flesh it out and to use it as a new normal paradigm for the study and understanding of human beings in all times and places.

A theoretical effort of this scope presents a problem with which I must crave the reader's indulgence. It requires that a system of interrelated ideas be presented in a linear fashion. The reader may find himself with questions or reservations about some material which may be addressed further along in the argument. I hope he or she will hear me out before drawing conclusions.

It was long ago clear to me that my approach to the study of human behavior and to a career in psychology was not in the mainstream of either the experimental or the clinical tracks. As a result, I have been somewhat of a loner in pursuing my task. However, I have received wonderful support from three people. I am indebted beyond repayment for the constant support, tactful criticism, and wise suggestions of my brother Bill. I also have had a ready ear, patient willingness to listen to or read lengthy presentations of my ideas, and many judicious questions which helped me continually to improve them from a greatly valued friend, Peter Kellogg. They both had the refuge of geographical distance from my preoccupation with my quest. My wife, Becky, had no such luck. She always listened, made many insightful observations, put in countless hours of skillful editing and computerizing, and provided the emotional support that alone made it possible for me to complete my task. If there is any merit in this work, credit for it is as much hers as mine.

— Part I —

Philosophical Assumptions of Human Science

1

Revolution in Social Science

Evidence is mounting that three developing concerns in social science have merged, generating changes of far-reaching implications. One is a growing dissatisfaction with the state of affairs in all the disciplines that comprise the social sciences. Criticisms encompass lack of progress in the discovery of laws and principles, absence of theory, accumulation of unrelated or unrelatable research findings, failure to deal with recent developments in the philosophy of science, doctrinal posturing, divorce from behavior in natural situations, overspecialization, ethnocentrism, and value biases.[1] These appear to reflect a growing doubt about the basic viability of the whole enterprise. While they have, to a limited degree, commanded response from mainstream social scientists, they have diverted little effort into new directions.

A second development, mainly in cultural anthropology and philosophy, concerns the possibility of the understanding of thought and experience across distinct human groups. A growing number of practitioners in these fields are wondering whether apparently vastly different worldviews, modes of thought, and structures of language constitute insuperable barriers to valid knowledge in social anthropology and history.[2] These concerns pass far beyond the previously mentioned criticism of enthocentrism in social science. They raise the question of whether it is possible to rise above ethnocentrism at all, not in the shallow sense that other peoples should not be understood in terms of the characteristics generalized from experience in one's own society, but in the much deeper sense that one cannot transcend the way of thinking about experience that results from development in his particular social group. Such a question gnaws at the very foundations of the long-held belief of social scientists that ultimately valid knowledge of human phenomena is the counterpart of the mastery of the nonhuman world by the natural sciences. So far, this gnawing has been either imperceptible to, or ignored by, most social scientists.

The third line of development runs through the decline of positivism in the philosophy of science and the controversy over Thomas Kuhn's (1962, 1970) analysis of revolutions in science to the awakening of some social scientists to its import for their disciplines. Kuhn's historical analysis of the natural sciences led him to suggest that these enterprises, instead of constituting a steady progression toward true knowledge of physical reality, reveal a cyclical process of conceptualization, doubt, and reconceptualization. It dealt a mortal blow to an already staggering positivism. It has been complemented by the increasing revelations of some of the more theoretically minded natural scientists about the uncertainty with which they hold their theories, their awareness that these theories are, or may be, only temporary ways of construing things. By this they do not intend the usual notion of possible error on the way to truth but rather a questioning of the notion of truth. Kuhn's effort has evoked a virulent reaction in some quarters. Yet twenty-five years of debate have revealed mainly the hardiness of his basic suggestions.[3] They have appealed to an increasing, if still small, proportion of social scientists who have strongly identified with and attempted to emulate their natural science colleagues. Nonetheless, most social scientists remain oblivious of this work or its implications.

These three developments—growing discontent with the product and the promise of social science, doubt about the validity of its aims, and questioning of the conception of science on which it is founded—appear to be converging to produce a profound reconsideration of the whole enterprise. In the last ten years there have been at least two interdisciplinary conferences of prominent figures to deal with the issues raised (Fiske and Shweder 1986; Secord 1982). These have served to sharpen the issues and to begin the process of the dissemination of them throughout the social scientific community. At the same time, they reveal the strength of resistance which so profound a change can be expected to generate. The change implied is nothing less than a revolution in social science of the very type Kuhn has identified in natural science. They reveal that social science is entering that period in the cycle of scientific revolution which Kuhn calls the revolutionary period, the period of doubt about the conceptualization of social science that precedes its reconceptualization.

Several of the views proposed imply radical reconception of social science. Most prominent among these is that social science is not and cannot be a quest for valid knowledge of reality. Advocates of this relativist position claim that the only knowledge possible is knowledge formulated or constructed according to the way of thinking of the scientist, a way which is restricted to members of his social group in his time. The implication of this view for psychology, for example, is that objective knowledge of human nature is unattainable. For socioanthropology it implies that scientists from one social group cannot understand the thought and experience of another except in their own terms, which will inevitably involve an indeterminate degree of distortion. Another view is that the social sciences should abandon their identification with the natural sciences because their subject matter is sui generis. Some are taking the position that the idea of social science itself must be rejected. They claim that those who study human phenomena must take their model from the humanities. Human understanding is a hermeneutic exercise, not a scientific one. Still others reject the traditional view that science can be value-neutral and conclude that social scientists should conduct their efforts so as to advance their personal values. Some advocate a redefinition of the concept of causality.

At the same time, there is increasing evidence of a breakdown of the traditional organization of inquiry into human phenomena. The boundaries between the natural science of human biology, the social sciences, and the humanities are vanishing. The status of the discipline of psychology most clearly illustrates this. Generally regarded as a social science, it sometimes is offered or defended as a natural science. More recently, a number of "halfway houses" between psychology and biology have been erected, including neuropsychology, biopsychology, psychopharmacology, etc. (Pribram 1971, x; Brewer 1981, 55). There are many psychologists who believe that psychology is ultimately biology and will disappear when neurophysiology becomes sufficiently developed. Koch (1974) asserts that psychology defies definition, that some of it is more in the nature of natural science, some of the humanities. Another example of this breakdown of structure is the encroachment of biology on socioanthropology in the form of sociobiology.

At the border between social science and the humanities, the boundary is increasingly hard to discern. At one conference on the state of the humanities, it was reported:

The attempt of a sub-division of the first conference to formulate a definition of the humanities . . . was not revived, because the majority preferred to encourage the recent trend in higher learning away from restrictive categories and to gather under the umbrella of humane studies all disciplines that seek an understanding of man. . . . Few of the participants felt any longer the need to defend their work from the encroachments of science—in fact, science was spoken of as an ally in a common cause. (Ackerman 1969, 606)

New fields of sociohistory and psychohistory are growing rapidly, paralleling the development of sociolinguistics and psycholinguistics.[4]

Within the social sciences the distinctions among disciplines have become equally blurred. Sociology and anthropology have merged. At the same time, the new discipline is unable to distinguish itself conceptually from psychology.[5] In fact, major branches are called psychological anthropology and social psychology. Strong movements toward behavioral science have emerged out of the policy sciences of economics and political science. Each owns up to a strong dependency on psychology. Some universities have instituted divisions and disciplines radically cutting across the old distinctions. While many applaud these developments, the significance of them for the present argument is that they reflect a major aspect of the reconceptualization of social science.

That all the views mentioned above are indicative of incipient revolution in social science is reinforced by another symptom of radical change—reaction. Among philosophers of science and that small proportion of social scientists who seem to be aware of these developments, strong resistance is manifest. It is expressed in two forms. One is rejection of change in favor of reforms within the traditional structure. Boundaries are fiercely defended and inadequacies, where recognized, are felt to be remediable by tinkering with the mechanics. The other is in the form of compromise. This consists of attempts to preserve as much of the old conception as possible while incorporating some of the new. Despite this ferment among some social scientists, the majority appear to be either unaware of the developments producing it or insufficiently appreciative of them to recognize their implications. Much of this must be attributed to resistance to the considerable threat that they represent. The nature of this threat and of the defense against it is clearly revealed in the following statement of two prominent social scientists, even though they reject the view as their own:

[T]here has been in the social sciences a vague sense of unease about the overall rate of progress. . . . Some have even talked of a "crisis" in social inquiry.

It is noteworthy that the prevailing positive mood among practicing social scientists is accompanied by an understandable desire not to be disturbed by worries about the foundations of the science or generalized concerns about a purported lack of progress. . . . [E]ach practitioner knows what progress means for him or her—it means doing even better what he or she is now doing. But beyond that, there may well be no common currency for measuring progress. . . .

Clarity of aim is an uncertain virtue in a healthy science: some activities that turn out to be important seemed aimless originally, and scientists who do have clear aims in mind are often aimed in different directions. . . . One cannot even say that it is always advisable to stick to the presumed facts or to insist upon agreement about the meaning of new concepts. There are times in the history of science when ignoring the apparent facts has paid off. . . . So it is quite understandable, perhaps even a form of wisdom, that most practicing social scientists do not want to be bothered by the crisis literature in the social sciences. (Fiske and Shweder 1986, 1–2)

The defensiveness of this view is clearly manifest in the contradictions within it. It starts by juxtaposing the "prevailing positive mood" with the "desire not to be disturbed by worries." It then reveals that "each practitioner knows what progress means for him or her" but that "there may well be no common currency for measuring progress." The criticisms being levelled are presented as virtues. Inability to predict, lack of consensus among scientists, unclarity of meaning of concepts, selective ignoring of facts are not things to be bothered about. They might "turn out to be important" or "pay off," although how this would be recognized, given no agreed-upon standards, is a mystery.

Having recognized the nature of the resistance to criticism, the authors of this statement of its rationale reject it, saying:

> The crisis literature raises to consciousness many of the assumptions that we as practicing social scientists take for granted about the nature of our science and our subject matter and the relationship between them. These assumptions have a decisive influence on what problems we select for study and how we go about conceptualizing and investigating them. . . . Those assumptions are too important to be taken for granted and too much a part of our ongoing research enterprises to be left only to philosophers to think about. (Fiske and Shweder 1986, 3)

Questioning the assumptions about the nature of science is an integral but undeveloped part of Kuhn's view of revolution in science. Unfortunately, some of the ambiguities in Kuhn's formulation lend themselves well to the kind of resistance being encountered. The most prominent and well-recognized of these ambiguities is in his concept of a "paradigm of science." The concept is central to Kuhn's thesis, so that his tendency to use it with a variety of meanings has weakened his case (Shapere 1964; Masterman 1970; Musgrave 1971; Suppes 1977). If his concept of a paradigm of science were to be clarified, the force of his contribution would be strengthened. One thesis of this work is that Kuhn's view, with such clarification, is very useful in understanding what is happening in social science today. A revolutionary period is beginning which is leading to a radical reconception of the whole enterprise. Recognition of this will provide a perspective on many current phenomena and expedite the process of reconception. This will rescue social science from its current chaotic condition and lack of authority in the society at large.

In making the case for Kuhnian revolution in social science, it will be useful first to specify the interpretation given to Kuhn's concept of revolution in science. A particular meaning of "paradigm of science" will then be emphasized by way of resolving its ambiguity. The model of scientific revolution can be revised to incorporate this meaning and applied to make the case for the present as a revolutionary period in social science.

CLARIFICATION OF "PARADIGM OF SCIENCE"

The interpretation of Kuhn's view of the structure of scientific revolutions invoked here is as follows: During periods of normal science, there is widespread agreement among scientists on a paradigm of their science; the paradigm includes theory, techniques, and procedures; theory is used to explain most observations, and puzzle-solving research is directed to that which remains unexplained; some research results constitute anomalies in the sense that they cannot be accommodated by the paradigm; anomalies inevitably accumulate to the point at which discontent with the paradigm produces proposals for alternative paradigms; this marks the inception of a revolutionary period; for a while, none of the alternative paradigms is sufficiently persuasive to gain a consensus among scientists; the majority continues to adhere to the old paradigm, although with increasing discontent; eventually, one alternative is proposed that does gain such a consensus; the old paradigm is abandoned and the science settles into a new normal period. Central to Kuhn's view of paradigms of normal science is that they are incommensurable. This means that they are not transformable into one another, not mere extensions or incorporations or improvements, but wholly different conceptualizations. They have different theories, techniques, and procedures. They redefine the science.

Any version of Kuhn's views involves a host of issues about which philosophers and historians of science have been debating for over twenty-five years. In various forums Kuhn has attempted to clarify and explain his views but succeeded only in raising more issues. It now appears that his work is serving more as a catalyst for the precipitation of new ideas, with implications much broader for academia than the history of the few natural sciences he addressed. It seems to be caught up in a larger dynamic.

It is very doubtful that most, if any, of the issues that have arisen can be resolved in the forms in which they have been drawn. The reason for this appears to lie mainly in the neglect of the role of philosophical assumptions in the natural sciences. Kuhn strongly implicated but did not develop the role of these assumptions. There has been widespread recognition of the idea that weltanschauungen, worldviews, or supertheories are involved in the controversy; but surprisingly little about them has informed the debates. The reasons for this and their implications will be addressed shortly. First, it is suggested that Kuhn's concept of a normal paradigm of science be divided into two distinct parts. The first of these is comprised of the worldview and the mode of thought held by the great majority of the members of the scientific community. The second is the conceptualization of the science that is derived from the beliefs of the worldview by the logic of the mode of thought. This conceptualization provides the bases of scientific practice. Kuhn's anomalies, then, are the observations and research findings that present difficulty of explanation either for specific theories developed by the science, or for one or more beliefs of the worldview which informs it, or for the logic of the mode of thought. Anomalies for specific theories of the science may lead to new ideas and reformulations presenting no threat to the worldview or the mode of thought. There seems no sound reason to include these in the notion of revolutions in science. However, those that cannot be squared with one or more beliefs of the worldview or the logic of the mode of thought have far greater consequences. As they accumulate over time, their threat to the normal paradigm is combined with threats from other developments in group life, including other sciences, and grounded in the gradual disintegration of the worldview of the group and its accompanying mode of thought. Thus a revolution in a science is always a part of a revolution in the way of life of the society in which the scientific practice exists. The period of revolution in the science coincides with a transitional period in the history of the society. Alternative paradigms which arise in the science reflect elements of a new worldview and a new mode of thought. The revolution cannot be completed during a single generation. Several generations are required because the changes involved are too ponderous and beset by reactionary efforts of generations still attempting to maintain the old worldview and incapable of a new mode of thought. Only after several generations, when the main force of the social change process is spent, can an integrated new worldview and a new mode of thought emerge,[6] from which a new conceptualization of science will be derived.

The ideas of "worldview" and "mode of thought" long have been used or, more accurately, alluded to in historiography and ethnography. They seem to have a special significance for those academics seeking to understand a diversity of human groups. Unfortunately, only very recently have there been any attempts to provide conceptualizations of them. They seem to be ideas whose time has come. They are now being used with considerable frequency even though they still are not adequately defined or explained. Worldview is never clearly embedded in a larger psychological theory and is often confounded with other terms such as "ideology" and "values." Mode of thought is involved much more rarely and mysteriously. A conceptualization of each is the subject of the next chapter. It will suffice for their use here to give worldview its common definition as the basic assumptions held about the nature of reality and to define mode of thought as the characteristic process by which thought is regulated.

If this conception of a paradigm of science is substituted in Kuhn's model, it can be restated as follows:

worldview and mode of thought → derived conceptualization of science → practices of science, including application of worldview to explain observations and puzzle-solving research into phenomena not already explained, refining worldview → accumulating anomalies for the worldview → alternative conceptualizations of science proposed without gaining consensus of agreement plus continued adherence of most scientists to the original conceptualization → worldview and mode of thought change → change in the conceptualization of science → new scientific practices

There is widespread agreement that today the American way of life (not to mention that of the rest of the world) is undergoing extensive and rapid change. There is constant reference to a technological or electronic revolution, the unpredictability of the future, changing sexual identities and their consequences for the family, the breakdown of sovereignty of nations, conflict between old and new orientations toward humankind's relationship to nature, the decline of traditional religion, and many more developments. The impact of Kuhn's suggestion that natural science is not what it is thought to be can be understood as one facet of this process of change. The issues that it has raised reflect the transitional process of reaction, compromise, and alternative paradigms. The inability to resolve these issues stems, on the one hand, from the reactionary effort to preserve the still implicit assumptions of the old worldview from which the conceptualization of the natural sciences was logically derived and from the resilience of the old mode of thought. On the other hand, it stems from the growing awareness, very unevenly distributed even among academics, of other anomalies for the old worldview, which suggests the usefulness of Kuhn's original views in one form or another. Powerful forces militate against resolution of the issues raised in Kuhn's work. Among these are the complexity and long duration of the process of change in transitional periods of the history of a society, the general implicitness of the widely shared worldview, and the totally unconscious use of the group's mode of thought. These last two combine to dictate a short-range perspective for modern Americans.

Given this perspective on the controversy, it is no longer a matter of Kuhn's current or original views of the nature of science. His was a major contribution which, along with other developments, has opened the door to alternative paradigms of natural science. Since the social sciences aspired to be like the natural sciences and borrowed from them the scientific method, the foregoing analysis applies to them as well. This work is addressed to the understanding of the state of the social sciences today and to dealing with their problems. No direct effort will be made to deal with the issues as they have been raised for the natural sciences. However, the following line of argument is relevant to almost all of them.

Applying this version of Kuhn's view of the structure of scientific revolutions to what is happening today in social science, the argument is that many anomalies have developed for the worldview upon which social science is based. They are generating alternative beliefs about the nature of reality and elements of a new mode of thought. Further, most social scientists still adhere to the old beliefs because no new formulation is sufficiently persuasive to them, but they do so with increasing feelings of unease. There is a revolution occurring in social science.

The case for this view follows. If it is cogent, it can have the effect of providing a broad perspective on many facets of the current situation and expediting the return to a period of normal science by focusing attention on what needs to be done. The case requires specification of the primary relevant beliefs of the current worldview, the identification of the major anomalies for it, evidence of alternative paradigms, and yet adherence by the uneasy majority of social scientists to the previous one.

THE INDIVIDUALISTIC WORLDVIEW

The worldview on which social science has been based can be labeled the individualistic worldview, as a case can be made that it has prevailed through the period of the history of Western civilization that historians often equate with individualism. It appears to have been widely shared in America throughout the nineteenth century and very likely considerably longer.[7] Anomalies for it have been accumulating for over one hundred years. Consequently, many social scientists today may only partially adhere to it, yet they carry on most of their work in a fashion largely derived from it.

The basic beliefs of this individualistic worldview relevant to the conceptualization of social science usually are articulated in terms of the Christian religion. Fundamental to it is the assumption of a dualism of substance in the universe—the spiritual and the physical. For social science, the importance of this is in its assumptions about human nature. This has long been referred to in philosophy as mind-body dualism. The human being is comprised of a spiritual mind (soul) and a physical body.[8] The mind includes a general capacity to reason, which is particularly important for determining moral and immoral courses of action in any situation, and a will to action that is free to select in any situation either a moral or an immoral course. With respect to amoral matters, this general ability to reason is regarded as capable of discerning the truth or falsity, the correctness or incorrectness, of arguments and conclusions.

Central to this view of human nature is the inherent conflict of the needs and passions of the body with the reason and will of the mind. The mind, while it transcends the demise of the body, must maintain the body to exist on earth. The needs and passions of the body frequently tempt the mind toward selecting immoral courses of action, often by corrupting the reasoning process. However, the will of the mind is capable of overcoming not only such temptations but the demands of the body altogether, as in martyrdom. Further, the mortal life of the body is brief compared with the eternal life of the mind (soul). Humans are the only creatures created in God's image. They have been placed on earth to further God's grand design for the universe, although they can understand only that part concerning moral choices in their lives. Hence humans, as temporary visitors on earth, can use their reason to study and master the physical world in playing their part in the grand design. Their lives are a struggle to live in accordance with God's commands, and part of that is the effort to perfect themselves (McLoughlin 1965).[9] The linear progressive view of the scientific enterprise is based implicitly on the belief in an omniscient god's grand design and on the optimism of the individualist's struggle to overcome his weaknesses in making himself more acceptable to his god.

From these key elements of the individualistic worldview, the conceptualization of social science is derived. First, it can be noted that these assumptions inform the long-standing, but now changing, trichotomous division of the structure of formal inquiry in the colleges of arts and sciences of American universities. There are natural science, which includes human biology (body, not mind); social science, which originally was the study of the arrangements free-willing individuals make in their interactions; and the humanities. Since the humanities deal with the nonphysical mind, they cannot be sciences. They analyze the ways in which humans have used and do, or might, express their human spirit (soul) in the arts and in literature to deal with the challenges, joys, and misfortunes of life. They also include attempts to refine the definition of the relationship of humans to God.

The distinctions among the disciplines of social science also are derived from the assumptions of the individualistic worldview, at least in their original form. This is a three-way division. Economics is the study of the arrangements humans make to provide for the material needs of the body. Political science is the study of the arrangements that develop to handle conflicts among people necessitated by the interaction of individualistic wills under pressure from the needs and passions of the body. Sociology, in the original sense of "the social," studies all other arrangements, such as the family, friendship, recreation, education, etc.[10]

The view of causality in natural science also is an integral aspect of the individualistic worldview. The essence of it is that observable events are the effects of particular causes. Nature can be analyzed into a multitude of cause-effect sequences. These constitute the facts of nature behind which are presumed to be discoverable laws. In this way the Cartesian view of nature as a myriad of separate particles interacting in time and space parallels individualistic social life with one crucial difference. Human life consists of a multitude of effects caused by individuals. Responsibility for consequences can and should be traced to the individuals who caused them. The difference between the natural and the social world is that, in the latter, human free will replaces deterministic laws behind events. In the social world, events are inherently independent, because the individual, by an act of will, can alter the cause-effect sequences—thus, originally natural versus social science. The individualistic mode of thought reflects this orientation to life. The syntax of the English language essentially is one of subject (cause)—predicate (behavior)—object (effect). Almost all experience is processed in this form. (For a more detailed account of this mode of thought, see Chapter 2.)

It follows from these beliefs of the individualistic worldview that humans are capable of objective—that is, value-neutral—study of the physical world but are susceptible to value corruptions of it. The natural sciences have developed the scientific method for this, and the social sciences have attempted to adopt that model. The essence of the model is controlled experimentation based on the assumption of cause-effect sequences of events. The canons of scientific method are dominated by the concern with the prevention of the corruption of reason. The practices in graduate schools of selection for intellectual and moral integrity, the necessity for familiarity with the mistakes and contributions of others, the fierce guardianship of academic freedom from corrupting influences, and the requirements of publication and replication all attest to this source of conceptualization of scientific method. Specific techniques, instruments, statistical analyses, etc., are only details within this context.

ANOMALIES FOR THE INDIVIDUALISTIC WORLDVIEW

With the recognition of the presence of the individualistic worldview behind the conceptualization of social science, it is not difficult to identify the anomalies that have challenged it and gradually generated the current revolution. As pointed out earlier, these anomalies have been accumulating for over a century from a wide variety of sources. For many academics and theologians, the beginning of this revolution was identified as the conflict between religion and science toward the end of the nineteenth century. It still is manifest today in the controversy over evolutionism versus creationism. The main sources of these anomalies can be summarized as follows:

1. *Evolutionary Theory.* The supporting evidence for this theory of the origin of species challenges the assumptions of special creation and mind-body dualism and suggests the possibility of naturalism. The challenge to special creation also entails questions about the possibilities of objective knowledge of reality.

2. *Neurophysiology, Neuropsychology, and Psychopharmacology.* The evidence for the close relationship between brain functioning and phenomenal experience undermines the assumption of mind-body dualism by promising to explain mind in physical terms.

3. *Behaviorism and Psychotherapy.* Evidence for the conditioning of human behavior and cure of mental disturbances by techniques of intervention challenge the assumption of human free will.

4. *Historiography and Ethnography.* Investigations of the nature of other human groups, particularly those regarded as primitive, have tended to challenge these prejudices at the same time as they reveal the varied influence of environment on human morality, motivation, and reasoning, threatening the universality of worldview assumptions of human nature in general and universal reason in particular. It also has introduced methodological holism in the form of reified culture.

5. *Child Development Studies.* Empirical and clinical observations of the relationships between childhood experience and deviance, morality, and personality challenge the assumption of human free will by implying their determination by particular early conditions of life.

6. *Indeterminism in Scientific Research.* The recognition that the investigator and the techniques used comprise a set of variables influencing research results challenges the assumption of the possibility of objective knowledge of reality.

7. *Marxist Analysis and the Sociology of Knowledge.* Developments in these fields pointing out the significance of interests and power in science and the interrelationships among the institutions of society have raised serious questions about the value-neutrality of scientific knowledge.

The cumulative effect of these anomalies has produced a profound challenge to the individualistic worldview.[11] The effect differs in social science from that in natural science. In the latter, anomalies appear to be most directly felt as challenges to the scientific theories being used. Social science has no such scientific theories. Lack of them is regarded as due to the youthfulness of social science. Consequently, in social science these anomalies for an implicit worldview have had their main effect through the creation of a set of very important but usually independently considered issues. Many of them scarcely enter the world of most social scientists but have been of great concern to philosophers of science. Some have been fundamental in one or another discipline for some time. This set of issues constitutes the main evidence for a revolutionary period in social science.

ISSUES CHALLENGING THE INDIVIDUALISTIC WORLDVIEW

As the worldview has been implicit, and as the anomalies have developed over a considerable period of time in a variety of areas, the issues that have developed have been formulated in a variety of ways with overlapping meanings. The following attempt to organize them inevitably is somewhat forced. It is designed with the intention of illustrating the revolution in social science via the juxtaposition of each with basic beliefs of the individualistic worldview.

I. Realism versus relativism of scientific knowledge. Essentially, this is an issue about whether scientific knowledge can be true knowledge about external reality or only a way of understanding reality that is relative to the way of thinking used, a way which varies in human groups across time or location. Included in this are several subissues or more specific forms of the issue:

1. Rationality versus irrationality of beliefs. Essentially, this refers to the question of whether or not there is a single, universal, rational basis of human thought to which questions of truth-falsity can be referred. It has produced such controversies as the existence of a rational bridgehead across cultures, the argument from technological superiority, and the distinction between propositional and semipropositional statements.

2. Progress versus reconceptualization in scientific knowledge. This issue is concerned with whether science is a process of progressively developing an increase in true knowledge of reality, with some backward steps or misdirections eventually being overcome, or whether changes in understanding constitute only different conceptualizations, which do not entail progress or regress, only replacement.

3. Indeterminacy versus determinacy of translation of languages. This issue concerns the possibility of understanding across human groups which use different languages. It includes questions about the nature of the *verstehen* experience in historical or cultural anthropological work. It also involves issues of the relationship of language to thought.

II. Reductionism versus emergentism of subject matter. This is an issue concerning how many and what kinds of objects or subject matter there are to be explained by social science. It can be divided essentially into two subissues:

1. Biological reductionism versus psychological emergentism. This is a controversy about whether mental or psychological phenomena such as consciousness, reflection, or thought can be entirely explained by the properties of the neurophysiological components of the brain or central nervous system or whether they constitute a process sui generis emerging from neurophysiological processes. This issue also involves controversies over whether the subject matter of social science is behavior or phenomenal experience and over the relationship between reasons and causes.

2. Methodological holism versus methodological individualism. This is a question of the nature of the "social." Are societies, cultures, and social structures something other or more than the interactions of the individuals who compose them exerting some sort of influence on members, or can they be entirely accounted for by the properties of the individuals interacting? It encompasses concerns about the unintended consequences of behavior and about the ontological status of language.

III. Human agency versus psychological determinism. Commonly referred to as free will versus determinism, the issue is whether humans have properties permitting them to transcend, in their decision making, the external influences on them, past or present, or whether reflection and self-monitoring are processes that themselves are determined by external influences. It encompasses concerns about the sense of being a person who has experiences and wills behavior and about the basis of human dignity.

IV. Natural science versus social science. This issue concerns whether or not the subject matter studied by the two divisions are so inherently different in kind that they require distinct conceptions of science. It includes the question of whether social science can be science at all or is hermeneutic in nature, incapable of discovering general laws and principles; the viability of the logical positivist approach to science; and the nature of causality.

V. Value-neutral versus value-influenced science. Essentially, this issue concerns whether social science can be free of value influences in the larger society or in the social scientist. It involves the issues of whether social scientists should explicitly pursue valued goals through their science and whether social science can reveal the bases of mystification or false consciousness and thus play a role in emancipating members of a society from such erroneous beliefs.

If these issues are juxtaposed to the basic beliefs of the individualistic worldview, it is possible to assess just how profound is the challenge to it (see Figure 1.1). The revolution in social science will not end until an alternative paradigm is proposed which either offers an integrated resolution of these issues or defines them away.

EMERGENCE OF ALTERNATIVE PARADIGMS

Alternative paradigms of science are theories based on premises inconsistent with those of the prevailing worldview and that constitute substantial components of a new worldview. They often implicitly suggest aspects of a new mode of thought. Two new paradigms have emerged from the social sciences reflecting the impact of the theory of evolution in taking the view that human behavior is determined rather than voluntary. One paradigm is represented in psychology by the psychoanalytic theory with its emphasis on the developmental determination of behavior, and by behavior theory with its emphasis on habit formation based on contingencies of reinforcement. In socioanthropology, the other paradigm postulates the existence of social systems or cultures that are distinct from their individual members and that constitute forces that socialize them and allocate them to roles. This paradigm strongly suggests a new systemic mode of thought. Microeconomics and the scientific study of politics represent alternative paradigms in these disciplines only to the extent to which they are based on the assumption of determinism in human behavior.[12]

These new paradigms have become prominent in their disciplines. However, while the variants they have spawned each have often fanatic adherents, none has captured a sufficient proportion of practitioners to replace the individualistic paradigm. The scientific method, based implicitly on the premises of the individualistic worldview, has been taken over from the natural sciences and practiced using the individualistic mode of thought. However, the deterministic view of human nature has not been explicitly accepted. Striking evidence for this was the storm of controversy among *social scientists* produced by the publication of B. F. Skinner's *Beyond Free-*

Figure 1.1
Relationships of Beliefs of the Individualistic Worldview to Current Issues in the Philosophy of Social Science

Individualistic Worldview	Issues in Social Science
mind-body dualism	emergentism vs. biological reductionism
	phenomenological experience as subject matter vs. behavior as subject matter
human free will	agency, reflectivity, emancipation vs. psychological determinism
	reasons as causes vs. reasons as effects
	methodological individualism vs. methodological holism
human reason permits valid knowledge of reality via the scientific method:	realism vs. relativism of knowledge:
	--determinism vs. indeterminism in science
--study of humans is logically divided into the natural science of biology, the social sciences, the humanities	--social science as sui generis vs. social science as natural science
	--social science as science vs. social science as hermeneutic
	--humanities as sui generis vs. humanities as social science
--science as progressive production of valid knowledge	--historical retention and increasing technological mastery of nature vs. culturally relative knowledge and cross-cultural and historical incommensurability of knowledge
--God-given human capacity for rational thought	--universal human reason vs. culturally relative reason
	--determinacy of translation vs. indeterminacy of translation
--science is capable of value-neutrality	--value neutral vs. value-laden science
cause-effect nature of natural events	causality as real vs. causality as a learned mode of thought
	causality as regular conjunction of events vs. causality by generative mechanisms

dom and Dignity in 1971.[13] Serious confrontation of the issues raised by deterministic alternatives to the individualistic worldview remain almost totally neglected in graduate study and introductory texts in these disciplines. The concepts of "culture" and "social system" have never established a secure ontological status. Economics and political science have remained primarily policy sciences. As a result, most younger social scientists today have developed and been trained in a mixed and inconsistent atmosphere. Many of them probably would deny thoroughgoing adherence to the individualistic worldview while espousing no integrated alternative to it. They tend to regard the theories proposing new paradigms as speculations to be tested for validity by the scientific method. Meanwhile, positivist research is accumulating at an increasing rate despite growing discontent.

CONCLUSION

This perspective on social science today has far-reaching implications for the future of all attempts to understand human phenomena. It entails radical change in the current view of the nature of science and in the structure of the pursuit and dissemination of knowledge in our academic institutions. Premised as it is on a cyclical but not repetitive view of history, it rejects both the notion of historical progress in the production of knowledge and the notion that it is possible to establish the validity of one view of reality vis-a-vis another. The holding of a worldview and a mode of thought dictates not only how experience is interpreted but also the scientific practices by which further knowledge is pursued. When a new worldview and mode of thought replace the previous ones, all experience is interpreted differently and additional knowledge is pursued through new practices. What are called knowledge and science by members of a society, then, are relative to the worldview and mode of thought possessed.

Revolutions in science are that part of the process of change in the way of life of a group that involve the practices by which knowledge is established. In transitional periods of the history of a human group everything changes. A new role and institutional structure develops, and a new "social character" with its variants emerges in the new generations of the population (Riesman, Denney, and Glazer 1950). This view of the history of "social character" follows from a theory of worldview and mode of thought. Chapter 2 is devoted to this theory. The relativism of knowledge derives from this view. A more formal statement of it and its relationship to the current view of knowledge is the subject of Chapter 3.

The primary impact on the social sciences of the view of knowledge and science presented here is the recognition of the occurrence of worldviews and modes of thought and their etiologies. With this recognition comes the realization that the social sciences are in a revolutionary period and that their central task is the resolution of the basic issues outlined earlier in the formation of a new paradigm of science. Primary in this task must be the resolution of the issues of subject matter. The issues are those of metaphysical dualism versus monism and determinism versus free will. Chapter 4 addresses these issues. It specifies the relationship between the sciences of psychology and biology and provides a psychological account of how beliefs in mind-body dualism and free will are determined by experience. A brief summary of the positions taken on the issues listed in Figure 1.1 is provided in Chapter 5.

The first five chapters, which constitute Part I of this work, present the case for a new, alternative paradigm in this revolutionary period of the social sciences. This new paradigm will be referred to hereinafter as "relativistic naturalism." While a number of the alternative paradigms currently available in the social sciences assume the naturalism of their subject matter, none are consciously relativistic in their view of knowledge. On the other hand, it seems almost certain that in the future a number of paradigms assuming relativistic naturalism will be spawned. Using this title is not an attempt to arrogate this perspective to one of its versions. Therefore, this paradigm is further identified as "a cross-cultural approach to human science." It is so identified for two reasons. First, because its purpose is to be able to explain the behavior and experience of humans, individually and collectively, across time and space, thus bridging all current disciplines concerned to explain human behavior and experience. Second, it is cross-cultural in that in its formulation it has attempted constantly to maintain a perspective on the diversity of cultural forms made available by the efforts of scholars in the fields of history and socioanthropology and in this way to minimize ethnocentrism.

Part II attempts two tasks. One is to provide the terms and principles, although only in brief and general form, that can constitute the foundations of both psychological and sociological theories for a new human science. Building on the distinction made in Chapter 4 between the sciences of biology and psychology, it explicates the relationships among all three sciences. Psychology is identified and defended as the foundation science. Chapters 6, 7, 8, and 9 expound psychological theory. Chapter 10 addresses sociological theory. The second task of Part II encompasses specification of the organizational structure of a human science designed to replace the current structure of disciplines in traditional colleges of arts and sciences and addresses the roles and problems of human science in the larger society. Chapter 11 is devoted to these topics.

2

Worldview and Mode of Thought

Relativistic naturalism is grounded in the recognition that all humans hold worldviews and modes of thought. The failure to realize this is responsible for the illusion of science as a method for developing valid knowledge of reality. The individualistic worldview includes no concepts of either worldview or mode of thought. The minting of these terms and their gradually increasing use in the last century is one expression of the disintegration of that worldview. They have been proposed by historians and socioanthropologists who have engaged in the study of human groups other than their own. Their deep sense that members of these groups see life and think about it in ways very difficult to interpret has not so far produced an adequate conceptualization of the terms.[1]

Mendelsohn (1968) traces interest in worldview to Robert Redfield and his circle and, in 1968, finds little use of the concept outside this circle. Kearney, making the first major review of world view studies, claims

world view is not a well-established field of study in the sense that it appears in course catalogs, or that there are recognized schools of world view theory or many scholars specializing in it. And yet, rather paradoxically, literature about world view and world-view-related subjects permeates anthropology. The major problem that I faced in preparing this review was to find a meaningful definition and organization of this material. (1975, 247)

The psychologist S. B. Sarason believes that

Psychology has never warmed to the significance of the weltanschauung, in part because of its embeddedness in European philosophy and in part (like Freud's unconscious) because it seems to lack the characteristics of a scientifically testable concept. (1981, 42)

The neglect of worldview inevitably has resulted in its confusion with a number of similarly weakly conceived concepts such as ideology, cosmology, theology, philosophies of life, and paradigms of science. There seems little likelihood of the resolution of several issues important to the future of human science without a theoretical conceptualization of worldview.

The extant literature on worldview reveals that there are several issues to be considered, such as its components and their etiology, whether or not it is widely shared, explicit or implicit, and how it is to be distinguished from related concepts. Unfortunately, this literature is not in a very useful form because it lacks embeddedness in larger theoretical frameworks with well-defined terminologies and guidelines for systematic study. For example, terms such as beliefs, values, attitudes, and assumptions are used without definitions. However, there are a number of clues to the nature of worldview of great potential usefulness. There seems to be a general consensus that worldviews constitute assumptions about the nature of reality, that they are similar to or include religious beliefs, that they often at least appear to be widely shared, that they can differ in content across cultures and over time, and often seem to be implicit in the thought of those who hold them. From psychology there are suggestions that at least some basic aspects of religion are established in early childhood and that religious beliefs are irrational in postulating unseen realms and beings (Erikson 1963; Freud 1961). There also is the notion that philosophies of life are characteristically, at least in Western civilization, established during adolescence (Allport 1961).[2] Perhaps more importantly, the paucity of attention to religion in psychology and the lack of interest in the idea of worldview give these the appearance of taboo topics, suggesting resistance to their examination.

A conceptualization of worldview must start from the recognition that it is psychological in nature. Worldviews are ideas, assumptions, beliefs. They are views that individuals hold. That they may be widely shared makes them no less psychological. Moreover, that some aspects of them are established in childhood but that philosophies of life are late-adolescent developments suggest they have a complex development. The following account is based on the conviction that the complex terms in a science should be related clearly to its basic terms. It cannot escape, therefore, representing a particular theoretical stance. Exposition of this stance is a diversion that cannot be afforded in the middle of an argument on the revolution in social science. (The psychological theory used is presented in Chapters 6–9.)

It also would be too great a diversion to attempt to review the literature and relate the positions taken to those of others. What follows is a conceptualization of worldview and its etiology which deals with the major issues. It takes the following form:

1. Worldview is systemic in nature and can best be understood in terms of the developmental learning of the individual.

2. Developmental learning of the individual is organized in a sequential fashion by the age-grading system of the society.

3. Worldview consists of both beliefs about meaning in life and death and a classification system including a system of beliefs about the categories of the classification systems.

4. Worldview is largely implicit in its functioning but is capable of becoming explicit.

5. The general components of worldview are based on the earliest structure in the experience of the child during the first few years of life, but learning in the subsequent years determines the specific content of them.

6. Worldview is widely shared among members of a society because they share the main organization of the sequence of developmental learning.

7. Worldviews change with the changing order in developmental learning based on changes in the society.

8. When social change is very rapid, there is insufficient order in developmental learning for the formation of worldview. The worldview of previous generations is questioned, rejected, and ultimately replaced in some succeeding generation.

9. Worldview is distinct from but related to ideology and mode of thought.

DEFINITION AND ETIOLOGY OF WORLDVIEW

Worldview is defined as the concepts and expectancies that constitute for the individual: (1) the overarching sense of meaning in life and death; and (2) the general system of classification of persons, things, and processes that he uses to categorize experience. It expresses the order that the developing person has learned from previous experience. Worldviews have a developmental course through the life span. They appear in their initial form around age three for reasons to be explained later in this chapter. They then occur in a series of forms characteristic of universal stages of human development. (The nature of these forms and stages is explicated in Chapter 9.) In the following discussion, the form of worldview characteristic of the stage of development following the major changes of puberty will be the focus because it appears to be the one most commonly referred to in the literature on worldview. In this stage, worldview becomes a well-organized, if largely implicit, system of very abstract and interrelated concepts and expectancies bringing potentially articulable order out of all previous experience. This system, then, provides a general basis for the interpretation of later experience and a means for pretesting the consequences of contemplated action. It constitutes the individual's understanding of the nature of the reality behind his everyday experience.

To account for the order in the experience of any given generation among those interacting in the society at the same time, it is necessary to break into the continual succession of living generations. Three to four generations are always contributing to the functioning of the society, with members of the oldest living generation having developed in interaction with three previous and now deceased generations.

Crucial to the understanding of worldview formation and change is the realization that what is here being called order in experience may vary markedly across human groups or within them over time on a dimension of order-disorder. The order also is changing at some rate of speed. Considerations of degree of order and rate of change will be taken up in detail later. The following explanation assumes the new generation to be born into a group with a high degree of order and a slow rate of change.

The definition of worldview assumes that humans have capacities to represent much of the order in their experience. There are various aspects of order and several different processes by which they can be learned. A belief is defined as a learned representation of the order in experience.[3] Two basic kinds of representations are involved—that of simultaneous order (concepts) and that of sequential or temporal order (expectancies). That is to say, humans can learn the patterns that occur together and also what sequences of patterns occur, that is, "what goes with what" and "what follows what." Worldview has its foundation in the developing child's learning of concepts and expectancies.

It is postulated that humans are capable of making abstractions from more concrete learning. The individual can learn what *kinds* of patterns occur together and what *kinds* of sequences occur. For example, from many very specific punishments in specific situations in which the child disobeys his parents, the child can learn the abstract belief that when he disobeys a parental prescription he will suffer some form of punishment. Moreover, abstraction of beliefs can occur at increasingly higher levels. One can abstract the common elements of already abstract concepts or expectancies, for example, the Individualistic beliefs that individuals are by nature acquisitive or that men have a strong sex drive. The results are classification systems and hierarchies of abstract beliefs.

The adult form of a worldview includes the highest levels of abstraction from previous learning that account for the repetitive aspects of experience of everyday life. The repetitive aspects comprise the order in experience. They are repetitive in the sense that they are common elements of many different activities and relationships. They are common both horizontally across activities and relationships of a given age-grade or stage of development and vertically through the age-grading system of development. This order should not be construed as a simple matter of conscious socializing of the child or of handing down the culture. Although many aspects of the child's experience occur because elders are attempting to direct learning, there is little basis for assuming a direct relationship between what they intend to do and what the child learns. Much of the influence on the child's learning comes from experiences of which the elders are unaware, even when they participate in it.

What is meant by the order in experience may be illustrated from child development in recent, not current, American society. For example, the child through every age-grade in many ways was involved, often vicariously, in many experiences in which males and females were differentiated systematically. It was not only in his own home that mothers and fathers, sisters and brothers, dressed differently, engaged or were encouraged to engage in different types of activities, and were related to in different ways. The same types of differences were repeated when he was in the homes of his friends or relatives, in his storybooks, in school, and in what he overheard of the conversations of others. As a given generation developed, little boys and little girls began to experience the other sex in different ways from their own sex. In adolescence they made the abstractions which constituted the worldview beliefs in the different inherent nature of males and females. These high-level abstractions made sense of a lifetime of experience and also fit with other abstractions as a part of a system of understanding.

Another example of this process is suggested by the experiences of American children with success and failure. Through the various age-grades, they were introduced to a series of activities in which success and failure in competition with others were common elements. Starting with sibling rivalry for attention from parents, they were encountered in table games, sports, academic quizzes and tests, competition for dates, and finally for entrance into college or for jobs. In each age-grade there were many competitive activities and relationships. Always the essence was winning and losing. Always one person's or team's success was another's failure. Always there was the temptation of self or others to cheat, whether it was in playing table games and saying, "I didn't go yet"; in baseball and saying, "It was a strike, not a ball"; or in school by looking on someone else's paper; etc. Vicarious experiences of the same components occurred through observing older children and adults, in storybooks, and hearing peers tell about their experiences.

It is not surprising, then, that the adolescent began to form the abstract beliefs that humans are by nature self-centered, competitive, and acquisitive, especially males, and that they have the reasoning ability to know moral from immoral action and the will to yield to or to resist temptation. These, too, made sense of a lifetime of experience. So well did these abstractions tend to summarize previous experience, at the same time corresponding closely to the views of older generations, that there was an inevitable sense that this was the fixed nature of things.

This is what makes the worldview a basis for the anticipation of future experience, for planning and assessing the "workability" of contemplated goals and plans of both self and others. There is virtually nothing that can happen after the formation of worldview that cannot be interpreted within its terms. It has categories for classifying all things and beliefs from which can be derived some form of explanation of all events. And it works because it is a summary of what really happens in the society.

In considering the American experience, it is easy to become sidetracked by the focus on individual differences in experience and personality. Children are thought to differ markedly in their experiences of success and failure, of love and rejection, etc. Unique self-concept development is thought to be the essence of life. This is misleading. Self-concept development goes on around the order in experience. Whether a child has much success or much failure, the success-failure structure of experience is the basic order. Whether there is much love or much rejection, the love-rejection structure is what is basic. Whether there are problems of sexual identity or not, sexual identity is the essence. Americans learn to think a great deal about the relationship of the object called the self to what is important in life. In this, a highly individualistic social system focuses on the different, indeed the unique, to the neglect of the shared.

What the child is steadily learning consists mainly of the categories of things, processes, and events and the principal ways in which to characterize them. The categories are organized into a hierarchical structure on the bases of the common elements which can be abstracted. The result is a system of classification and beliefs about each category that permit the individual to derive expectations logically for a great many anticipated situations. He also can derive various scenarios for all kinds of hypothetical situations. This learning will be heavily weighted on the human side. That is, the worldview inevitably will emphasize people and their main characteristics thoroughly as a result of the constant interaction among members of the group through life. The elaboration of learning about the nonhuman world depends upon the roles it plays in everyday life. In groups which live very close to nature, so to speak, such as the pygmies of the rain forest or other groups with limited technology aiding their hunting and gathering or agriculture, such learning will be extensive. In groups with highly developed technologies, much learning will occur around these artifacts and processes rather than around natural phenomena. In any case, the process of abstraction of common properties at ever higher levels will culminate in the conjunction of the order in the person's experience and the expressions of worldview of older generations. The crystallization of worldview constitutes an assimilation of the worldview already prevailing. The stability of the society makes the generalizations of older generations meaningful to the younger who have shared the same general order.

WORLDVIEW AND RELIGIOUS BELIEFS

One major aspect of worldview does not appear to be covered by the kind of order in experience in the foregoing account. It is the religious beliefs. These beliefs are usually regarded by social scientists as transcending experience and irrational in nature. How can the god or gods of the group with their particular characteristics be said to be abstractions from the order in everyday experience? How can the rituals of religious practice be traced to developmental experience? These considerations often seem to be behind the common view that religion is handed down from generation to generation and even that it exists independently of particular people. This assumes that merely telling children about things suffices to produce the most intense conviction. It is true that, from the early years, the religious ideas and practices of the society are part of the child's experience. This tells us little about how learning represents such experience. In what sense children prior to puberty are religious remains opaque. That being Christian, Moslem, Jew, Baptist, Methodist, or Episcopalian becomes part of the child's identity is both undeniable and superficial. Few American children, who might even fight over religious slurs, can articulate the differences between these identities. Only in adolescence does religious conviction become conscious, articulate, and intense. This is partly due to the development of new capacities for thought and reason (Piaget and Inhelder 1969). But why should such capacities lead to this consequence? Why wouldn't they lead to the rejection of beliefs for which there is no direct confirmation in sensory experience and which require remarkable assumptions, for example, the existence of invisible gods and realms of existence. These beliefs do make deep sense to the adolescent, once he has considered them. The question becomes one of the basis for this meaningfulness.

Before suggesting how religious beliefs reflect the actual order in developmental experience, it is important to make clear what is meant here by "religious" and what is not. It does not refer to religious practices and customs. These are behaviors that are determined by other aspects of learning besides worldview. It is not theological doctrine, except for clergy and a small percentage of believers. Such highly systematized and articulable belief systems require a process of reflection rarely engaged in by the majority of members of a society. The case is similar for philosophical systems not ordinarily regarded as religious beliefs. What is meant here by religious beliefs is that subset of beliefs in the worldview that explains the meaning of life and death and provides the overarching framework within which the other beliefs of the world view take their meaning. All human groups appear to have such beliefs. There seems no reason to doubt that all human beings will have some way to understand the birth of new life and the end of lives in their familiar physical forms or that the experience of these will be of great importance. However, the term "religious" as conventionally used has ethnocentric meanings, diverting attention from the essence of these beliefs to particular forms of them. Here religious beliefs include any set accounting for these phenomena whether they have any supernatural components or not. In this sense, atheists may be godless, but they have religious beliefs.

The religious beliefs of the worldview are just as much abstractions of the order in experience as other beliefs. However, they have a special basis in experience. They are founded in the order in experience in the first few years of life, probably the first three. While some social scientists, particularly psychoanalysts, have suggested a childhood basis of religious beliefs, there has been little attempt to conceptualize this learning and its variations across social systems.

PRIMARY WORLDVIEW

This approach assumes, with some others, that human development proceeds from the gross to the differentiated. Early experience is regarded as of a special kind, because it does not occur in the context of any previous learning to which it can be assimilated. The child starts with no concepts, beliefs, attitudes, values, rules, norms, etc. He starts from scratch in representing the order in his experience. He knows no language in which to organize experience and with which to recapture and reexperience it. Nothing experienced is a thing among things, a kind of thing, or a different kind of thing. It is probably impossible for adults to recall experience under these conditions. The very small child usually is regarded as commencing to recognize very specific objects and to accumulate a repertoire of object identifications and little anticipations and skills. Such a view recognizes only that part of the order in the child's experience which is represented by objects. There is clearly a great deal more order than that. There is order in the behavior of whatever caretakers relate regularly with the child. There is order in the routine of the environment of the child. There is order in the physical surroundings to which he is exposed. There is order to his experiences of his body. There is no sound reason for assuming that the child's early learning cannot represent at least the major features of the overall order in the relationships among these orders. The argument here is that the child does represent this order. The representation is primary worldview. It is the underlying structure informing all later learning.[4]

Since primary worldview can vary markedly in different societies, any conceptualization of it must focus on its possible dimensions or components. Anthropologists have made a useful start on categories of worldview. However, they have not suggested the kind of distinction being proposed here between primary worldview and other aspects of order in experience. This distinction emphasizes the sequential nature of human learning and its process of differentiation. Of great significance for world-view is the idea that the past is always immanent in the individual's present. That is, the gross early structure remains even as it is elaborated, much like the unseen structure of a building. This provides the psychological foundation of the meaningfulness of apparently irrational religious beliefs about the overarching meaning of life and death in worldview.

The dimensions of primary worldview would seem to be the following:

1. The number of significant other "figures" in the sense of distinct relationship(s) to others who determine the conditions of life;
2. The attributes of each "figure";
3. The dominant emotional quality of the relationship to each "figure";
4. The role of the child in the relationship(s).[5]

Number of Significant "Figures"

All age-grading systems have their particular arrangements for the care of the newborn, although they can differ markedly. Some person or set of persons interacts regularly with the child in the first few years of life. However, the child has no initial reason for distinguishing among these persons except on the basis of how they relate to or treat him. The child's initial classification is of different relationships, not persons. Hence, if two or more caretakers treat the child in substantially the same manner, he learns initially a relationship to one "figure." If those he deals with relate in very distinct manners to him, he learns two or more relationships. This is a primitive sort of learning involving only gross dimensions of experience. While there is strong evidence that infants in the first half year of life can identify their caretaker by face and probably smell, touch, and sound, this does not provide a basis for the differentiation of relationships unless each caretaker has a distinct relationship which the child also can discriminate. What is significant for worldview here is the role of this dimension for the number of gods, powers, or superordinate essences attributed to reality. Primary experience in human development starts with "what," never "why." This "what" is the bottom line of understanding or meaning. Humans do not normatively ask why gods exist, or spiritual powers, or nature, or the group itself, if that is the superordinate essence. They just exist, and all meaning starts from that fact.

Attributes of Each "Figure"

The manner in which the caretakers relate to the very young child varies substantially across human groups. Partly consciously, but mainly unconsciously, they structure his experiences with them in particular ways. Certainly most fundamental are their powerfulness, omniscience, capacity to bestow benefits and punishments, and to appear and disappear mysteriously. Of particular significance would be their benevolence or malevolence, or the ratio of malevolence to benevolence, as assessed by the child's experiences of comfort-discomfort, stress-security, pleasure-unpleasure. Another dimension, very probably, is consistency-inconsistency in the sense of the child's capacity to bring order out of his experience. His life can be subject to varying degrees of capriciousness and of intensity of comfort and discomfort. Equally important will be the child's growing sense of his capacity to influence these "figures"—that is, the degree to which his actions are systematically related to theirs. Where there are two or more significantly different "figures" in the child's experience, they can relate differently to him on any one or combination of these dimensions. This will not be a matter of chance for new members of a society. The number and form of relationships will be a reflection of the order in that society. This component of worldview establishes the general nature of the characteristics of the gods, powers, or other superordinate essences.

Dominant Emotional Quality in Relationship to Each "Figure"

The way in which the young child is treated will select from the limited range of his emotional capacities a particular one or pattern which will dominate his early experience. Erikson (1963) has suggested the importance of trust and mistrust in the first year of life and its relationship to the conceptualization of a god. Some clinical psychologists, focusing on the emotionally disturbed, point to depressive, paranoid, and schizoid "positions" in early development. Much American psychology of child development focuses on love and rejection, security and insecurity. However, there is little attention to cross-cultural differences that might help to dimensionalize this component of worldview. In the worldview, this component contributes some of the characteristics of the superordinate essence but more significantly indicates the major significance of the relationship of them to the individual. Life in the worldview is emotionally "all about" certain kinds of emotional experiences, such as love-rejection, security-insecurity, certainty-uncertainty, suspicion-trust, etc. Note, however, that the worldview consists only of beliefs about this aspect of the nature of things. Feelings or motives concerning superordinate essences are not part of worldview but of other aspects of personality.

The Role of the Child in the Relationship

There is no reason to assume, and most psychologists do not, that the child is born with a sense of self. The child experiences but has no initial sense of something doing the experiencing. Psychologists generally assume that the child lacks any sense of the extension of his physical body. Instead, the child learns to identify himself the way he learns to identify any object. The earliest experiences of a relationship are not of the self and some other, but of the correlations of experiences that can be identified. Some clinical psychologists, most notably psychoanalysts, have emphasized the complexity of the individuation of the child from an initial embeddedness in a maternal matrix. Symbiotic schizophrenia, for example, is understood as the failure of the complete separation of self from the mother as a distinct entity. Sometimes identical twins, raised together, speak about themselves in ways that suggest an identity which encompasses them both. This is only to suggest that even body-image development is a matter of learning.[6]

More significant to worldview is that the *physical* entity of the individual, once learned as an object among objects, acquires, through learning, *psychological* characteristics. Most of the psychology of personality today is about these psychological attributes of the physical person—masculinity or femininity, selfishness or unselfishness, rigidity or flexibility, degree of aggressiveness, etc.

Clearly, the ways in which self-concept is developed or dimensionalized are culturally relative. In very early learning, the self may vary in its significance for experience in general. That is, significant others may invoke the self frequently or infrequently in relating to the child. They may attribute to it many or few characteristics. The child may learn that the self plays a very large or very limited role in the determination of his own experience. This is reflected in the rather recent concern of American psychologists with whether people think in terms of internal or external control of events (Lefcourt 1982). A very different set of experiences will produce the learning that the individual is responsible for all major aspects of his fate in life from that which produces the learning that one is a pawn of forces beyond one's capacity to control. A child can be significant to or relevant in the lives of others in many different ways, in many ways, or in few ways. How this self-concept is structured at the outset will be crucial for the individual's understanding of his relationship to his gods, powers, or other superordinate forces.

Primary worldview is the child's first and lasting sense of the meaning of his experiences, or the nature of it all, including his place in it. It is very general and inarticulable. It is a framework within which all later experience takes its meaning. Hence later experience is a differentiation and elaboration of meaning. In this sense, it is much like Freud's view of Oedipal relationships taken in its broadest sense of prototypical forms of relationships in terms of authority, love, and gender. However, it differs in two important ways. First, it moves the basic prototypes back to the first three to four years. This makes Freud's prototypes of family relationships more like the first stage of differentiation of primary meaning structure. Secondly, it is more general than Freud's, deliberately avoiding ethnocentric bias in specification of relationships.

In the absence of literature in social science and history that is readily amenable to illustration of primary worldview, an effort has been made to provide an example in Figure 2.1. It is based on a comparison of major aspects of early childhood experience in older and preceding generations of the American middle class and the central beliefs of the Christian religion shared by members of that class, perhaps particularly among Protestants.[7]

Primary worldview itself does not determine the specific beliefs of the worldview even with respect to its religious aspects. It provides only the gross framework within which specific beliefs are shaped by later experience. Hence, in the illustration given, children of those generations could have formed that primary worldview and yet never developed the Christian worldview. They could even be atheists. Nevertheless, their overarching view of life would reflect the same qualities of primary worldview. Their superordinate essence might not have been the Christian God but the state, or the brotherhood of man.[8] They still would judge their lives on the basis of their adherence to what was good or bad to this "figure" and be concerned about its ultimate judgment of their contribution to it.[9] Individuals with atypical experience in the early years of life, and thus with different primary personality structures, would be expected to have worldviews with some significant differences from the norm.

While the primary worldview provides the overarching framework within which all later learning is a differentiation and elaboration, it does not dictate many aspects of such learning. Which aspects it does not dictate depend on the nature of the initial framework. The one just illustrated, for example, does provide a framework of authority-subordinate learning but not male-female differentiation.[10] The differentiation of this framework is determined by the nature of the age-grading system. The child's developing interactions with others and objects is the basis for the classifications of persons and things and of the basic relationships among them.

The age-grading system will structure the age-grade in which the worldview is crystallized so that it happens in a particular way. This might be extensive rituals with heavily condensed symbolization expressing the major beliefs. It might be by admission into previously secret or adult-only organizations whose activities and organization within and across organizations manifest and express the overall order. It might be by a sense of urgency about the child's preparation for the adult stage of life. This produces parental pressure on the child to be realistic and sensible and to take a long-range view of life. This is guided by continual, if fragmented, expression of beliefs of the worldview in a context designed to help the child make the appropriate abstractions. However, in some societies this

Figure 2.1
Relationships of Individualistic Primary Worldview and the Conditions Determining It to General Beliefs of Christianity

Individualistic Primary Worldview	General Beliefs of Christianity
1. Number of Significant Figures Determining the Conditions of Life	
One--the parent figure. Given the conjugal family structure and its division of labor by sex and the private home, the child's life is dominated constantly by his relationship to his mother. Father, grandmother, baby-sitters, and older siblings are minor caretakers who treat the child in substantially the same manner as the mother. The deep emotional investment of mothers in their children produces very close supervision and interaction.	There is one God who created the universe and everything in it.
2. Attributes of Each Significant Figure	
Parental figure is source of all love, pleasure, and solutions to problems; judges all behavior; must be obeyed; punishes bad behavior but does not stay angry.	God is omnipotent and omniscient. God is loving but sits in judgment on every person with respect to their moral conduct. He can intervene in the life of the individual at any time to bestow blessings, punishments, or challenges. God has a grand design for the universe. No one can know this design, but everyone knows how he should conduct his life as part of it. God is displeased with misconduct but is forgiving if the sinner is truly repentant. God cannot be deceived.
Parent figure determines all conditions of the child's life. It takes care of all his needs, organizes his life into a schedule of eating, bathing, sleeping, playing, bodily moves him around at will, administers punishments and pleasures, anticipates his actions, understands his feelings, readily discerns his early efforts to deceive in order to avoid punishment. Parent is loving but willing to punish child condi-	

tionally upon good or bad behavior as a means of ensuring child learns proper lessons and develops upright character. Punishments are tailored to perceived capacities of child and replaced with love when child is perceived as having learned the lesson.

3. Dominant Emotional Quality of Experience

Love and rejection by parent figure. Child is completely dependent physically and psychologically on this figure. No one else plays more than a minor role in his experience. Parental disapproval produces strong feelings of rejection accompanied by various discomforts. Attempts to maintain parental love and avoid rejection are most central to child.

The meaning of life and of death is the anticipation of God's ultimate judgment which will result either in basking for all eternity in the love of God or being rejected and suffering eternal discomforts. Life's blessings and trials are manifestations of God's approval and disapproval of how the individual is conducting his life at the time.

4. Type of Identity Established

The child himself determines whether he is loved or rejected by the parent figure by how he regulates his behavior. Parent figure characterizes the child as good or bad, obedient or disobedient. Anger is generated in child by discipline but parent figure does not allow it to be expressed against parent. Child becomes anxious about permanent loss of love and learns to turn his anger against himself by accepting that punishment is his own fault, and that he has no one to blame but himself.

God gave every human a soul comprised of the capacity to know right from wrong and the free will to choose between moral and immoral behavior. The individual is subject to many temptations from the needs and passions of the body. These can be resisted by an act of will. If the individual yields to temptation, he earns God's disapproval; but if he repents and resolves to avoid such behavior, then God is forgiving. God's ultimate judgment is determined by how the individual has chosen to conduct his life. Acceptance of Christ as the Savior signifies the individual's subordination of his will to that of God.

33

process occurs less through language than ritual, providing a worldview less articulable in words but more expressible in other forms.

INTEGRATION AND STABILITY OF WORLDVIEW

With the assumption of development in a relatively stable society, it follows that the formation of the adult form of world view normatively produces an integrated and comprehensive set of very abstract beliefs.[11] It is integrated because it is a summary of the order actually experienced. The relationships among persons and things have been experienced both horizontally across many activities within each stage of development and vertically through the common elements of different specific activities and relationships through the succeeding age-grades. Categories of things, persons, and processes have been built into a hierarchy of increasingly abstract concepts. Virtually every type of experience that can occur in the society has been included in one or more of these categories. This includes deviant behavior. Consequently, the individual is virtually psychologically shockproof at the level of abstract understanding. Whatever befalls him makes some kind of sense. There is a continuous experience of social consensus about these interpretations of experience to reinforce the new worldview. The individual, having grown up in his social order, comes increasingly to recognize significant aspects of that order in his own feelings and thoughts.

The result of this integration and comprehensiveness of adult worldview is a strong stability to it, a sense of the naturalness of it, and an intense conviction about it. The order is continually experienced as being confirmed. It is just "the way things are," the nature of reality. As a summary of order, it provides the foundation for reasoning about all later experience and for contemplated actions as well.[12] It seems very likely it is partly this worldview formation that marks in all societies transition to a new stage of development, which corresponds to what in America is called adulthood. In individualistic generations of Americans, the postpubertal individual eventually was observed to base his actions and decisions on similar assumptions to those of older generations who had already formed the worldview. This distinguished him markedly from younger generations who lacked this basis of action.

The profound sense of overarching meaning gained is, psychologically, an externalization of the inchoate primary world view of which later experience is a differentiation and elaboration. This is why the apparently irrational religious beliefs are adhered to with such conviction. The religious aspects of the worldview and their expression in institutionalized forms express and make conscious sense of the individual's primary worldview. This gives the worldview a psychological depth which accounts for the intensity of conviction.

UNIVERSAL COMPONENTS OF WORLDVIEW

Any attempt to identify universal elements of worldview must be careful to avoid ethnocentric bias. The variety of ways of life across human groups is extensive, including diverse forms of family structure and early child-rearing practices. Nevertheless, the foregoing account of the etiology of worldview points toward the identification of some basic universal components.

All worldviews can be expected to specify one or more superordinate essences or beings and their properties. They also will account for the relationship of the individual to each of these forces or beings, including the dominant emotions. These elements will identify the meaning of life and death however the particular events of birth and death are conceived.

Another universal element of worldview is an abstract system of classification of things, processes, and people. In the individualistic worldview, for example, this level of classification includes entirely spiritual beings, humans, animals (fauna), plants (flora), and inanimate things.[13] Most significant among these classes will very likely be that one which includes those who hold the worldview. This will probably include all or almost all of the members of the society. This class will be significant because its subclasses at the next level will reveal the bases of most of the important relationships of members. For example, in the individualistic worldview these subclasses appear to be male-female, adult-child, sane-insane, and four races. The various combinations of these categories constitute the bulk of the system of social stratification. In other groups the caste-type categories may be quite different, although some may be universal.

The third universal component of worldviews is a system of abstract beliefs defining the characteristics of each category of humans. These result from the summaries of previous learning discussed earlier. In the individualistic worldview, for example, women have a maternal instinct; men have a powerful sexual drive that is inherently heterosexual; nonwhite races are subhuman beings—savages having reason but either lacking the capacity for morality or, being childlike, requiring missionary work to teach them morality; an adult is one who has learned right from wrong, an achievement which occurs usually by age eighteen; the insane are those bereft of their reason, etc. All behaviors ultimately are traced to these defining characteristics and variations of them. Conversely, the individual can derive general, guiding expectations in contemplating future actions with specific others from this belief system.

A fourth component is an abstract system of beliefs concerning whatever is not included in the belief system about people, or what individualists would call the world of nature. This will include beliefs about the relationships of this realm (or realms) to humans. It will be heavily colored by the natural features of the local environment, geographical and climatological. This component may be divided into various major categories including space, time, and number. In any case, the worldview will include the total realm of experience. This permits the holder of a worldview to have some way of understanding or thinking about everything he encounters, at least at an abstract level. However space and time are conceived, they will provide, along with beliefs traced to primary worldview, beliefs concerning the origins and history of all categories.[14]

In summary, worldviews seem likely to include the following components:

1. Identification of one or more superordinate essences or figures, the relationship(s) to which give life and death their primary meaning.
2. The key properties or characteristics of these essences or figures.
3. The dominant emotional qualities of life.
4. The role of the individual in the relationships.
5. The most abstract levels of a hierarchical system of classification of things, processes, and people.
6. A system of abstract beliefs that provides the key characteristics of each category at these levels of the classification system.
7. Beliefs concerning the origins and history of all categories.

WORLDVIEW CHANGE

Worldview changes across generations, not within them, except in the developmental sense of elaboration and integration explained in Chapter 9. Once members of a generation have formed a worldview, there is no psychological basis for its change. If change in their society increases in rapidity during their adult years, they will try to understand it in terms of their worldview. If this presents them with difficulty, the strength of their conviction about their worldview will decrease or increase defensively. They will be keenly aware that things are changing, but they will have no other interpretation of the changes, nor will they be able to construct one. They will have a feeling the "the world is going to the dogs," or that the gods are angry, or that some demon or spirit has entered the scene. In some cases the worldview itself may have provision for such change, as in millenarian views. It is likely that the older generations will be disposed to criticize the younger for their failure to adhere to the true or proper way of life.

The basis for change in worldview must be change in the order in experience for new generations. This must constitute a significant departure from the old order and be widespread through the social system. Inevitably, the general processes of social change are involved. Sociologists and anthropologists have long been concerned with this topic. The important issues of periodicity in history, or of duration of structure, are inherent. It would seem fruitful to assume that social systems are always changing but vary in the rate of change. When the rate is slow, worldview can be assumed to be stable. There are subtle modifications of systems of classification at more intermediate levels of abstraction. However, when the rate of change is rapid, it is less a matter of new order in experience than of less order in experience. Mixtures of old and new activities and relationships preclude hierarchical abstractions of common elements for several generations. In these transitional periods what occurs is the progressive breakdown of the meaningfulness of the old worldview without the development of any replacement. Transitional generations have a very difficult time "getting it all together."

Beyond the manifestations of this problem of finding overall order in experience, other characteristic phenomena of transition can be expected. There will be greater conflicts and "gaps" between living generations. Groping for new order will produce a diversity of cultlike groups and movements led by charismatic individuals who temporarily provide for the members a form of meaning heavily dependent on the resources of the leader. A greatly increased interest, concern, or fascination with death can be expected. There will be expressions of a desperate and defensive reactionary adherence to old beliefs by some members, while others are critically examining and making explicit the assumptions of the old worldview.[15] There will be subtle changes in the meaning of words and the increasing minting of new ones. A popular form of transitional and very superficial worldview will appear, based on the idea that continued change is the only order that exists. Within the intellectual stratum of the society, or whatever may correspond to it in nonliterate groups, new philosophies will be spawned. Change will be occurring simultaneously in all major institutions, although not necessarily at the same rate or in the same forms.

From the standpoint of learning in members of any new generation, there will be little order to be abstracted. Only when the rate of change slows down will a new order begin to emerge. Psychologically, it will be registered first as a new primary worldview. The new age-grading system will then provide the order in the differentiation and elaboration of this structure. In the meantime, at the earlier stages of the transitional period, the efforts of older generations to facilitate formation of worldview in the younger will be increasingly unsuccessful. Their interpretations of experience will be progressively less meaningful to generations developing without the old order. Somewhere among the cults and philosophies of the transitional period, the outlines of the new worldview will begin to appear. Particular life histories and the historical moment will come together in decisive expositions of views which first express well the order which the majority have begun to experience (Erikson 1975). These views will be externalizations of the new primary meaning structure and express the new classificatory systems. A new worldview will prevail, perhaps, only after a prolonged struggle among alternative formulations.

WORLDVIEW AND IDEOLOGY

It is useful to make a sharp distinction between the concepts of worldview and ideology. Worldview is defined in terms of beliefs about the nature of the reality behind appearances. Ideology is defined as beliefs about the way in which reality is currently expressed in appearances, attitudes toward that expression, and beliefs and attitudes concerning preservation and change in it. Ideology is about how one's society (or world) is actually functioning and what should be done about it. Worldview has nothing to do with attitudes or values, with what should or shouldn't be.[16] It is about the limits on what could be. It defines the possible. Ideology defines the actual, the desirable, and the undesirable. (For a more complete discussion of ideology, see Chapter 8.)[17]

MODE OF THOUGHT

Like worldview, mode of thought is a weakly conceptualized term introduced by historians and socioanthropologists to social science.[18] It, too, stems from the awareness of something basically different across human groups. Mode of thought can be understood as the characteristic form in which experience is processed and thought regulated. The worldview of a person defines the nature of the *content* of thought. The mode defines the nature of the *process* of thought. Mode of thought, then, would be manifest in any attempt to articulate any aspect of a worldview. However, mode of thought encompasses more than speech utterances. Although a great deal of human thinking is linguistically driven, whether expressed or latent, a significant proportion of it probably is not. This is not a reference to dreamlike thought or to Freud's idea of primary process. It refers to thought directed by the order in nonlinguistic experience. Obviously, the longstanding issues of the relationship between language and thought are involved in such a suggestion. These issues constitute a useful means for clarifying the idea of mode of thought.

The view that language structures thought is strongly suggested by the recognition that different human groups use different grammars and that the essentials of the local grammar are learned by children by the age of four. There can be no doubt that linguistic experience plays a tremendously significant role in the development of a mode of thought. Language provides the developing person with perhaps the vast majority of his categories. It also serves to direct much of his attention selectively to the environment in general and, in particular, to the order in which the environment is to be perceived. Whatever the person learns, he can communicate to others directly and quickly only by using the order his language provides. However, if language were all that structured thought, some very dubious conclusions would follow. External reality, for example, would play no more of a role than to provide objects to be selectively identified. Secondly, it would mean that language would remain unchanged, except perhaps for the addition of new nouns, whatever the nature of changes in the patterns of interaction among members of the group. Thirdly, it would provide no place in the explanation of human behavior for experiences which defy articulation in language, thereby excluding many of those important aspects of human communication embodied in art, music, dance, and ritual. Finally, the idea that language structures thought would imply that during virtually the first two years of life, when the child can hardly be said to have any linguistic competence, he also has no structured thought.

These implications seem unnecessarily restrictive. It is more promising to consider that linguistic order interacts with the nonlinguistic order in experience to structure most, but not all, thought. The question arises, In what does the nonlinguistic order exist? The answer probably is best approached by considering what any visitor to a totally strange society would observe. Without being able to speak its language, he could only observe the patterning of activities of its daily life. It is true that some of it would not reveal any coherent pattern. On the other hand, a great deal of it certainly would, although the observer would find himself rather selective in what he thought he understood. Still, he could observe repetitive patterns of activities in a general round of life.

What is most important in nonlinguistic experience for the development of a mode of thought is the nature of this pattern. The key to it lies in the learning of the unit of experience or of meaning. The flux of experience has to be divided and organized in some manageable and coherent fashion. Learning the basic unit of thought would seem to be determined by such elements as the duration of time intervals between significant experiences, the number of interactions or sequences of events during these intervals, the number of persons or objects involved in the interactions, the forms of interaction, the role of passive or active participation by the child, the pace of events, etc. The key idea in all this concerns intervals of significant experience. Significance can be conceived in terms of experience that signifies the occurrence of disorganization or reorganization of thought.[19] The mode of thought consists in the types of units and the ways in which these units are internally organized.[20]

At this point, the analysis of modes of thought inevitably breaks down because the analyst has only his own mode to use for the task. This is the essence of the idea of Kuhn's notion of the incommensurability of paradigms. The incommensurability lies in the modes of thought, bearing in mind that they also process the different content of their accompanying worldviews. All that can be added here is that the mode of thought is determined by the interaction of the nonlinguistic order of the elements within the units of significant experience and the syntactic order of the linguistic experience. It is most important to note that such interaction requires some compatibility between the two orders. A particular syntactic order cannot make sense of every nonlinguistic order. A nonlinguistic order cannot be articulated thoroughly by just any language. If the two orders are sufficiently different, then the developing child will have difficulty both in understanding what is said to and around him and also in making himself understood with any clarity.[21] This is the basis for change both in mode of thought and in language.

One further observation about modes of thought can be offered. They have dimensions or characteristics that can be identified, but the specification of these is inevitably distorted by the system of classification of the analyst. The best that can be done to generate some support for this conceptualization of modes of thought is to provide an example. The example must be an analysis of the analyst's own mode of thought. What follows, then, is a brief analysis of the mode of thought which has accompanied the individualistic worldview, middle-class variant. It will be called the individualistic mode of thought. It is pragmatic, judgmental, and comparative in character.

Its pragmatism lies in the division of experience into a series of mostly unrelated short-range sequences of cause and effect. Events consist of a subject and an action with respect to an object. The subject is understood as the cause and any change in or of the object as the effect. Events are unrelated except through a common property of the causal agent, for example, its carelessness/carefulness, laziness/industriousness, aggressiveness/helpfulness, power/impotence, etc. However, since these characteristics can change, the relatedness of events is limited and short-range. Thought in the individualistic mode is highly fragmented. Tasks and goals are approached one at a time, with little thought devoted to the relationships among them, for example, "I'll cross that bridge when I come to it." The flexibility inherent in human free will precludes a long-range perspective and makes the present situation all that counts. There is no systematic organization or field-type analysis in the individualistic mode. Individualists are atheoretical.[22]

Pragmatism in this sense is reflected in the syntax of the English language. Sentences have the subject-predicate-object structure.[23] It is very much a nominalizing language; "The walk did me good," "The rain ruined our picnic." Speech demands a subject. When there is no known subject, it provides one in the form of the pronoun "it," as in "It is raining." Individualists do not think there is something in the sky doing the raining. Their mode tempts them to think the clouds are the causal agent.

The judgmental characteristic of the individualist mode of thought lies in the constant disposition to hold subjects responsible for the effects they have on objects. This is the foundation of the concept of causality. It is an assumption about the nature of relationships.[24] The main types of judgments are in terms of morality—that is, good and bad—and efficiency—in other words, successful and unsuccessful. There is a strong animistic quality to these judgments, with the result that it is difficult to avoid the idea of responsibility for effects even when the causal agent is nonhuman or even inanimate and therefore, by definition, incapable of willing the effects. In their most unguarded moments, Individualists curse and/or physically abuse their cars, tools, doors, and pets. Disposed to punish the "bad" rain but knowing it will have no effect, they can't help blaming the weather forecaster.

The comparative characteristic of the individualistic mode of thought lies in the inability to make judgments except in terms of comparison. There is no absolute standard for judgments. Causes and effects are bigger and better or smaller and worse. There must always be something against which to compare experience. This quality generates the concern of Individualists with records and recordkeeping. Even the weather and the stock market set records. As a result, this characteristic harbors the disposition to assess experience in terms of progress and regress. The combination of pragmatic, judgmental, and comparative characteristics gives the Individualistic mode of thought a linear, progressive, and cumulative, by small increments, perspective, such as, the gradual development of facts and principles in social science.

It does not seem difficult to trace the establishment of the individualistic mode of thought to the first three or four years of life, when not only the learning of the general structure of the language but also the learning of Individualism occurs. What the small children of individualists experience is a fragmentation of life into simple and short-range sequences of causes and effects. This is due to the concern of mothers with the development of the child's character. Regarding the child as having a free will, they want to ensure that the child understands that he is responsible for the consequences of his behavior. Almost every action of the child is assessed in terms of its significance for his proper development. As soon as the child, mainly by the development of his means of locomotion, is understood as actively engaging his environment, he is treated as ready to both literally and figuratively stand on his own two feet.

This produces that period of life which has been called "the battle of wills" and "the terrible twos." Its essence is the child's learning that he should assess himself as good or bad depending on the effects he causes and strive "every day in every way to become better and better." His life is divided into short sequences of these causes and effects. As he learns, he observes that other persons, animals, and things also are judged. The child quickly learns to assess her dolls or pets in this fashion, by projecting her budding self-assessments to them. Moreover, assessment of the self as the central object in life is constantly done in comparative terms at least by age three. The child's behavior is compared either to his past performances or to the performances of others such as his siblings and later peers. Comparison to one's own past performance provides the basis of the quality of progress and regress in life. It is called "self-improvement" or "backsliding." Comparison to the performances of others is the basis of social status in life and underlies the concern with upward and downward mobility.

The nonlinguistic order in the child's experience exists mainly in the types of activities with which the child is provided. They consist mainly of a regular series of short-range tasks, increasingly competitive in nature, each judged by the parent. Very common are behaviors with respect to eating a meal, taking a bath, getting dressed, greeting adults, trying to walk, investigating objects in the environment such as lamps, light sockets, things under the sink, stairways, etc. As the child is introduced to more formal activities, he begins to learn the idea of a goal to be strived for. This idea is in the activity, or in the reaction of others, and need not be established through speech. For example, before he can understand speech, the child is often given blocks and then shown that they can be piled in a column. His disposition to imitate provides the organization of his behavior. However, even when not imitating but just exploring the properties of the blocks out of curiosity, the child finds the parent interrupting his activity in ways which signify action and goal. Even a race with Daddy from the back door to the car establishes the sequence with no words necessary. The differential behavior of the parent provides the foundation for learning a competitive goal even before the child understands the words "You won" or "I won." Punishments, rewards, the sudden involvement of or change of reaction by the parent, and modeling all contribute to the nonlinguistic order in experience.

The linguistic order begins to accompany these experiences before it has any meaning to the child. However, the systematic occurrence of speech patterns and particular events permits the child to begin to relate the two. Much speech serves the function of punctuating the beginning and ending of sequences. As the child learns the references of nouns and processes, the speech signifies the order in which they are processed—subject-predicate-object, and then various qualifiers and transpositions. Once the child's thought can be evoked by speech, the immense potentialities for subvocal speech reflection on past events frequently replaces the situation-determined evocation of ideas. This new plane of experience vastly elaborates thought, but always in the same mode.

To suggest the possibility of change of mode of thought, some aspects of experience among the current generation of small children are instructive. Those children experiencing the most change today are surely the ones whose career-oriented mothers regularly take them to day-care centers or nursery schools. Here the structure of experience cannot be the same as in the traditional individualistic family. The adults are not the child's parents and have not the same investment in him. They have the responsibility for regulating the lives of a group of children of roughly the same age as a business enterprise. They cannot give anything like the same individual attention to each child. Their assessment of the children, still largely individualistic, is not based on the same criteria as are a parent's.

Inevitably, the child will find that he engages in group activities very frequently. Group activities have group, not individual, goals. They are inherently cooperative activities, except when groups compete against each other or their own past performance. Although the individualistic adults try to assess the effects individually, the activities often cannot readily or coherently be fragmented in this way.[25] Too much depends on interactions to assess individual responsibility. The interactions take on the quality of a system organized to attain the group goal. More frequently the responsibility has to be understood in group, not individual, terms. The pragmatic characteristic of thought begins to give way to the field or systemic. The judgmental quality transfers to the group and is rarely as immediate as with individual tasks. Comparison is less likely if all the children are engaged in action toward the group goal. Even if self-improvement of the group remains a standard, much more attention must be paid to the complex processes which it requires. The units of experience of the child are longer in duration and more complex in composition. Analysis is less significant than synthesis in attaining goals. A new mode of thought is incipient. However, during this transition from what sociologists have called the entrepreneurial to the bureaucratic society, children encounter both individualistic and new, more systemic organization of experience. Such inconsistency does not establish a new mode of thought, but probably no coherent mode or, at best, a compartmentalization of thought by settings. The mode may be more Individualistic at home and more systemic at the nursery. There is no way to integrate these two incipient modes. As the family as an institution disappears and public group child-rearing institutions develop, the individualistic mode of thought is destined to vanish and be replaced by some form of a more systemic mode.

Some of this process of change of mode of thought has been manifested in the discontent among some elements of current younger generations in the United States. They focus on the unacceptability of what they refer to as the "linear thinking" of older generations. Some social scientists have made similar observations:

Our language is oriented to the assertion of orderly relations of antecedent and consequent, or cause and effect, and largely biased in terms of linear relations.

Consequently, we are unable to express in language the ongoingness of multidimensional organized complexities such as organisms and personalities. (Frank 1970, 241)

I believe that scientists and scholars, as well as the children on the street, are shifting to a new way of thinking—a way that is dynamic rather than static, close-looped rather than linear, and the process is accelerating. (Senders 1978, 643–44)

Two manifestations of the changing mode of thought are the increasing concern with ecological systems and the need for long-range planning in government and business. The foregoing entails that worldview and mode of thought are intimately related. As what people think about changes substantially, the way they think about it also changes.[26] This view not only is consistent with the ideas of periodicity in human history and with structure in society but goes a considerable way toward defining what these terms mean.

3

Relativism of Knowledge

With the concepts of worldview and mode of thought presented in the previous chapter, the argument for revolution in social science proposed in Chapter 1 can be resumed. There is a revolution occurring in social science in the sense of a transition from one worldview and mode of thought to another. As the conception of science or, rather, the formalized means to the understanding of experience, is always a logical derivation from a worldview, the revolution entails transition to a new conception of science. The focus of this change currently is manifest in the issues of realism versus relativism of knowledge.

In their present forms, these issues have become stagnant and offer little possibility of resolution. The fault lies with advocates of both positions. The realists have proceeded from unexamined assumptions. The relativists have not provided an adequate conceptualization of the key ideas of ways of thought and of the incommensurability of them. Utilizing the concepts of worldview and mode of thought presented in the last chapter, it is possible to clarify the issues and offer resolutions of them.

The key to the central issue lies in the recognition that it is about *sources* of knowledge. For the realist, the scientific method is the only source of valid knowledge. For the relativist there are both knowledge and mode of thought prior to and determining of the scientific method. If worldview is understood to be this prior knowledge, then the issue can be restated as follows: Does the scientific method produce knowledge of reality or does knowledge of reality (worldview) produce the scientific method? To put it in less ethnocentric terms, do the practices by which members of a human group consciously and systematically attempt to understand experience determine their view of reality, or do their worldview and mode of thought determine their investigative practices? The many forms of the issue currently being debated and the various arguments advanced can be clarified and resolved more readily using this definition.

In attempting these resolutions the realist position is explicated first. Several problems of this position are identified. The relativist view of knowledge is then presented. The relativist conception of science and its major implications are explained. The possibilities of commensurability or incommensurability of worldviews and modes of thought are addressed.

THE REALIST VIEW OF KNOWLEDGE

Realists recognize two forms of knowledge—common sense and scientific. The latter is regarded as valid knowledge of reality. Common sense is regarded as knowledge acquired in daily living via weakly controlled or biased observations. It is rarely understood as systematic in form, consisting, instead, of unrelated beliefs about the relationships among things.[1] It may be shrewd or foolish. Only testing via the scientific method can reveal which. This method consists of the following steps: (1) hypotheses concerning the causal relationships among two or more observable phenomena; (2) experimental test of the hypotheses by use of scientific procedures; (3) establishment and accumulation of facts by confirmation of hypotheses; (4) intuitive discovery of principles underlying sets of facts; (5) accumulation of valid principles by experimental testing of them; (6) construction of microtheories via intuitive relating of sets of principles explaining sets of facts; (7) verification of microtheories by deriving hypotheses and testing them experimentally; (8) intuitive construction of middle-range and then general theory capable of explaining the total set of facts; and (9) verification of general theory by deriving hypotheses and testing them experimentally. Verified general theory constitutes ultimate valid knowledge about human reality.[2]

There are two major problems raised by the realist view of knowledge. One concerns the treatment of commonsense knowledge. The other is the inadequacy of the rationale for the scientific method. They will be taken up in this order because it will be shown that the latter rests on the realists' failure to understand the former.

Realism and Common Sense

The problem that arises for the realist position from its recognition of commonsense knowledge stems from its peculiarly cavalier attitude toward it. Regarding it as a set of relatively unrelated hunches or inadequately based beliefs utterly obscures for them the role it plays in life. In fact, this attitude stacks the cards heavily in favor of the authority of scientific knowledge. It does so only by ignoring the basis on which daily life is led, for it is commonsense knowledge (worldview) that guides the overwhelming majority of human behavior, including that of the social scientist. It provides the bases for the way he raises his children, interprets the behavior of those around him, understands what his government is doing, anticipates the future, etc. The most important decisions he makes throughout life are based on common sense. Yet he appears to regard it as a lot of questionable speculation that should be subjected to scientific verification. Such verification will be established only in the indefinite future. He sometimes tries to justify his view by pointing to examples of research that do not confirm commonsense ideas.[3] The glibness of this treatment of commonsense knowledge by the realist is matched by his remarkable lack of interest in understanding where it comes from or what its characteristics are. For scientists who generally show so great a concern for rationality, this seems a glaring inconsistency.

A second aspect of the problem for realists in their treatment of commonsense knowledge is their neglect of its central role in the conduct of science (Smedslund 1980). There are key steps in the scientific method in which common sense appears to make fundamental contributions. First, there is the question of the source and nature of hypotheses. Realists claim that hypotheses are really just hunches or notions that occur to the scientist about relationships among variables. They usually assume that their origin lies in some chance or semicontrolled observations. What are never considered are the classification systems that define what variables there are and what sorts of relationships among particular variables are considered.[4] For the realist, the systems are either taken for granted or ignored in favor of the operational definitions that stand for them. Which notions get tested also doesn't matter to the realist, for all relationships among variables are regarded ultimately as manifestations of the principles underlying observable events. If confirmed by experimentation, they contribute to the store of facts to be explained. On the other hand, the realist is content to assume that, whatever their origins, the hypotheses tested somehow constitute unbiased sampling of relationships.[5]

Commonsense knowledge also plays a role in the selection of operations and procedures in experimentation. Realists are very concerned about these aspects of science. However, many of the key controversies and unsolved issues in every social science come from them. There are, for example, serious doubts about the assumption that behavior in the laboratory is representative of behavior in natural settings, the adequacy of criteria of validity of measures, the uniformity of approach to the experiment among subjects engendered by instructions and administrative procedures, the representativeness of sampling of populations, and the assumptions behind statistical analyses. It requires little reflection to realize that a host of implicit assumptions is entailed. When controversies arise, there seems to be the implicit assumption of some agreed upon framework of thought for discussing them. Only their cavalier attitude toward commonsense knowledge allows realists to neglect its role in both everyday life and in scientific practice.

The rapid development of a transitional period in American history has obscured the recognition of the place of worldview in social science. The changing experiences of younger generations and the accumulation of anomalies has so weakened the conviction of social scientists in one or another aspect of the individualistic worldview that they are disposed to think of their research as the means for establishing conviction. The increasing decline of order in experience produces the possibility of questioning all aspects of the prevailing worldview. Yet the paradigm of normal social science retains its individualistic bases. The result is that research on virtually any hypothesis is acceptable, but, whatever its results, some social scientists can readily suggest weaknesses in the design based primarily on the neglect of potentially contributing variables. Some of the impetus for these criticisms comes from the old implicit framework and some from experience of a changing society. At the same time, the behaviors of members of a society that, taken together, constitute a pattern which is the group way of life are treated as if they were independent fragments. Inevitably, the researcher is neglecting a great many contributing variables. The primary finding of all this research is that more research is needed. The more any researcher becomes involved in his area of specialization, the more aware he becomes that more research means a great deal of research—indeed, a program of research that will take many years. What such a realization means is that the implicit interrelationships of all variables comprising the determination of behavior in a situation, even the strange situations of the social scientist's laboratory, are gradually becoming explicit. However, working in a transitional period in which both old and new patterns of interaction are occurring, the social scientist can become only bewildered, which strengthens his belief that only scientific research can end the confusion. It is an utterly vain hope. What is happening is that inconclusive research continues frantically pending the end of the transitional period when a new worldview will emerge among younger generations. It will reveal the futility of the vast bulk of the research of previous generations and reject the whole normal paradigm. The new normal paradigm will be used to solve the puzzles which remain for the new worldview.

Realist Rationale of Scientific Method

The realist's justification for the validity of scientific knowledge, rarely thought about except when teaching introductory courses, presents another serious problem. For them it is simply an exercise in logical thought. The reasoning is essentially as follows: Any belief may be true or false because it may be based on inadequate or biased observation and reasoning. Without carefully controlled observation, we may arrive at an incorrect conclusion. We have to be on guard against believing what we may prefer to believe. Only conclusions arrived at by the scientific method avoid these errors. Scientific research ensures that only one conclusion can be drawn properly because it controls for other possibilities. The training and requirements for publication of research are the surest safeguards we know of against the introduction of personal bias, deliberate or inadvertent. No other basis for arriving at knowledge can make these claims.

Logical exercises occur only with given premises. What the rationale never provides are these premises. They are taken for granted because they are implicit. Only a little reflection is necessary to recognize that these premises are derivations from the beliefs of the individualistic worldview. They are: (1) All normal human beings have the capacity for rational thought; (2) this capacity permits valid knowledge of physical reality; (3) it can be corrupted by sloth or other temptations of the human passions; (4) the exercise of moral willpower can resist these temptations; and (5) as temptation is ubiquitous and often subtle, individual research must be subject to verification by others. Moreover, in case the individual fails to resist temptation and departs from these criteria, the requirements of review and replication reveal it and prevent false knowledge from being officially disseminated.

The two problems just discussed for the realist view—its disinterest in the origins, nature, and role of commonsense knowledge and its obliviousness of the premises from which its rationale of scientific knowledge is derived—focus attention on the key assumptions on which it is based. These are the assumption of a universal human reason and the assumption that this reason can know physical and social reality. The issue of realism versus relativism of knowledge is about the validity of these assumptions.

Realism and Universal Reason

Realists have properly criticized relativists for their failure to provide a clear conceptualization of the idea of different ways of thought among different human groups or of the idea of incommensurable paradigms of science. It should be recognized that the realists are guilty of the same failure from their side. Nowhere have they provided a conceptualization of the universal human capacity for reason. It is a belief that simply has been taken for granted. No doubt this is at least partly due to the impact of the theory of evolution. With its emphasis on the survival or extinction of species, it tends to emphasize species-wide characteristics conducive to survival. As a result, much thinking in the social sciences about humans has been disposed to postulate fixed traits. It is an easy, if dubious, leap to the assumption of universal reason and equally easy and dubious to the assumption that that capacity is the one which is manifested in Western

civilization. A quite different conception of human reason will be presented shortly. What is important here is that it be recognized that realists
have just as great a responsibility as do the relativists to present a case for
a particular view of human reason consistent with the theory of evolution.

Realist Conceptions of Natural and Social Reality

The realist view of reality is rooted in the dualism of the individualistic
worldview even though many realists today reject or question it. In that
worldview there are physical and spiritual substances. Only the former are
subject to scientific study. The human being is comprised of both—a spiritual soul/mind existing temporarily in a physical body. When the body
dies, the soul/mind lives on in another nonphysical realm. Human reason
is part of the soul/mind. Therefore, it implicitly exists outside the physical
realm and can be applied to that realm objectively, that is, as a nonparti-
cipant observer of it. This is the implicit basis of the realist conception of
natural science, which includes human biology. In the individualistic
worldview, the human being is partly of both worlds—the physical and the
spiritual. Hence, social science is fundamentally different from natural science. It can study and *describe* the arrangements humans make to meet
their physical needs (the economic), manage the conflicts which individual
needs and passions engender (the political), reproduce, raise, and train
children, etc. (the social). However, it need not scientifically *explain* all
this because it is based on free will. The individualistic worldview contains
all that is necessary to explain these arrangements, given the environmental conditions. Individualists have no difficulty explaining communist, fas-
cist, or democratic governments, free enterprise or collectivistic economies, Machiavellian behavior or the contemplation of the spiritual by
religious hermits, nunnery, or prostitution, etc.

The realist's view of knowledge rests on residual beliefs of the individualistic worldview. That worldview establishes what exists to be scientifically explained and the basis on which it can be explained. It separates
human thought from the physical world. It defines human thought as universal and as a process familiar to that of individualists. On the other hand,
the physical world is regarded as existing independently of the social world.
It has its own principles or laws of functioning. All humans, no matter
which group they are members of or which particular physical environment they live in, encounter the manifestations of the same physical laws.
It follows that their attempts to apply the same universal human reason to
the understanding of these laws provides a basis for establishing the validity of the various views they develop. The reason they do not all come to
the same conclusions is that some do not make full and uncorrupted use
of reason. Many allow their reason to be distorted by emotions or pref-
erences or just do not use it to make the carefully controlled observations

necessary for proper conclusions. Nevertheless, possessing the capacity for reason and being exposed to the operation of the same physical laws, there must be a basis for a dialogue between any two human groups which has the potential for assessing the validity or invalidity of particular views. Whatever the language used by any group, the fact that they must have some way of talking about widely shared aspects of physical reality must provide a rational bridgehead across the language barrier. Moreover, the technological mastery of nature constitutes evidence of valid knowledge of its laws.[6]

As social scientists, gradually abandoning the dualism of the individualistic worldview, identified with the natural scientists, the same arguments are regarded as applying to their knowledge. The laws of human nature also can be discovered. The behaviors of the members of all human groups can be understood. Only the human emotions or passions can prevent mutual understanding among reasonable men, and all humans have the capacity to be reasonable.

What is remarkable to note about realists is that, even as the anomalies for the individualistic worldview moved their thinking away from dualism toward physical monism and thus made social science over in the image of natural science, *the separation of mind with its universal reason from physical reality persevered.* The possibility of discovering the truth about reality extended to human phenomena but the universal reason by which this could be accomplished was not regarded as part of the subject matter. Even today there is no psychology of rationality although there is a psychology of problem solving and an interest in the differences between child and adult thought.[7] There was no socioanthropology of rationality until the idea of relativism of knowledge was introduced although there has been an interest in the relationship of language to thought and in the difference between primitive and civilized thought.

Two pesky problems have arisen for the realist view of social science, neither of which has yielded satisfactorily to reason. The reason they arose and will not go away is that they challenge, in an indirect fashion, the paradoxical separation of the mind fre   nature. One problem is the issue of the subject matter of social science. This is couched in terms of experience versus behavior (Wann 1964). The phenomenological position that what most requires understanding is what individuals experience consciously rather than the mere movements of their bodies implicitly challenges social scientists to examine the workings of the conscious mind. The full implications of this challenge for the separation of mind from nature never have been grasped. Attention has been diverted to the scientific impossibility of observing experience and the dubiety of accepting verbal reports of experience as valid accounts of experience itself. Realist scientists are able in this way to ignore consciousness and focus on the task of explaining observable behavior. The preeminence of behaviorism has masked, if thinly, the unsatisfactory resolution of the issue.[8] The resolution has been to regard experience as epiphenomenal and therefore irrelevant to the understanding of behavior. The phenomenologically inclined have resisted it strenuously but ineffectively. In psychology a profound schism between experimentalists and clinicians developed. The realist scientist, thus, was left free to apply his "objective" capacity for reason to the discovery of the laws of human nature.

The other problem for realist social science comes from the phenomena of indeterminism, first in physics and then in its own disciplines. Indeterminism in physics has its main effect in its challenge to objectivity in the scientific method. It suggests that scientists are part of the subject matter they are investigating. How they conduct their research is a factor in its results. Most realists are able to ignore the idea primarily because it appears to be a phenomenon applicable only to the strange new world of subatomic physics. Those who do not ignore it find it a nagging, if peripheral, concern. Indeterminism burst on the scene in psychology with the "Rosenthal effect," later called "experimenter effects." Rosenthal (1964) revealed that characteristics of the experimenter himself played a role in the behaviors measured. In social anthropology it also was being recognized that the presence of the participant observer anthropologist was changing the nature of the culture he was studying. In these disciplines as in physics, perhaps more so, it has been possible for most realists to ignore the problem by treating it as mainly a matter of methodological ingenuity in particular kinds of research. The implications of indeterminism for the implicit dualism of reason and nature remains opaque for most realists. However, indeterminism has become an anomaly much more disturbing for others.[9]

Summary of the Realist View

The realist view of knowledge is seen to rest on two shaky foundations. First, it fails to recognize the role of worldview and mode of thought in human life in general and in the conception of science in particular. Second, it assumes implicitly a dualism of the rational mind and physical nature which allows for the belief that the mind can objectively, and therefore validly, discover the laws of nature, including human nature, by use of the scientific method copied from the natural scientists.

THE RELATIVIST VIEW OF KNOWLEDGE

The relativist challenge has developed slowly from a variety of sources. All of them, in one fashion or another, attack these two foundations of realism. However, they have lacked a conceptualization of mind adequate to support the challenge. Relativistic naturalism attempts to overcome this weakness with its conceptualizations of worldview and mode of thought. Its approach is based on the following points, which will be taken up in the order listed:

1. Physical monism is assumed. It entails that mind is included in physical reality. (The main issues of dualism versus monism are addressed in the next chapter, so the case for monism will not be presented here. For convenience, mind can be defined as central nervous system if it is recognized that no dualism of mind and body is intended, as the central nervous system is in constant and complex interaction with the remainder of the physical organism.)

2. Mind is comprised of a system of very, but not infinitely, flexible capacities for the representation of experience which can develop in a variety of forms dependent on the characteristics of the environment over time.

3. The environment of the developing individual is composed of human and nonhuman components *experienced as a matrix.*

4. Worldview and mode of thought are products of the interaction of the environmental matrix and the flexible capacities of mind.

5. There are two forms of knowledge—worldview knowledge of the reality behind experience and substantive knowledge consisting of explanations of the experienced manifestations of that reality.

6. The relativist conception of science is the systematic application of an explicit worldview to defined domains of observations for the purpose of constructing explanations of each domain. Research is conducted into phenomena that are not explainable in this manner.

7. There are laws of the functioning of both human and nonhuman components of physical reality that set limits on the forms that environmental matrices may take. The commensurability or incommensurability of worldviews and modes of thought is a function of *types* of environmental matrices.

8. There are limits to the understanding possible across groups even with commensurable worldviews and modes of thought. These are produced by indeterminism in the interaction of human groups.

Mind as Flexible Capacities

Central to relativistic naturalism is a view of human nature radically different from that of realistic individualism. It assumes that the human mind consists of a set of very flexible capacities which can develop in many different ways. (For a more complete account of flexible capacities, see Chapter 6.) How they develop depends on the order in the environment of the developing individual. The basic idea is that these are capacities for representing order and then processing these representations of it in interaction with it. The manner of processing is the mode of thought which itself is learned. An example of these capacities is representation of simultaneous patterning of objects and settings regularly encountered. These are forms of perceptual learning or object identification. There are also capacities to represent sequential patterning in experience, the relative probabilities of patterns and sequences, and similarities and combinations of patterns and sequences. And there is the capacity to represent the significance of experiences. Here it will have to suffice to point out that, in this view, emotion is most of what is significant in experience. (A conceptualization of emotions is discussed in Chapter 6.) Because the emotions can be conditioned, humans can learn attitudes toward a very broad range of things or concepts.[10]

That human capacities have great flexibility seems obvious from the wide range of environments to which humans can adapt, including considerable variations of conditions over time. Other evidence leading to the notion of flexible capacities are the noncyclical and polymorphous nature of human sexuality, the long period of dependence during which children learn the ways of their group, the diversity of human languages, and the long life span during which the behaviors of the individual change in many ways. Such observations, far from suggesting a fixed and universal form of human reasoning, suggest that the form of reason itself depends upon the flexibility of reasoning set by the nature of the capacities, but they are such as to permit a variety of worldviews and modes of thought. The flexible capacities of mind are one component of an interaction. The other is a conceptualization of environmental influences on human learning which can be used to understand the development of worldviews and modes of thought.

The Environmental Matrix

In the relativist view, unlike that of the realist, human experience is not dichotomized into encounters with the natural and with the social. The social is no less natural than the nonsocial. The individual is always born into some form of *relationship* of a group of humans to their nonhuman environment. Central to the relativist view is that the human and nonhuman aspects of environment are in constant interaction. The members of a human group are behaving in ways that alter their nonhuman environment over time. The latter operates so as to alter the ways of the human group over time.

A key difference between the realist's and relativist's views of reality is that relativists recognize that *the developing child's experiences of the nonhuman aspect of reality are always embedded in the matrix of the combined human and nonhuman environment.* The child does not learn about each separately. At birth he does not know there are two such aspects. He brings with him only his flexible capacities for learning about his environment. Just as the human and the nonhuman aspects of that environment are integrally related, so his learning constitutes an integrated understanding of them. That is to say, his way of understanding his nonhuman environment is never independent of his way of understanding his human environment. Thus, for example, while Individualists classified their environment in human, animal, plant, and inanimate categories, in other societies, bushes, trees, rocks, etc., may be regarded as animate.

The central point in the relativist view is that worldviews are constructed systems of beliefs about the reality behind appearances. The abstractions made by humans are understood as what explains the actual environmental matrix they encounter, including the sequence of it through the life span. The matrix of human and nonhuman environment in which any member of a human group develops is different from that of members of any other group and can change during his lifetime. The constructions possible to humans, therefore, do not even necessarily entail the idea that there is a fixed reality behind reality, that is, a set of laws or principles which apply always and forever.[11]

The realist dichotomy of the social and the natural which lies behind the ideas of a rational bridgehead and technological mastery of nature is the source of the greatest difficulty in resolving the issue of realism versus relativism because it refocuses attention from observation of the physical environment to the theories of modern physics and chemistry. Realists are so transfixed by the apparent mastery of nature which these theories provide that they fail to realize that they provide no explanations of natural phenomena at all. Were they to attempt to explain what is observable, they would quickly realize that the natural environments of many different human groups are very different. Moreover, they would note that these natural environments cannot be distinguished from the social life of the groups who live in them. Of course, for realists, both "the natural" and "the social" are just manifestations of the combinations of elementary particles under particular conditions. However, this does not explain why there are particular combinations in particular places and why they change the way they do over time. Not much interest exists for such explanation, and the reason is that realists are still fundamentally individualists. They are interested in manipulation and control of the environment, not in understanding it.[12] That is why the ecological movement is new and part of a developing new mode of thought.

Worldview and Substantive Knowledge

Relativistic naturalism recognizes that the effort to understand experience starts with a body of knowledge—the worldview—as well as with a mode of thought. Worldview consists of beliefs about the nature of reality—the principles behind appearances, for example, what kind(s) of substances there are that comprise every apparent thing, what classes of things there are, what human nature is, etc. This is a knowledge of possibilities, not actualities. It provides the range of possible explanations but no actual explanation of particular experiences. Thus it constitutes a set of intellectual tools for the construction of explanations given whatever materials the experiences provide. It is theoretical in that it is comprised of the terms and the propositions relating or defining these terms that are brought to all experience. Although experiences vary greatly, these tools remain the same. This theory is used to construct explanations of ranges of experience, that is, substantive knowledge. The beliefs of the worldview will establish what constitutes a meaningful domain of appearances to be explained.

The constructed accounts of actual experiences—these explanations, understandings, interpretations—are substantive knowledge. They tell us what we know about things and events as they have happened or been encountered, in other words, how to understand appearances.[13] For example, in relativist psychology the explanation of a person's personality at some period of time is substantive knowledge of that particular individual. He has that personality; that is why the total set of his behaviors occurred during that period. In relativist socioanthropology, the explanation of the role and institutional structure of a society is substantive knowledge of that particular society. Members of two different societies using different worldviews and modes of thought will develop different substantive knowledge about a common neighbor society which they observe. Substantive knowledge is relative to the tools with which it is constructed.

Relativist Conception of Science

The views of human nature, of the physical environment, and of knowledge in relativistic naturalism provide the basis for the derivation of a conception of science radically different from that of realism. The term "science" here refers to formalized, systematic efforts to understand appearances. This definition applies to realism as well as to relativism, but the latter recognizes that the task is one of the application of worldview.[14] The relativist conception consists of the following steps: (1) explicit worldview and mode of thought; (2) applied to worldview-defined domains of observation; (3) in order to construct explanations of each domain (substantive knowledge); (4) employing puzzle-solving research to phenomena which resist such explanation.

Scientific knowledge for the relativist is based on explicit, not implicit, worldview. The human scientist is always aware of the belief system that he is using to explain observations. He has critically examined it and consciously decided to use it in preference to any other. He has precise definitions of its terms. He has examined the internal consistency of its beliefs and formulated it in the most consistent way he can. Finally, he has carefully formulated it so as to include sufficient terms and beliefs to explain the broadest range of human phenomena of which his science is aware. Precision, internal consistency, and comprehensiveness are the criteria of the relative usefulness of belief systems. They replace the realist criterion of truth-falsity. This approach is not foreign to current realist social science. Members of every discipline are keenly aware of the relative merits of the various schools of thought with respect to these criteria of usefulness. A substantial amount of literature in each is devoted to criticism and defense of these alternative worldviews (or segments of them) on these grounds. However, realists use these only as criteria preliminary to the primary criterion of verification by experimental research.

Scientific vs. Lay Knowledge

If every individual holds a worldview and uses a mode of thought, and if these are very widely shared among members of a society, then it would appear that all members of a society are scientists producing scientific knowledge. It is worth noting that much of the work of academics in the disciplines of the humanities is as much an attempt to produce substantive knowledge, that is, explanations of observations of human phenomena, as is that in the social sciences. In relativistic naturalism, everyone does what scientists do, but only scientists do it with maximal precision, systematization, and comprehensiveness, in other words, with explicit worldview and mode of thought applied to intersubjectively agreed-upon units of observations.

Naturalistic Observation

The relativist scientist is trying to explain the same subject matter as the lay person—appearances of everyday life. He has his worldview and mode of thought to apply. There is, therefore, unlike the case in realist science, no reason to conduct experiments in order to establish the facts to be explained. For the relativist, such experimentation is merely observation of people in strange situations, that is, atypical environments. However, the relativist does need to carefully and systematically identify the appearances to be explained. The methodology of relativist human science is concerned with how these identifications are made. (This methodology is discussed in Chapters 10 and 11.) Once made, the worldview is applied to construct explanations of meaningful domains of the appearances. This is what the lay person and the realist scientist do in their everyday lives outside the laboratory but with an implicit worldview and without benefit of intersubjective agreement.

In establishing the observations within a domain which are to be explained by the application of worldview, the important issue arises of what constitutes an observation within a meaningful domain of observations. In the relativist view, an observation refers to behavior, including speech, on which there can be intersubjective agreement among human scientists. This behavior includes movements and utterances only. A general example might be that person X carried the sheaf of papers from desk X to counter Y and handed them to person Z, saying "Here are the A vouchers." Observations include only movements and utterances because inclusion of other aspects of observers' experiences, such as the intentions, feelings, thoughts of the observed person, etc., are aspects on which intersubjective agreement will be very unreliable. There are many possible inferences or interpretations of a sequence of movements and utterances even for members of the same stratum of the same human group. These cannot constitute the "data" of science. On the other hand, there seems little difficulty with intersubjective agreement on the movements and utterances themselves except, perhaps, for those that are extremely rapid. Special training and the use of equipment such as recorders or film, where necessary and possible, should minimize ambiguity.

It follows that relativistic naturalism is positivist only in the sense that it assumes that it is possible for those who share an explicit worldview and mode of thought to establish intersubjectively agreed-upon domains of observations, the explanation of which constitutes substantive knowledge. Such domains of observation are, therefore, empirically grounded but not by means of the experimental method. The observations are always guided by what their worldview dictates as things to be observed, meaningful domains, and the operation of their mode of thought. (See the discussion of roles and role analysis in Chapter 10.) Substantive knowledge is always knowledge only for those who employ the same means of constructing it.

Another important issue raised by this emphasis on observations as behavior and utterances concerns the place of phenomenal experience in human science. For reasons long advanced, such experience cannot constitute the observations to be explained by human science. No one can observe it except the person having the experience. Verbal reports of experience are unreliable for the following reasons: (1) The reporter may conceal some aspects of his experience; (2) the operation of defensive procedures may produce reporting only of the defensive derivative of the experience; (3) verbalizing is too ponderous a procedure to be able to report all of experience before it is forgotten; and (4) linguistic competence is never sufficient to verbalize all experience.

However, this does not mean that phenomenal experience is excluded from human science. It is excluded from the observations to be explained, but it is inevitably included in the worldview applied to explain the observations. That is, the existence and nature of phenomenal experience is and must be part of any worldview. For example, the idea that X is feeling grief because X has lost to death someone close is an inference based on the belief that there is an unobservable emotion called grief which occurs under specified conditions. That such beliefs are part of worldviews can be attributed to the phenomenal experience of every individual which is projected to others in a form mediated by the reflective capacity as it is developed in his group. (For a discussion of reflective capacity, see Chapter 4.) It follows that the worldview of phenomenal experience is relative and that the explanation of phenomenal experience is included in human science by inference from observed behaviors in situations.

Relativist human science is, therefore, interpretative science. It is interpretative because it starts with worldview knowledge and its attendant mode of thought which serve as the tools for the construction of the understanding of appearances. There is no possibility that these tools will not be applied to this task. Worldview knowledge and mode of thought cannot be suspended. However, relativist science is not interpretative in the sense in which that term has conventionally been used. It is not intuitive, subjective, or artful in the sense of providing a *verstehen* experience, as in the humanities. That kind of interpretation is what occurs when an implicit worldview is employed. Relativist interpretation is scientific in that it consciously and systematically applies an explicit worldview to carefully and systematically identified appearances. It is keenly aware of the forms of explanations at which it will arrive and of the way in which they are reached. Moreover, unlike current hermeneutic exercises in academia, interpretations of particular domains of observations occur within an explicit context that relates them to interpretations of all other domains. It is not, for example, interpretation of unrelated or only implicitly related fragments of history, or of isolated cultural patterns or customs, or of specific acts of individuals. The domains of meaning established by the worldview are domains within the overall context of meaning. This context is explicit.

Puzzle-Solving Research

Relativist science does recognize an important place for research. Its role, however, is not to establish truth but to assimilate unexplained observations to substantive knowledge. It is not based on the individualistic conception of causality. The great majority of this research aims at the refinement of theory. That is, it provides sets of specific terms and principles which account for variations within the terms and principles of the worldview. For example, the individualistic worldview assumes that humans are capable of remembering past experiences and also of forgetting them. Research on human memory fills in the specifics of which kinds of experiences under what types of conditions are remembered or forgotten. The refined worldview can then be applied to the explanation of observed variations of actual rememberings and forgettings.

Some research is addressed to accounting for anomalies, observations that appear to contradict or defy the beliefs of the theory. For example, individualists believe that humans are capable of perceiving reality veridically. Yet they perceive an unbent stick when placed in water to be bent and unbent when withdrawn. They also perceive puddles of water on the road during very warm days and yet they perceive no water as they get to the spot where the puddle was anticipated. Their worldview provides no way of explaining these observations. Research serves to modify the worldview by addition of terms or principles accounting for exceptions to the belief in veridicality of perception.

With the use of explicit worldview as compared to implicit worldview, the modification is one that preserves the internal consistency of the worldview. And the research itself is regarded as the provision of additional observations within the larger context of observations of meaningful domains. These observations are not treated independently but are added to the others, and explanation is of the total set. Relativist science does not discover isolated laws or principles which eventually may be integrated. It refines and elaborates the system of principles already in use. Of course, such research may only add to the list of anomalies observed. It also follows from the relativist view of science that the two kinds of knowledge humans have, worldview and substantive, are integrated. The substantive knowledge of appearances is valid knowledge in the sense that it is, except for anomalies, consistent with the abstract knowledge of the reality behind appearances that comprises the worldview. Consequently, substantive knowledge is knowledge on which action can be based with confidence. Substantive knowledge makes sense of appearances. Combined with worldview knowledge, it reveals what can be anticipated in the way of appearances, given hypothetical conditions.[15]

Commensurability of Knowledge

The relativistic naturalist, basing his reasoning on the beliefs in physical monism, psychological determinism, and flexible capacities for reason, rejects the possibility of knowledge of the truth about reality. Rejecting the belief in a universal human reason, the relativist believes that there can be no criteria that are independent of one or another worldview and mode of thought for the establishment of the validity of knowledge, including technological mastery of nature, nor a rational bridgehead across all human groups. For the concern about truth-falsity of knowledge he substitutes concern about the commensurability or incommensurability of different forms of knowledge across human groups or within a group across time. This concern moves attention to important new issues of the limits of human flexible capacities, the limits on the forms of appearances which the nonhuman environment can take, and the limits on the interaction of the two.

There is no rational bridgehead traceable to universally shared nonhuman reality because there are multiple human environments that include human groups and can be classified and characterized in many ways.[16] The argument for validity of knowledge based on technological mastery is equally ethnocentric. This is especially the case for the realist's dichotomy of physical and social realms of experience. If physical reality comprises both, then serious questions concerning mastery in Western civilization are raised. For example, the problems stemming from pollution of air and water, the cluttering of space, additives in foods, nuclear waste, creating stronger strains of bacteria, etc., must be included in the realist's balance sheet.

If different groups develop different worldviews and modes of thought because they develop in different environmental matrices, what are the possibilities that attempts to communicate with one another can result in a genuine and thorough understanding? Can there be limited forms of understanding? Is it possible that ways of thought are so incommensurable that nothing more than superficial understanding is possible? What are the conditions which enhance or interfere with the possibilities of understanding?

It would take another treatise to address all these questions. It will have to suffice to suggest some considerations which may point the way to more complete answers. One consideration concerns the limits on the flexibility of human capacities to develop different forms of reason. As humans are a species that has evolved out of the physical environment of the planet, these capacities cannot be infinite. They must be limited by the forms of learning and linguistic structures and processes of the central nervous system. If these capacities evolved to permit humans to cope with multiple environments through the human life span, then there must be some limits set by the capacities to organize the effects of experience into a useful system of thought and planning. There must be some limits set on the flexible capacities by the necessity to integrate their development.

Another major consideration must be the limits of the possibilities for the appearances that physical reality can take. Just as in humans there must be some capacity for representing order, there must be order to be represented. The known habitats of human groups do not vary infinitely. Nevertheless, they not only vary and vary across time, but can be varied significantly by their human inhabitants. There is, then, a habitat-inhabitant interaction which has double limits. There are almost certainly only a limited number of general forms that environmental matrices may take.

It seems very likely that these can be classified into types. The issue of commensurability-incommensurability of ways of thought then can be approached in terms of types of human-nonhuman environmental matrices. It seems likely that members of groups within a type will have considerable possibilities of commensurability of knowledge. The types may constitute a gradation of differences that entails a gradation of commensurability. For very different types there may be so great an incommensurability that virtually no understanding is possible. However, it should always be borne in mind that intergroup contact, no matter how limited initially, can produce a diffusion of elements which changes each group over time at an increasing rate and toward commensurability.

It is important to realize that understanding of one group by another is not the same as each group having a way of thinking about the other. Worldviews and modes of thought always provide ways of explaining experience. These ways determine how to relate to the other group. The greater the discrepancy between the types of environmental matrix, the greater the likelihood of conflict between two groups.

Indeterminism in human science sets another limit on commensurability. Any attempt to explain the behaviors of another group requires interaction that inevitably alters the behaviors of both groups over time. The subject matter of human science is not fixed. Nor are the worldview and mode of thought applied. Perhaps the greatest challenge to relativist human science is that of formulating an explicit theory that can make indeterminism determinate by principles of the dynamics of interaction between or among types of environmental matrices.

4

Naturalism of Subject Matter

Relativistic naturalism resolves the issue of mind-body dualism versus physical monism in favor of the latter. The basis of this position is the acceptance of the evolutionary theory of the origins of humankind. Our species has evolved out of the interaction of the mutated nature of previous species as it has been selected by its adaptability to its physical environment. Such interaction presupposes principles of physical function and process in the species, its environment, and in the relationship between the two. There is no necessity for, nor sound reason to, introduce the notion of spiritual substance into this process. The logical difficulties presented by postulating interaction between purely spiritual and purely physical substances are obviated. The now vast and growing evidence from observation of central nervous system processes and their relationships to self-reports of experience, limited as it is by the realist method, powerfully supports the view that phenomena of mind can be explained in physical terms.

The most profound obstacle to the acceptance of the position of physical monism today is the lag which occurs between a changing environment and persevering linguistic syntax and vocabulary. The small child inevitably will have to use the vocabulary and the syntax to which he is exposed even as the changing matrix of human and nonhuman order in his experience is rendering them less valid communications about it. The references of words change so that the words often are interpreted differently across generations. New vocabulary begins to emerge which is not integrated with the old. Nonlinguistic forms of communication increase in frequency. Yet the old worldview continues to intrude itself, enjoying the advantage of being the only fully developed form of meaning available despite its growing inadequacies. Thinking and speaking in terms of mind-body dualism and its corollaries continue to provide obstacles to the naturalist position. The naturalist cannot escape the responsibility inherent in his view to explain how the apparent duality of experience voiced in the terms of the individualistic worldview is only a manifestation of physical matter.

The task requires the resolution of three of the key issues generated by the anomalies to the individualistic worldview. It can be accomplished by taking the position of biological reductionism rather than emergentism, determinism rather than agency, and reasons as effects rather than as causes. They are discussed in this order.

THE RELATIONSHIP OF PSYCHOLOGY TO BIOLOGY

The existence in academia of the two disciplines of psychology and biology derives directly from the individualistic worldview. Biology is the natural science of the human physical body. Psychology was originally a social science of the spiritual mind. Through introspectionism psychologists tried to understand the relationships between phenomenal experience and physical stimulation. It was not long before the anomalies for mind-body dualism discussed in Chapter 1 produced a profound split in psychology between phenomenologists and behaviorists. The latter, partially abandoning the individualistic worldview, embraced determinism in human behavior, relegated phenomenal experience to the realm of the epiphenomenal, and initiated the issue of whether psychology is a natural or social science. Today one can find proponents of the view that psychology is a temporary science pending sufficient development of neurophysiology to replace it. One also can find those who regard the two sciences as independent, their final results to be compared eventually to reveal what relationship, if any, there may be. There also are those who take the view that psychology deals with phenomena that are emergent from the physical processes of the brain and that cannot be reduced to biological terms.

Relativistic naturalism takes the position of biological reductionism. It is that both psychology and biology are natural sciences in the relativist view of knowledge, that they are related on a dimension of abstraction-reduction, and that both are useful but for different purposes. This resolution is inescapable once relativism of knowledge is recognized. Worldview is prior to any formalized approach to knowledge and therefore determines its nature. Fundamental to all worldviews are abstract beliefs about human nature and variations of human nature among groups or individuals. These beliefs are regarded as the nature of reality and regulate everyday understanding of experience. Worldviews have their bases in the common elements of everyday experience through human childhood until the years following the major changes of puberty. They are based overwhelmingly on observed behaviors and very little on observations of biological functioning under the skin.

It follows that psychological explanation is prior to biological explanation. It also follows that establishment of biological science is a derivation from the psychology of a worldview. Biological science in attempting to explain human behavior takes its direction from the psychology of the worldview.[1] When a neuropsychologist investigates brain functioning, he is not simply "going in" to see what is there. He is looking for the physical bases of what he already thinks is there. He may assume, for example, that the brain contains structures and processes for the basic survival needs or drives such as hunger, thirst, etc. (Pribram 1971). He may assume that there is some mechanism by which the mind can direct the brain to control the body (Penfield 1975). He may assume that there are certain properties that correspond to particular personality characteristics, such as extraversion or introversion (Powell 1979). He may decide to look for the physiological bases of some set of emotions (Weil 1974). There is no way in which he can suspend some such framework for thinking about his subject matter. He is inevitably providing a biological account of psychological states and processes. Biology is the elaboration and refinement of the psychology of the worldview. It is a reduction of psychological terms to biological terms.[2]

For two reasons there is no possibility whatever that biological explanation will replace the psychological. One is that the psychological is prior and constitutes the main form in which experience is interpreted. The other is that biological explanation as a refinement of the psychological cannot explain any range of behavior without becoming impractically lengthy and complex.[3] Psychological explanation, arising in worldview as a shorthand for the commonalities in experience will remain the practical level of discourse. It is biological explanation at its most abstract levels of conceptualization. Biologists will always need such abstract levels just as the family doctor must explain to his patients the very complex states of their bodies in such general terms as migraine headache, mononucleosis, high blood pressure, encephalitis, etc. For special purposes, it is useful to move to the physiological language of biology. Both levels are needed and useful. Those who use the reduced level will often find it useful to move back and forth across the two levels, depending on the purposes of their discourse.

This view of the two sciences as related on a dimension of abstraction-reduction signifies the rejection of the idea of emergent processes of the brain. The concept of emergent processes can be understood as a characteristic transitional period effort to synthesize elements of the old worldview with those of an incipient new one. It has arisen out of the impact of the naturalistic view of human nature produced by the theory of evolution. If humans are entirely physical beings, a problem arises of how to understand phenomenal experience such as choice and consciousness in physical terms. The essence of the concept is that the physical components of the brain, in their complex interaction, produce these phenomena even though the phenomena, in turn, cannot be accounted for in terms of the properties of these physical components. That is, emergent processes are not reducible to the physical terms of neurophysiology. Significantly, these emergent processes are often referred to as mentalistic. Thus the concept serves to preserve the old mind-body dualism in a quasi-naturalistic form. It is not surprising, therefore, to find that some who espouse such views also continue to adhere to the belief in free will (Popper and Eccles 1978; Bandura 1989, 1991). Others are willing to abandon free will but view consciousness as an emergent process (Sperry 1985).

There is nothing wrong with attempting such syntheses. What else could be expected of responsible scientists and philosophers in the face of accumulating anomalies for the prevailing worldview? However, attempting syntheses and successfully achieving them are quite different matters. There is always the danger that the attempted syntheses become seductively satisfying so that critical examination is eschewed (Jaynes 1976, 13; Globus et al. 1976, 123). The problem with the concept of emergent processes is that it replaces the old dualistic dilemma of how the physical body can interact with the spiritual mind with a new dilemma of how the physical brain can produce phenomena that cannot be accounted for in physical terms. One possible explanation for the occurrence of this new dilemma is that it is due to the use of incompatible elements of two modes of thought—the individualistic and an incipient new one. The individualistic mode of thought analyzes experience into many discrete interacting parts with cause-effect relationships. In the natural sciences this is the Cartesian view of reality. The universe consists of a myriad of atoms combining and recombining in time and space. This appeared to serve very well as an approach to knowledge as long as the spiritual mind of humans was excluded from its purview. The human body could be approached in this way, leading most recently to a view of it as a sort of machine with replaceable parts, as in transplants and genetic engineering. However, when the phenomena of mind became subject to study by the scientific method, something strange happened. Rather suddenly, although there were precursors in biology and gestalt psychology, the idea of the whole being greater than the sum of its parts became very appealing to many academics. This appears to be a departure from the Cartesian model. It seems to be part of a new way of thinking reflected also, perhaps, in the rise of ecological concerns and international interdependence among nations. If the brain consists of physical components, what transplant or synthetic part could be introduced to cure problems of consciousness? Presumably, a whole new brain would be necessary, a solution certain to produce considerable revulsion once it moves from the realm of science fiction to medical consideration. What complications are introduced by the anomalies of unconscious processes so powerfully introduced by psychoanalytic theory of human behavior, or by recognition of aphasias, or by split-brain research?

It is not proposed here that the reducibility of the psychological level of conceptualization to the biological has the merit of preserving the Cartesian model and incoporating the mind into it. Far from it. This view is part of a new worldview which will have its own mode of thought, very much along the lines of the ecological interdependency type of thought just beginning to emerge. It will replace, not incorporate, the Cartesian model and be incommensurable with it. Thus, the dilemma presented today by the concept of emergent processes within a general Cartesian context will be obviated. What are now called mentalistic phenomena will be recognized as only biological explanation at its most abstract level of conceptualization which is reducible to less abstract levels.

Psychological explanation, then, is naturalistic explanation. This level of conceptualization will be used in the following account of the phenomena which lead individualists to the belief in a spiritual mind. It potentially can be reduced to the physiological level of explanation. It is not suggested here that this is currently possible except minimally. Nor is it claimed that what follows constitutes more than a very general account which points to the direction which a more adequate naturalistic account could take. A major goal of this book is to encourage interested social scientists, biologists, and humanists to participate in the formulation of theory for human science. If what follows has cogency, it will provide a viable alternative to mind-body dualism and can be elaborated more fully in the future.

NATURALISTIC EXPLANATION OF SPIRITUAL MIND

Attentional Processes

The key term in a naturalistic account of mind is "attentional processes." This is because, for the individualist, mind is synonymous with consciousness—what the person is aware of—and attentional processes determine the content of consciousness.[4] Because he regards mind as human reality, and because he believes mind is always functioning except under very rare conditions, for example, when asleep or in a coma, he feels no need to explain consciousness any further. Neither does he feel that the various altered states of consciousness now of interest to psychologists and biologists require any changes in his view of human nature, although some hypnotic phenomena are perplexing. He believes that the body, when functioning normally, influences the mind in many ways. Altered states of consciousness are readily understood as due to abnormal functioning of the physical body, such as in drugged, injured, or surgically impaired states. Consequently, any attempt to account for mind in naturalistic terms constitutes an attempt to explain consciousness.

Attentional processes become key ideas because they have considerable potential for doing so. They suggest an integral relationship between what we are conscious of and what we attend to. For individualists this idea carries no threat because what we attend to is a matter of free will. However, naturalists consider attentional processes as physical capacities subject to formulable principles of functioning. If the phenomena of spiritual mind can be accounted for, even in a general way, in terms of attentional processes, the great mystery of consciousness is at least substantially clarified and a naturalistic alternative is identified. Attentional processes are now receiving a great deal of attention in the new cognitive psychology. Unfortunately, it occurs in the realist vein. Consequently, the approach is fragmented and lacks a conceptual context of the functioning of the total person. The following discussion of attentional processes borrows heavily from cognitive psychology but carries well beyond it by suggesting their place and function in a larger context.

Attentional processes constitute one set of capacities of the person as a physical organism. They function to select some of the momentary information that enters the ongoing organization of the total body. The selected information serves to maintain or modify the ongoing organization of the body and therefore the observable behavior of the person.

Attentional processes have at least the following properties:

1. The amount of information that can enter in one unit of attention is very brief, but attention is extremely labile. Consequently, for relatively stable sources of information, the attentional processes can select large amounts. However, for fleeting sources of information, only limited amounts can enter before much information becomes unavailable.

2. Attentional processes include direction to particular sources and inhibition of other sources. Since amount of information in any unit of attention is limited, which sources of information are attended to and which are inhibited are critical for ongoing organization. This property is what is commonly referred to in such expressions as "concentrating on something" and "shutting out distractions." It includes the capacity to inhibit extero- and interoception at the periphery of the nervous system—a person may not see, hear, feel, taste, or smell in environmental conditions which, under other conditions, would produce such experiences.

3. Attention to particular sources of information may be directed innately or by conditioning. That is, humans are born with innate capacities to have attention directed by certain conditions such as large changes in the intensity of stimulation, by movement, or by contrast and contour in vision, etc. They also can learn to direct and inhibit their attention in particular ways under particular conditions.

4. Attention can be directed to conditions affecting exteroceptors, interoceptors, or states and processes of the central nervous system itself. That is, attention can be directed to thoughts, images, and feelings. It also can be inhibited selectively with respect to them.

5. The vast majority of the functioning of attentional process in humans is conditioned (learned). The organization of conditioned attention is very intricate. It is determined by the environmental matrix in which the individual develops. That is, there is order and pattern in the way in which any person's attention is directed most of the time. Therefore, the information used is highly selective.

A naturalistic account of the individualistic idea of mind leans heavily on attentional processes. However, it also draws on processes and principles of the learning of concepts and beliefs about the self, memory, and the role of speech in learning.

Components of the Individualistic Idea of Mind

There appear to be four distinguishable aspects of spiritual mind in individualistic thought. In the academic literature two or more often are confounded and given one of the following labels. This account, therefore, differs somewhat in the use of terminology.

Subjectivity is the sense that one exists as a being who is constantly having experiences, including the experience of self. This has been called the idea of the "constantly observing 'I'."

Dualism refers to the experience of being a composite of a physical body and a nonphysical mind. The experience that thoughts and some images and feelings, such as awe, inspiration, wonder, and hope, occur independently of bodily states, while there are other experiences directly related to bodily states and external events, such as hunger, fatigue, lust, anger, fear, etc. This includes the experience that bodily states can strongly influence thought and that thought can control the behaviors of the body, even to the extent of causing death, as in martyrdom.

Choice is the experience of deliberation, problem solving, and decision making as a process distinct from but related to bodily and external events that terminates in the establishment of a goal to be attained or a course of action to be implemented. It includes the experience of strong doubt, uncertainty, conflict of goals, and vacillation accompanied, during the process, by the sense of being the one who must make the decision and afterward as the one who has made it.

Will denotes the experience of investment, intention, determination to attain goals or to implement courses of action even in the contemplation or anticipation of great difficulty and discomfort. This sometimes includes the determination to implement a course of action other than that expected by others only because they have such expectations.

Subjectivity

The environmental matrix of the individualist is usefully characterized as competitive, comparative individualism. Individualism means that each

adult member of the society is regarded and regards himself as responsible
for his fate in life. In assessing his fate he uses the comparative mode of
thought. He thinks in terms of being better or worse off than before or
than others and aspires to higher status. He understands his fate as a matter of his own characteristics which can be changed by the exercise of his
will. His fate in life depends on how he fares in constant competition with
others and himself for rewards which are inherently scarce. The members
of each individualistic generation learn to understand themselves, others,
and the meaning of life in these terms.

To do so requires that early experience heavily emphasize the self as a
focus of attention. There is no reason to assume that a child will ever
develop on his own a concept of the self. Its development requires that
his physical entity frequently be the focus of attention and that the child
learn how to think about it. The basis of subjectivity in individualistic
thought is the conditioning of the child's attention to the concept of himself. He must learn to observe his behavior, characterize it in a variety of
ways, assess its worthiness, reason out how it can be improved, and resolve to achieve these improvements.

This learning develops around the primary socializers' frequent direction of the child's attention to himself by characterizing his behavior and
its consequences as something caused by him and revealing his characteristics. The characteristics are judged as desirable or undesirable, and the
directions for changing them are indicated. Perhaps this is most clearly
revealed by the nature of the report card in American elementary schools.
The competitive comparative achievement in school subjects is commonly
indicated in one section in terms of letter grades. The grades constitute an
achievement status system, so that the child understands how he compares
with others and with his own past performances. Another section of the
report card indicates the characteristics he has and doesn't have which
account for his level of achievement—for example, concentrates well, is
careful, is thorough, pays attention, accepts criticism well, etc. It must be
recognized that a similar process of characterization of the child has been
going on in the home for several years prior to formal schooling. These
ways of thinking about self and others are supplemented by vicarious experiences of observing assessments of siblings, peers, and figures in storybooks.

The central feature of this learning is that the child has his attention
conditioned to move from observation of the effects of his behaviors—
such as spilling something, making something, helping with something—
to his behaviors—helping, spilling, making—and then to himself—you did
X. The self is simultaneously characterized in a variety of ways, each of
which is judged as desirable or undesirable, which for the child means
acceptance or rejection by important others. This learning is constantly
elaborated in the form of suggesting or commanding ways to change the

self. The result is an increasingly complex self-system of thought to which attention is directed frequently as the child at first observes his behavior and later anticipates behavior. The nature of the thought process is something like the following sequence: experience . . . I caused it . . . it means this about me . . . it is desirable or undesirable . . . what should I do about myself. So fundamental is this learning that the individualist directs his attention to himself following many experiences in which he only observes the behaviors of others or of anything. There is a sort of transition from "I caused X" to "I observe X" in these cases. This is the basis of subjectivity.

Yet such learning is relative to the environmental matrix of individualism. Individuals in other societies can have their attention conditioned in quite different fashion. It may be such as to make the self a much less significant element of thought. The whole process is largely linguistically directed, with the result that the individualist becomes capable of talking to himself, overtly or subvocally, in a similar fashion to the way in which his socializers spoke to him. It appears that subjectivity depends on such speech, and that is where individualists get their view of human rationality. The speech has the structure of the mode of thought, and even subvocal speech captures attention. Thus the person, whenever his thought is so driven by speech, regards himself as reasoning. However, languages differ in their syntax as well as in their vocabularies and do so systematically with other characteristics of the total environmental matrix. The functions which speech serve vary markedly in different groups (Hymes 1979). There is no reason to assume that it is universal to humans to have subjectivity as individualists understand it.

Equally important in understanding subjectivity is that it is illusory. The individualistic child's attention is not conditioned to his self-system for every behavior or experience, only for those regarded as significant by his socializers. Thus in many instances the child has experiences which do not condition attention to his self-system. They are merely experiences much as one might assume occur to animal species lacking linguistic capacities. A tiger may be assumed to have the experience of seeing a deer in a grove of trees or of drinking at a water hole. There is no reason to assume the tiger has the experience "I am seeing a deer in the grove" or "I am drinking at the water hole." There is no reason to believe that animals without speech have a self-concept at all. So, with humans who do have a self-concept, there is no reason to assume that it is constantly evoked by experience. The remarkable thing about the learning of a self-system is that it results in the person having two basic types of experience—those that include and those that do not include the evocation of the self-system. What is remarkable about this is that when the experience does not invoke the self-system, the individual not only does not experience subjectivity, but he is unaware that there is no subjectivity. A person cannot have an experience and at the same time think "I am not aware that I am having this experience." To have that thought would be to be aware of having the experience. As a result, subjectivity appears constant when it is not.[5] The individualist's belief in subjectivity is an illusion, although possibly among all humans in various groups, his subjective experiences are the most frequent.

One of the reasons why individualists are convinced about the "constantly observing 'I'" is that part of their self-system is that they have a self-system. That is, they are aware that this "constantly observing I" is sometimes observing the self. They call this "self-consciousness" and believe it is a characteristic which can be too highly or too little developed. Small children often manifest a spontaneous lack of self-consciousness which would be inappropriate in an adult. On the other hand, an adult may be too self-conscious, with the result that his preoccupation with thoughts about self hinders his attention to the task at hand. The difference to the individualist is between having the experience "I see X working diligently" and the experience "why don't I work diligently?" In many cases the latter thought directs the person's attention away from the work reinforcing the experience of not working diligently. Depressive rumination in individualists may be the most extreme example of such self-consciousness. However, it is not evidence for the "constantly observing 'I'." It is evidence for the human capacity to reflect on reflection.

The reflective process is almost certainly dependent on the linguistic capacity of humans. It is essential to the development of a self-system. It is thinking about experience. Humans learn how to think about experience. Tigers do not. Tigers think in the sense of forming percepts, expectancies, attitudes, scripts. But they do not think about these thoughts. Humans do. To do so, they have to have experiences from which they learn how to think about such thoughts. They have to learn to characterize, to classify experience. This is what sharing the language of one's group produces. Whatever the actual nature of the states and processes of the human body, members of all human groups learn to characterize them in one way or another or, rather, some of them or some parts or combinations of them. It has its basis in the human ability to abstract common elements from experience and represent them. However, which common elements of many complex experiences are abstracted will vary with the human group. Each has its own system of classification. The child in any group will hear his experiences characterized in systematic form. That is because his socializers already have learned to classify experience and believe that the child has the same types of experience. For example, all groups will have terms for what we call emotions. They will not classify such feelings in the same way, but they will have some way.[6] The child will be aware of having feelings, and he will hear words which represent the way others characterize feelings. If a dog, let us say, has knocked a child down and made him cry, the next time a dog approaches the child, the child will show some effects of that experience. Others may think the dog will not knock the child down, and so they say, "Don't be afraid, it is a nice doggie." "Be afraid" is their way of characterizing the child's complex current experience. The child will learn to believe that he has the capacity to experience the emotion of fear. It is important to note that the characterization is not of overt behavior of the child but an inference from his behavior about an unobservable inner state or process. The child's attention probably is innately directed to emotional states, but he has no way of thinking about them at first. From such experiences the child learns to characterize these states. That constitutes the beginnings of the reflective process. Then, however, the child can learn to think about these inner states, about what they mean. This is reflection on reflection. The sequence in this learning is something like: the experience of an emotional state . . . I am afraid . . . I am a sissy if I am afraid in this situation, or why am I frightened so easily. It is a hierarchical, not a linear process, in that it moves to more abstract levels of characterization. Reflection on reflection occurs because human attention can be directed to thought, and a reflection is a thought. Potentially, the process is endless. There might be reflection on reflection on reflection. In actuality, it is doubtful that humans normatively ever do more than reflect on reflection.[7]

It is not hard to imagine how the individualistic child learns to reflect on reflection. As his behavior is characterized, it is judged as desirable or undesirable. For him this amounts to being rejected-punished or accepted-rewarded. Before he has any way to reflect on these characterizations and judgments, he can only dwell on their consequences. Individualistic parents use such terms for this as pouting, sulking, showing off, etc. They react to such behavior, providing the child with ways of thinking about his reflections on self—such as, "Nobody likes a show-off," "Don't be a baby," and "Pay attention." Later on, he finds himself characterized as a daydreamer, or moody, or too self-conscious. He learns that he should do something constructive to improve his character. If he does not translate his reflection on reflection into action, he is too self-conscious. If he does not reflect on reflection enough, he lacks the necessary self-consciousness.

It is important to emphasize that of all the states and processes that an individual can experience, which aspects of them he learns to characterize and reflect on will be relative to his environmental matrix. They also always will be selective in the sense that not all of such experience will become part of the self-system. For example, there appears to be little reflection on imagery in individualists. There is some talk about imagination, but it seems more related to problem solving than to imagery. Individualists often think they know what someone is thinking but rarely, if ever, what is his imagery. In other human groups reflection on imagery may play a much larger role. There is the suggestion from the lives of artists, musicians, and hallucinatory persons that imagery can play such roles.

To summarize, the subjectivity of individualists results from a very highly developed self-reflective process which includes reflection on self-reflection. However, it is an illusion inevitable in self-reflection that there is a "constantly observing 'I'." The admonishments to "think about what you are doing" or even about "what you are thinking" and to "take responsibility for your actions" condition the individualist's attention to his self-system a great deal of the time. But it is selective, not constant, and a result of development in a particular environmental matrix.

Dualism

Individualists are introduced to the terms mind and body very early in life. However, what these terms mean must be established by a long, complex history. The key appears to be in the communication of three related but distinct referents of the terms "you" or the child's name. These referents are (1) the child's physical body, excluding the idea of brain, (2) the child's mind as distinct from his body, and (3) the two taken together.[8] Consequently, the child learns to think of himself as comprised of two distinct but related components.

The experiences which produce these conceptual distinctions in the child are many and rest on quite specific distinctions. The child learns early that "you" refers to a particular object which corresponds to a body image, but the word occurs in many different contexts. Sometimes he hears speech about "your foot," "your ear," "your tummy." Sometimes he hears speech about "your mind," "your thought," "your imagination," "your intentions," "your expectations," "your ideas," "your feelings." The latter have no physical referents for the child. That both types of referents are spoken of in the possessive form "your" implies that both are aspects of himself. In addition, sometimes the child's body is punished, and at other times the punishment does not involve any localized bodily pain but hurts all the same—that is, psychological punishment, such as rejection or deprivation of pleasures. Sometimes the child experiences only the word "you" accompanied by a pointed finger or eye contact—"I'm talking to you," "he means you," or "what are you up to?" In these cases there appears to be a third referent that is not clearly distinguished from or encompasses the other two.

These early experiences provide a strong foundation for the clarification of mind-body dualism in later years. Then, more sophisticated terms are introduced to the child, such as spunk, initiative, drive, stick-to-itiveness, heart (as in "you gotta have heart"), or in sayings such as "sticks and stones may break your bones but names can never hurt you" and "beauty is only skin deep." It is likely that only in adolescence does all this experience become integrated with the set of experiences around formal religious terms like body and soul.

This learning is all reflective and dependent on speech. Memory processes play an important role. They recapture past events which can be reinterpreted in the more sophisticated ways developed later. A key aspect of the whole process is the juxtaposition of explanations of the behavior of nonhuman creatures in different terms. This process initially is badly confused for individualistic children by the anthropomorphism of children's stories as well as the inconsistencies of trying to get across moral lessons by attributing goodness and badness to the family pet or other animals, germs, etc., which threaten or help humans in one way or another. Nevertheless, over time it becomes clear to the child that the behavior of other creatures is explained in a fundamentally different fashion. Terms like "mind," "imagination," "thought," and "feelings" are not appropriate. Other terms like "instinct," "survival," "nature," "made that way," "savage," "dumb," etc., are substituted for properties of mind.[9]

At the same time, a distinction emerges between terms like "want," "need," "desire," and other terms formerly distinguishing mind from body. While these terms have no clear physical referents themselves, they often are coupled with references to states of the body, such as hunger, fatigue, sweet tastes, pain, thirst, and sexual stimulations. They constitute the initial basis for the idea of temptations of the body. These are interpreted for the developing child as physical states that may dispose him to do or to think bad or wrong things. At the same time, he is learning that another nonphysical part of him can resist these passions—for example, "You lied instead of telling the truth because you were afraid you'd be punished," or "You got mad and hit your little brother instead of telling Mommy he ate your lollipop." These feeling states in this way become attributes of the physical body and distinct from other states referred to as "behaving yourself," "doing right," "thinking it over," "remaining calm," "self-discipline," "reason," "sensibleness," and "knowing what is right and wrong." The essence of mind as distinct from body thus becomes reason, which can decide what is right or wrong, sensible or foolish. In this development the learning of the ideas of choice and will play important roles.[10]

Choice

The essence of individualistic choice is the sense of having a choice rather than of choosing. Choice is the awareness of and consideration of alternative possible goals or courses of action. It has to do more with the process of deliberation, anticipation of consequences, and arriving at a decision than with the final settlement. It includes the sense of the freedom to select any of the goals or courses of action. It has the quality "I could do this or I could do that. What do I want to do?" In this sense, it is what often is implied by the term "free will," which would be better rendered as "free choice." The definition of free choice is: The behavior of a person in a situation is as likely to occur as any other behavior that the person considers at the time and of which he is capable.

The choice is free and it is made by an act of will alone. The phrase "any other behavior that the person considers at the time" refers to the alternatives which occur to the person in the decision-making process. The phrase "of which he is capable" distinguishes fantasized goals or courses of action, the skills or opportunities for which the person lacks, from those requiring skills or opportunities which he has. The definition is contrasted to that for psychological determinism, which is: The behavior of a person in a situation could not have been other than it was, because it was the product of the interaction between what the person brought with him to the situation from previous experience and the properties of the situation.

The phrase "what the person brought with him to the situation from previous experience" refers to his total bodily state at the time, which includes the potential for a new bodily state in the given situation. It also includes the possibilities for the occurrence of *ideas* of alternative behaviors. However, the basis for the behavior which occurred rather than any other also is included. That is, the decision is predetermined by the cumulative and sequential interaction of the inherent capacities of the person (defined to exclude free choice) and the environmental matrix in which he develops. The properties of the situation (objectively defined) play a key role in determining the subjective definition of the situation.[11]

The challenge to relativistic naturalism is to provide an explanation in physical terms for the individualist's *belief* that he has a free choice. The explanation has two main elements. One is the learning of multiple expectancies, each with its own significance, in a situation. The other is learning to reflect on the memory of the decision-making process and its resultant determined behavior in terms of having a free choice. Obviously, this approach implies substantial segments of a psychological theory. To explicate them here would be a diversion of attention. This is the subject matter of Chapter 6. It will have to suffice to point out that an expectancy is a learned representation that, given a situation, particular behavior will lead to another situation; a goal is the anticipated situation which currently regulates the individual's behavior; goal setting is a process determined by the relative significance to the individual of each alternative expected situation, and the significance of an anticipated situation is the strength of pleasurable or unpleasurable emotion conditioned to it.

The belief in choice rests first on the capacity to represent temporal sequences of experiences as expectancies or anticipations. Since situations can be very similar, the individual can learn several expectations for situations which are very similar. For example, the very small child can learn that when he sees the cookie jar, if he reaches in it, he will have a cookie and then can eat it and enjoy it. He also can learn that if he tries to do so, he will have the cookie taken away and be spanked, which he will not enjoy. Once the child has had both kinds of experiences, when he sees the cookie jar, both expectancies can be evoked. This is easy to observe in small children, especially when the parent is present. They see the cookie jar, they make an initial move toward it and then hesitate and look toward the parent. In effect, they are thinking, "Will I have the cookie or will I get a spanking?" The choice can be conceived in terms of going to or not going to the cookie jar. The deterministic explanation is that the relative significance of the enjoyment of the cookie and the unpleasure of the spanking determines what he does, other considerations being equal.

At this point the child can be understood to have a problem to solve, a decision to make. He does anticipate both possible consequences. His hesitation represents thinking it over, deliberating. More complex problems are only quantitatively different in that either more possible expectancies of current action and consequences or longer range implications are considered. The basic process is the same. For the determinist, no free choice occurs. The relative significance constitutes a sort of weighting process which is decisive. How, then, does the individualist come to *believe* that he has made a free choice? The answer is in terms of the learning how to reflect on this process.

There can be little doubt that such learning takes considerable time and many different experiences of the decision-making process. Individualist parents are deeply concerned that the child, beginning by age one at least, take responsibility for his actions. Their primary concern about development of their children is that they learn the proper moral lessons which are necessary for them to have good, upright character when they become fully independent at the end of adolescence. Parents are responsible for their children's character, and their children's behavior reflects on them. They also are, normatively, strongly attached to the child and believe that only by getting across the proper lessons can their child lead a happy and constructive life. They punish the child for its own good, and it often does hurt the parent more than it hurts the child even if the child cannot yet appreciate that.

To get across such lessons, in the context of their belief that the child inherently has a free will, these parents pay close attention to the child's responses to their efforts. They see him as, if not exactly a little savage, one who wants what he wants when he wants it. He must learn not only that such an approach to life will lead to his future unhappiness but that it often is immoral. What one can have, how one goes about getting it, and in what circumstances must be learned in order to lead a moral and constructive life. Parents often anticipate what the child has "in mind." They may provide it or warn against it. This inevitably gets the child's attention. Rewards and punishments in particular situations result in the child's learning of alternative expectancies. Once learned, they occur in the child's thought in the given situation. The parents are keenly aware of the child's experience of a choice. They look him in the eye and wait for his next move. They repeat the warnings "No, no, mustn't touch," "I said no," and "Don't you dare." Inevitably, the decision-making process runs

its determined course. The child's goal is set, and he implements it. If it
is the wrong choice in the eyes of the parent, the punishment usually
follows. The parent tries to make the child reflect on what has happened.
Believing he freely chose to disobey or defy, the parent says so. If the
child sulks or pouts about the punishment, the parent understands that he
is angry about not getting what he wanted. He also understands that the
child is angry at the parent. The child is morally wrong to be angry at the
parent. The parent punishes for the child's good. Therefore, the reflection
encouraged is "You have only yourself to blame," "You deliberately de-
fied me," "You knew that was wrong." At the same time the child hears,
"You could have asked me," "You could have waited till dinnertime," etc.

What the child learns is how to think about the decision-making process
which occurred. When it occurred, it involved no reflection. One expectancy occurred, then the alternative. The weighting process produced the
goal which then regulated his behavior. All he experienced was two or
more expectancies and the result. For example, a small child is spanked
by his grandmother for hitting her. She observes the child's hurt feelings
and asks him, "Why did you hit me?" The child responds, "Because I did
it." He had as yet no way to reflect on his behavior beyond thinking that
he was the agent. Later on he would answer, "Because I was naughty."
Finally, "It was my fault." All this occurs in the context of many other
experiences with respect to others vicariously in which what happens is
explained in terms of free choice.

It should be noted that the learning of the individualist of how to reflect
on this decision-making process is highly selective and limited. His attention is drawn to the alternative courses of action and to the resultant decision. However, other key specifics of the determinants of the decision
are ignored. They are ignored, of course, because his socializers believe
the determinant *is* his free will. The child experiences thoughts of eating
the cookie with a pleasurable feeling and thoughts of the spanking with an
unpleasurable feeling. His thoughts fluctuate between these two anticipations for an interval of time dependent on the relative strengths of the
feelings. The closer they are in strength, the more vacillation. Eventually
one becomes regnant and is acted upon.

A determinist parent could teach the child to reflect differently on his
experience. He could say, for example, "You thought about how nice it
would be to eat the cookie and you also thought that you wouldn't like a
spanking. You wanted the cookie more than you feared the spanking, and
that is why you went to the cookie jar. I am going to spank you, and next
time you will fear the spanking more than you will want the cookie; and
then you won't go to the cookie jar." The child would be learning that his
behavior was determined by particular processes rather than a matter of
his free choice.

The individualist learns to reflect on this process by thinking, "I decided

I wanted the cookie more than I didn't want the spanking, and I could have decided the other way." As a child, he reflects only that he was naughty and so he was punished. Later on, he will reflect that he yielded to temptation and brought the punishment on himself. Why his will is sometimes weak and sometimes strong, the individualist has no way of reflecting on the other than that it was his choice.

Will

The individualistic idea of "will" is distinct from that of choice, even though choice is ordinarily understood as due to an act of will. The functional significance of will for individualists is the experience of effort in the attainment of a goal. Will is really willpower. It is a matter of preserving the goal already chosen against the temptation to abandon it in favor of some other. They call it "stick-to-itiveness," "hard work," and "perseverance" in the face of obstacles and temptations, as exemplified by the children's story *The Little Engine That Could* (Piper 1990).

The foundations of will are the reflective learning of the young child as he undertakes tasks toward goals which are *not initially goals that would have occurred to him.* He undertakes them at the exhortation of significant others because he has learned the goal of their love and approval. Individualists often regard these as chores which have to be done, although that would not cover all of them. Learning how to kick a football is not a chore in this sense. It is, however, something which Dad wants his son to accomplish. The child learns that his father disapproves when he gets bored or tired or distracted during the lesson. He wants the approval of his father more than the other potential goals which occur to him, at least some of the time. The reward of his father's approval for success, or at least improvement, strengthens the significance of the goal. Then it becomes his goal; and when Dad comes home from work, the son says, "Dad, watch me kick the football." Before the goal is one which provides pleasure for the child, it is an imposed activity resting on fear of disapproval. The child thinks of other goals he would prefer to be seeking. He learns how important a certain goal is to Dad by pursuing one of these other goals and then experiencing his father's disapproval.

In this case, "will" is how the child learns to reflect on the process of anticipating his father's disapproval as alternative potential goals in the situation occur to him. These alternative goals capture his attention and prevent momentarily his attention to the imposed goal. His attention has to be conditioned back to the imposed goal. The father initiates this process by saying, "Pay attention to me," "Don't be looking over there," etc. The awareness of the alternative goals, of the expectancies of the father's disapproval, and the consequent attention to the imposed goal constitute a process which the individualist learns to think of as the exercise of willpower. Later on, the goals often are not imposed by significant others, but they involve *temporary* lack of significance compared to other possible goals. The individual finds his attention moving toward these other goals. Yet he has learned that the *long-run* significance of the goal is greater than the short-run significance of the other goals. He has learned to condition his attention back to the long-range goal when he is distracted by short-range goals. This process he understands in terms of willpower. Some psychologists understand it in terms of "delay of gratification" and believe that it is a capacity that may or may not be developed in a child. For the individualist, the child who delays gratification is exercising his willpower, and the child who does not is weak-willed or yielding to temptation. Significantly, one is weak-willed by an act of will for the individualist. All acts are willed.

Conclusion

Such learning involves the most complex and subtle processes of human functioning and becomes very intricate and extensive. A fully adequate psychology awaits the collaboration of many academics who take the stance of relativistic naturalism. If the brief account rendered suggests cogently the direction which a fully adequate naturalistic account might take, it has served its purpose.

BEHAVIOR AND CAUSALITY

At the outset of this chapter, it was pointed out that a basic difference between relativistic naturalism and realistic individualism is in the conceptualization of behavior. Central to individualism are the dualistic view of the person and the linear cause-effect mode of thought. In combination, this produces a view of behavior as the effect caused by the mind. This sequence is for the individualist what makes the person responsible for his behavior. Some philosophers suggest that reasons are causes of behavior. The mode of thought appears to be preserved in more recent hybrid views which reject spiritual mind in favor of physical brain or central nervous system. Thus behavior still is regarded as an effect caused by the functioning of the brain or central nervous system. A similar preservation of dualism without spiritual mind is expressed in the idea of psychosomatic problems.

Relativistic naturalism rejects both spiritual and physical dualism. It does not employ the linear cause-effect mode of thought. Rather, it regards the human being as a single, living, dynamic system. It emphasizes process rather than state. It rejects the nominalizing mode of breaking systems down into discrete interacting parts so characteristic of the individualistic view of the human machine. All that goes on within the human body is integrally interrelated. The individualistic emphasis on transplantable parts and localized effects is replaced with an emphasis on systemic processes, rhythms, balances, and harmonies.

Behavior is the observable manifestation of the organization of the total body. Behavior relates the body to its environment. The person is constantly in interaction with his environment. Even when the person remains as motionless as he can for some period of time, he is behaving. There is a complex organization within the body that maintains this behavior. Feedback from movement or posture, as well as from the environment, is a constant and integral part of total bodily organization.

Relativistic naturalism, unlike realistic individualism, does not conceive of learning as occurring in the mind but in the total body. Since all the processes of the body are in constant interaction, the impact of environment is on all of them. The effect is something like what medical doctors refer to when they say that a transplant is rejected by the body, or when they refer to the side effects of the administration of drugs. All the processes of the body become tuned to particular harmonies, rhythms, and balances, which are affected by impact on any part of the body. These harmonies normatively have a range of functioning within which variations in the environment are assimilated. Moreover, they are processes, not states. The nominalizing mode of thought of individualism implies that human behavior, like a movie, consists of a series of states in time frames that, when speeded up, gives the impression of motion. The states are states of mind which dictate behavior for individualists but program it for hybrid views. In relativistic naturalism there are not states, but processes. However, among these processes, some have stability in the sense of repetitive form. These are the stabilizing aspects of bodily organization. They are not independent processes, but components of the total process.

Unlike individualism, relativistic naturalism does not regard the human being as an autonomous unit in nature. Rather, he is an integral part of nature. Yet he is a unit in the sense that he functions on organizing principles characteristic of his species, that is, his human nature. What is organized are the bodily processes as they are influenced by environment. Thus the human being is a system integrally related to a larger system.

This view of human nature precludes the division of the person into a mind and a body related in terms of cause and effect. The mind does not cause the behavior of the body for its reasons, and the body does not sometimes cause the mind to function irrationally with the result that the mind causes the body to act immorally or incompletely. In relativistic naturalism the human being is a single complex unit of processes.[12] Behavior is only the observable manifestation of total bodily functioning. What causes behavior, then, is what causes total bodily functioning. This is an interaction between the inherent capacities and principles of human nature and the order in the environment of the person. Human nature limits, selects, and organizes the impact of environment, while what it has to organize is dependent on the nature of the environment. The human capacities to learn preserve selectively the impact of previous environments. Current environment is always interacting with the total bodily organization of the person at the moment including this learning. This interaction of what the person brings with him from his past experience as organized by his human nature and the nature of the current environment causes his behavior. It causes his behavior because it determines current total body organization of which the behavior is the observable manifestation. It is important to note that environment determines behavior in two ways, first by its contribution to learning in past experience that is included in current total bodily organization, and second by how current environment interacts with this organization to effect a new organization.

Individualists think mind causes behavior partly because they are aware that one can remain in one bodily posture while many thoughts occur. Moreover, the thinking often is of a decision-making nature, so it appears that the individual, when confronted with a problem, deliberately ceases behaving until the problem is solved and then implements the decision. In relativistic naturalism the assumption of an unchanging posture on the occurrence of a problem is understood as an inherent and/or learned reaction to the complex impact of environment on total bodily organization. The complexity of human learning is such that the impact of a particular environmental situation that occurs to a complex organization requires time to work through, not entirely unlike the time it takes a one-armed bandit to spin through its predetermined wiring to arrive at the final settings on the gears. The whole process is predetermined by the organization of learning. The final working out constitutes a new organization with its manifested behavior just as the observed pictures in the windows of the one-armed bandit manifest a new setting of the machine which will interact with the next coin inserted in it.

The individualist's strong sense that he deliberately set out to solve a problem and reached a decision is due to the subjectivity and choice aspects of "spiritual mind" explained earlier. They are learned ways of reflecting on selected aspects of the predetermined working-through process. What greatly complicates that process and makes it appear to be self-directed is the role of subvocal speech. Had the person no speech (or speech substitute, such as sign language), the working-through process would be much more rapid. It would be accompanied by fleeting awareness of (attention to) unconnected thoughts, images, and feelings. This may be what occurs with monkeys or chimps when faced with their equivalent of a problem. The capacity for speech, however, alters the process significantly. It initiates a dialogue with self based on feedback. It should be noted that this dialogue is predetermined by learning. The dialogue makes specific aspects of the process available to attention in a systematic fashion based on the grammar of the language. It also serves another very important function—making available to reflection the memories of the material brought to consciousness. This allows the person to reflect later on those aspects of the process. The fact that a great deal, probably the vast majority, of the working-through process is neglected by this dialogue produces the sense that what one is conscious of is all that has occurred. The person thinks that what he has been conscious of constitutes the whole process, when it has been a highly selective but systematic portion of it accompanied by learned ways of thinking about that selective portion. The individualist learns to reflect in such a manner that he thinks of these portions as his reasoning and of the end product as the free choice of his spiritual mind which then directs the behavior of his physical body. However, as the accumulating anomalies suggesting unconscious thought and motivation indicate, these conscious reasons often are not the bases of behavior. They are only the conscious part of a much more complex process of working through the impact of current environment on total bodily organization. In relativistic naturalism the behavior of the person reflects his total bodily organization at the time of the environmental situation. That interaction determines a new total bodily organization and the new behavior is only the observable manifestation of it.

The individual's reflections on those selected aspects of bodily organization that capture his attention at any time are functional in total body organization. In this limited sense, reasons are causes of behavior. That is, they contribute to total body organization, of which behavior is the overt expression. They are not epiphenomenal accompaniments. Neither are reflections on behaviors after the behavior has occurred. They are functional aspects of reorganization. It is only the individualistic belief in the free choice of one's behavior that produces the idea that these reflections constitute the total organization and, therefore, are the causes of behavior.

Summary of the Philosophical Assumptions of Relativistic Naturalism

The application of a modified version of Kuhn's model of revolutions in science has been used as a means to introduce a cross-cultural approach to human science based on a relativistic view of knowledge and a naturalistic view of human nature. Kuhn's concept of a normal paradigm of science is interpreted as comprised of two parts. It starts with a worldview and its attendant mode of thought. A worldview is a system of abstract concepts and expectancies concerning the nature of the reality behind appearances. A mode of thought is the process by which experience is processed and thought is regulated. The second part is a logical derivation from the worldview, using the mode of thought of the procedures by which explanation of experience is constructed. The vast majority of experience is explained through application of the beliefs of the worldview. Special means (research) are derived to attempt to accommodate experiences that resist such explanation. These means may be successful, unsuccessful, or generate new anomalies. The accumulation of unexplainable experiences begins to raise issues concerning the nature of reality. It occurs because the society is entering a transitional period from one pattern of group life to another as a result of the operation of one or more major forces for change—technological changes, cultural diffusion, natural catastrophes, etc. What Kuhn identifies as revolutions in science constitute the reflections of this process of change in those institutions of the society that are primarily responsible for formal or official forms of explanation. They are only one aspect of the transitional process which can be understood psychologically as the disintegration of the prevailing worldview and mode of thought and the gradual learning of new ones over a number of generations.

Application of this modified version of Kuhn's model to modern social science reveals that it is now in such a revolutionary period. Reconceptualizations of the nature of reality and new modes of thought are the bases for the relativistic view of knowledge. The recognition of the operation of the individualistic worldview from which the social sciences were derived and of the profound issues that have been raised for that worldview provide the basis for the naturalistic view of human nature. In this way the stage has been set for relativistic naturalism as a replacement for the current division of human studies, consisting of human biology in the natural sciences, the social sciences, and the humanities.

At this point a brief summary is offered of the positions taken by relativistic naturalism on the issues facing current social science listed at the end of the first chapter. Here it is necessary to point out that it is inherent in the relativistic view that issues posed in terms of one worldview and mode of thought cannot be addressed directly by another. A new worldview is a reconceptualization of reality. A new mode of thought reasons differently. Questions are not posed in the same fashion or terms. What follows, then, does not constitute the resolution of each issue listed but a brief account of the stance of relativistic naturalism relating it to these issues. Presentation of a complete new worldview and mode of thought is beyond the scope of this work, which endeavors only to make the case for the abandonment of the approach used in current social science and the establishment of a new one.

PHYSICAL MONISM

Relativistic naturalism assumes that reality consists of only physical substance. With respect to humans, mind-body dualism is rejected, including the notion of emergent processes. The human is entirely a physical being. What is understood in the individualistic worldview as the spiritual nature of the mind is interpreted in terms of the operation of the human attentional, reflective, and emotional capacities. As physical states and processes, these capacities operate on principles of physical matter. It follows that there is no issue of whether human science takes human behavior or phenomenological experience as its province. Although any person's verbal reports about his phenomenological experience must be understood as behavior, his actual phenomenological experiences, which are not coextensive with his verbal reports, are physical events and so are included in the new human science not as subject matter but in theory and explanation.

The individualistic assumption of human free will is rejected. Human behavior is determined by the interaction of the physical properties and capacities of the individual with the physical conditions of his environment in a sequential, integrative process through the life span. This is a very complex and continuous process which does not imply that the individual's personality or developing nature is ever fixed. (See Chapters 7 and 9 for an account of continuities and discontinuities in human development.)

RELATIVISM OF KNOWLEDGE

The individualistic assumption of a universal human reason is rejected. Relativistic naturalism assumes that human nature consists of a set of very flexible capacities that can be developed into different worldviews and modes of thought by different environmental conditions. Limits on the types and the flexibility of human capacities and limits on the variety of environments on the planet are reasons to expect that there may be degrees of commensurability among some worldviews. However, others may be incommensurable. This applies as well to modes of thought of generations of groups that are historically related. It follows that the establishment of knowledge is not progressive beyond the bounds of the prevalence of a particular worldview and its attendant mode of thought. This view entails that any attempt of those using one worldview and mode of thought to translate another written or spoken language into its own terms is likely to involve distortion of an indeterminate nature.

Issues concerning the similarities and distinctions among the natural sciences, the social sciences, and the humanities must be recognized as issues formulated in individualistic terms. Relativistic naturalism rejects this trichotomous division of the study with respect to human reality, including its definition of science. It is replaced by a new human science based on three sciences—biology, psychology, and sociology—which are related on a dimension of abstraction-reduction and which are alternative, not complementary, forms of explanation of the same observations (see Chapters 4 and 10). The new human science consists of disciplines based on distinct or related human groups geographically and historically (see Chapters 10 and 11). Each discipline is scientific in the relativistic sense that it is the systematic application of a worldview and mode of thought to the explanation of defined domains of observations, with "puzzle-solving" research into unexplained observations.

Acceptance of the theory of evolution entails indeterminism in science. The scientist cannot be other than a participant within any setting. The functions of human science are not those of the social sciences, as will be explained in Chapter 11. The overwhelming proportion of the work of human scientists is the establishment and explanation of intersubjectively agreed-upon observations of naturally occurring behavior and speech. Indeterminism is recognized as inevitable in the establishment of domains of observations. The observing human scientist is a participant in what he is observing. However, there are reasons to believe that the effects of the scientist on what he observes in his own society can be minimized sufficiently to provide intersubjectively agreed-upon domains of observations from which useful substantive knowledge can be constructed by those who share a particular worldview and mode of thought. (See the discussion of methodology in Chapter 11.) Indeterminism in the observation of members of other societies is a more serious problem. However, scientist observers can establish intersubjective agreement on their observations. (The issue of value-neutral versus value-laden science is dealt with in Chapter 11 following the explanation of the structure of the new human science.)

CAUSALITY AS MODE OF THOUGHT

It follows from the relativism of knowledge based on the application of a learned worldview and mode of thought that ideas of causality are relative. Relativistic naturalism rejects the individualistic view of causality. In taking a field mode of thought, it eschews causal notions entirely. In the field approach, what is observed is understood as the expression of the state of the total field of forces. No identifiable component of the field is autonomous in its nature. Rather, the nature of each component at any time is a resultant of the interaction of all components. Therefore, it is meaningless to attribute causality. There are changes over time in the total field, but these, too, are attributable to the interactions of all forces in the field.[1]

This approach also rejects the individualistic view of reality as a whole consisting of discrete parts. The total field has parts only in the sense of components whose nature never is totally independent of the nature of all other parts. Thus, it is meaningless to pose such an issue as whether the whole is greater than the sum of its parts. Part-whole distinctions in general are eschewed. Neither is there an issue of methodological individualism or holism in the sense of reified entities.

It is meaningless to ask whether reasons are causes of behavior. The environmental conditions of life over time interacting with the capacities of the individual person determine what his personality is at any particular time. However, specification of the determining conditions requires characterization of the total field. A person's behavior is only the overt manifestation of the interaction of the state of development of his total physical organism at the time and the state of the rest of the field in which he behaves. The way in which the person is reflecting on his incipient behavior is only one aspect of this total bodily organization.

CONCLUSION

Relativistic naturalism recognizes itself as a relative view of knowledge. Given that this is a transitional period in the history of American society, it is offered as an alternative paradigm to realistic individualism. Its philosophical assumptions have been presented. Part II offers some general guidelines to other major aspects of a worldview in the hope that they will generate sufficient interest among other scholars to create a programmatic effort to establish a more comprehensive one.

A good deal of effort already has been expended on the task as the revolution in social science has developed. In every social science alternative schools of thought have been proposed and debated. Criteria of adequacy have been sharpened. Strengths and weaknesses have been recognized. A staggering range of observations of human phenomena has been reported. Yet in no discipline is there a consensus of agreement on theory. Realist social science perseveres despite the anomalies and the discontent. To continue this course of action is both fruitless and socially irresponsible.

Probably the greatest obstacle to the accomplishment of the task is the individualistic mode of thought. It tends strongly to specialization and technical refinement. Members of the society with strong theoretical interests have been shuffled to the periphery of science. There is increasing evidence of an interest in changing this situation. There is more concern to foster interdisciplinary research, which inevitably requires relating of previously separated ranges of ideas. There is the recognition of the importance of cross-cultural research, which makes similar demands. There are journals appearing that encourage theoretical contributions. There is increasing concern about overspecialization and about turning out technicians in our graduate schools. The time is ripe for the development of a new paradigm.

The case has been presented that the psychological level of conceptualization in worldview is primary. For this reason, the following four chapters will attempt a general outline of a new theory of psychology. Chapter 6 addresses the main features of human nature. Chapter 7 deals with the vital but most neglected subject of how to conceptualize systematically the environmental influences on the developing individual through his life span. Chapters 8 and 9 present a universal approach to the conceptualization of personality and its development through the life span.

Chapter 10 makes a case for the necessity of sociological theory and addresses some central issues in the field. No attempt is made to address biological theory, mainly because of the lack of adequate background of the author, but also because of its current nascent state being greatly diminished in usefulness due to its lack of an agreed-upon psychological theory from which to proceed. The concluding chapter outlines the organization of the new human science and suggests the basic methodologies it might employ. It then addresses the role of human science in the total society and some of the key issues concerning that role.

— Part II —

Theory and Structure of Human Science

6

Human Nature

An adequate theory of psychology must be one that can be applied to the explanation of the behaviors and experiences of any individual in any society, past or present, and at any point in the human life span. While description of the person is an important function of psychological theory, it is explanation that provides the basis for social problem solving and for understanding changes in the person over time. From the range of ideas that have been proposed, from the assessments of strengths and weaknesses of previous theoretical efforts, and from consideration of the contributions from socioanthropology and historiography, it is clear that, to be able to explain behavior, a general psychological theory requires three primary dimensions.

The first is a conceptualization of human nature. There must be terms and principles for the description of properties that the individual person brings with him to life as a member of the human species. This dimension must include the potentials for properties to mature in or out at various times in the individual's life. It also must address the possibilities of individual variations in human nature.

The second dimension is a conceptualization of environmental influences on the individual throughout his life span. From conception the person always is in an environment that has many forms of influence on him. Many possibilities for differences in environment exist across individuals or for one individual over time. There must be a way to conceptualize these environmental influences so that they can be taken into account systematically in explaining behavior and experience at any point or period in the life span.

The third dimension is personality development through the life span. This is a conceptualization of the results of the interaction of human nature and environmental influences. The individual's behavior changes in

Figure 6.1
General Tridimensional Model of Psychology

```
                                  Environmental Influences

                                  through the Life Span
─────────────────────────────────────┬──────────────────────────────
Human Nature:                         │
                                      │
   The individual's variant of        │   Personality Development
                                      │
   his species characteristics        │
                                      │
```

many ways through his life span. There must be a way of conceptualizing
the organization of the human organism and changes in that organization
over time in order to explain why the individual behaves and experiences
as he does under particular conditions at any point in his life. There can
be no adequate explanation of observed human behavior without conceptualizations of these three dimensions, which are represented in Figure
6.1.[1]

There are those both inside and outside the field of psychology who
will regard this model as impossible to use. They take the views that each
individual is so uniquely and complexly different by nature from every
other and that environmental influences are so complex and unique to
each individual that no conceptualization could do justice to them. These
views reflect both the individualistic obsession with individual differences
and the neglect of the possibilities of order in environmental influences.
Together they constitute a denial of the possibility of human science and
so merit no further consideration here.

The myriad issues beyond those already addressed in previous chapters
can be located within or across the three dimensions of the model. This
chapter suggests an outline of an approach to the conceptualization of human nature and addresses the most fundamental issues related to it.

The key to an approach to human nature is given in this query: "The
great natural variation of cultural form is . . . the ground of [anthropolo-
gy's] deepest theoretical dilemma: how is such variation to be squared
with the biological unity of the human species?" (Geertz 1973, 22) The
key is in the idea of the biological unity of humankind. Psychological theory must conceive the nature of our species in a fashion which gives it the
potential to explain "the great natural variation of cultural form" while
preserving the unity of the species. This rules out attribution of cultural
form to genetic variation among human groups. It also puts a severe strain
on any assumptions about inherent dispositions of a teleological nature in
the species, for example, instincts or behavioral tendencies which serve to
reproduce the phenotype, because these are too rigid to account for cultural diversity.[2]

This variation is a great deal more than what is implied by the expression one man's meat is another man's poison. That is a way of describing individual variations within a cultural form. Rather, it refers to such fundamental differences in group patterns of behavior as religions, family and kinship structures, competition or cooperation in everyday activities, normative sexual practices, martial or peaceful orientations toward neighboring groups, child-rearing practices, languages, reverence for or exploitation of natural resources, social stratification, etc., and, more fundamentally, patterns of all of the above in ways of life so different that in many cases they may be incommensurable.

Interpretation of human evolution will have to be far more sophisticated than the ideas of adaptation to the environment in which a species evolves or of characteristics ensuring reproduction. These are basic necessary assumptions that account for no more than the existence of the species. They are more useful as criteria of extinction than as bases for explaining the actual behaviors of homo sapiens. Apparently, human genetic endowment is such as to permit the development of such common, often normative, behaviors as martyrdom, fasting, celibacy, abortion, contraception, fatal curiosity, risk taking, thrill seeking, self-deception about the reality of danger (drug-induced or otherwise), many varieties of knowingly lethal initiation of contact with others (wars, raiding parties, feuds), exhaustion of basic resources, misogyny, homosexuality, and suicide.

It seems inescapable that there is nothing in human nature that ensures that individual humans will do what is necessary for survival or reproduction and nothing that ensures that humans will not behave so as to terminate their existence, individually or collectively, wittingly or unwittingly. This conclusion introduces what will be referred to hereinafter as the "evolutionary paradox." The paradox is that, while the evolutionary process determines the existence of species adapted to survival and reproduction and the extinction of those species not so adapted, it has produced in the human a species highly adapted to survive but readily capable of behaving so as to endanger, even preclude, its survival and/or reproduction.

Quite clearly, evolution of human nature has been a complex, intricate, and long-term process of great subtlety. It has produced the genetic bases for planning, imagination, reflectivity, symbolism, playfulness, imitation, duplicity, probability, compulsivity, memory, curiosity, dreaming, humor, reverence, timing, spacing, numerology, dance, art, music, and intricate, rapid, and orderly interaction with others and with the nonhuman environment, etc., and all in a great multiplicity of forms.

Humans are poor tree climbers, slow runners, unprolific breeders, and weakly armored for physical struggle with other predatory species, offensively or defensively. Therefore, it seems they have evolved to rely on their wits. They can find ways to live in every type of environment on this planet and for limited times, at least, in some environments beyond it.

Moreover, they can systematically alter their environments for their own use and, perhaps just as often, to their own detriment. Any conceptualization of human nature, it would appear, must place heavy reliance on its great flexibility. The only way in which the great diversity of cultural forms can be accounted for is to assume that the process of evolution for humans has produced a being so intricately tuned to environmental influence that he has capacities that make him extremely adaptive. However, the cost of this adaptability is that it can produce byproducts in learning that may be maladaptive for individuals and even subgroups. Yet the same capacities permit learning about these maladaptive possibilities. Complexity, subtlety, and flexibility appear to be the essence of adaptability.

Equally subtle and complex must be the nature of human motivation. No simple notions of activation, energization, survival drives, or instincts extending individualistic views of nonhuman species to humans in order to accommodate evolutionary theory will suffice. The individual is a constantly functioning organism always in some form of interaction with his environment. There is no need to consider what gets him into action much as a dozing tiger is seen as being roused by hunger or thirst. Instead, what needs to be accounted for are changes in the patterning of the behavior of a constantly behaving being. In addition, the bases of such changes must have the potential to account for the full range of behaviors observable. Simplex notions of human motivation in terms of survival drives or instincts or behavioral dispositions ensuring reproduction of the phenotype have been totally inadequate to this task. They are proving increasingly inadequate to account for the behaviors of many other species as these are more carefully observed in their natural habitats. Of central importance in these considerations must be the functions of emotion. The tendency to dismiss emotions as epiphenomenal or irrational diversions from adaptive functioning or processes too complex for computer simulations of the mind is a lame excuse for not dealing with aspects of human functioning of obvious importance to any layman.[3] There is a profound inconsistency in accepting evolutionary theory of human origins and regarding emotions as having evolved either for no functional role or to function maladaptively.

A conceptualization of human nature also must do justice to the complexity and organization of the individual's interactions with his environment over time. This must include recognition of human development from very simple forms of interaction in infancy to those elaborate forms in later life which reflect long-range planning for the attainment of multiple goals in programs permitting considerable flexibility. It is the recognition of this development from simple to elaborate which requires that human science provide a system of basic terms and principles that permits generation of more complex terminology of behavior and yet preserves the developmental integrity of explanation. That is, the complex terms of personality must be reducible to the basic terms of the science, a property that has always been absent in the gap between experimental psychology and clinical theory. The theory of human nature must be adequate to explain at one and the same time the complexity of the individual person that is manifested in the organization of his behavior over time and the specificity of his momentary interactions with his environment. No simple mechanical models of stimulus and response, flowcharts of information processing, or profiles of personality traits will serve for this task. It requires something in the nature of a field conceptualization capable of encompassing both the organization of the total human being at any moment and its dynamic continuities and discontinuities over time.

The remainder of this chapter suggests an approach to the conceptualization of human nature which addresses the considerations just discussed—flexible capacities, human motivation, and field organization of behavior. They are taken up in the order listed. The adaptive functioning of the emotions is revealed in these accounts. The integration of basic and complex terminology and the continuities and discontinuities in the dynamics of behavior are addressed in Chapters 8 and 9.

FLEXIBLE CAPACITIES

One of the first tasks for human scientists is to generate a taxonomy of the basic capacities from which can be derived the full range of human behaviors and subjective experiences. It will have to be a system radically different from and more sophisticated than the chapter headings in any standard introductory textbook in psychology. It will have to be different from the processes currently being considered in computer simulation of the human mind. The following list is an initial attempt to suggest such a taxonomy:

attention	organization
recognition	imitation
generalization	discrimination
postication	anticipation
probability	imagination
significance	speech

One approach to the conceptualization of these capacities is through the focus on interaction with the environment. Fundamentally, all behavior occurs in a three-dimensional context of space, time, and significance. The evolutionary process can be understood in terms of how it has equipped the human being for these three dimensions. In addition, the environment of humans is very substantially one of other human beings living in groups. The human species is born virtually helpless and lives through a long period of dependency upon others, not becoming capable of reproduction for about fifteen years. Consequently, it must have evolved capacities particularly designed to deal with this social dimension of its environment. All of the above listed capacities can be conceived within this four-dimensional context.

The Space Dimension

The individual always exists in a physical setting (including other people) of considerable complexity and therefore one that changes in multiple ways with great rapidity. Inevitably, humans have evolved to be able to deal with this complexity and rapidity. One form this evolution has taken is the development of multiple modes of registering the external environment. The essence of the capacities involved in the space dimension is recognition. To function, the person must interact with his current physical environment. This environment is always a pattern recognizable in all exteroceptive modes. As many aspects of the pattern may have significance for the person's continued functioning, he must be capable of recognizing them. The pattern can be regarded as a physical setting. Any change produces a new setting. Recognition capacities must therefore be able to handle the complexity of settings and the multiplicity of settings. The specific capacities involved in recognition in the space dimension are at least the following:

1. *Attention*. This very flexible capacity permits the individual to register rapidly many aspects of a setting and a multiplicity of changes in a setting.

2. *Generalization and Discrimination*. These twin capacities permit the individual to recognize similarities or differences in settings or aspects of them attended to. Together they provide the capacity to classify settings or aspects of them, including the development of systems of classification.[4]

3. *Imagination*. This is the capacity for imagery in the visual and other sensory modes and their potential combination in synesthesia.

The Time Dimension

The essence of the time dimension is the representation of sequencing in the experience of the environment. The individual exists in an environment with many dynamic properties. Changes in the environment occur in accordance with principles of the functioning of physical things, including humans. Thus, there is order in change. The capacities of the time dimension permit the person to deal with this sequential ordering. They include at least the following:

1. *Anticipation*. This capacity allows the person to represent changes in the environment that have been experienced such that he can represent changes before they occur. He can represent what follows what in experience.[5]

2. *Posticipation*. This capacity allows the person to represent environmental conditions that have preceded current experience such that current experience can evoke them. He can represent what precedes what. This knowledge can then be combined with anticipation to deal with the future.[6]

3. *Probability*. Sequencing of changes in the environment, while having order, usually is too complex for totally consistent order. This capacity allows the person to anticipate or posticipate multiple possible orders in terms of the relative frequencies with which they have been experienced.[7]

The Significance Dimension

The capacities which represent the space and time dimensions permit learning about many aspects of experience, but they treat them all alike. They are simply states, events, or processes which occur. They provide no information concerning the differences or potential differences in their consequences for the individual. The significance dimension adds something beyond recognition and sequence. It represents experiences that make a difference. It identifies what is important and what is relatively important.

There are two general types of significance. The first concerns experience which has direct significance for the survival of the person. It has long been of central concern to psychologists. Humans have evolved to register in a special fashion experiences which signify states or processes of the body about which something must be done. These have been called "sources of drive" and include the traditional ideas of hunger, thirst, fatigue, pain, lack of oxygen, extremes of temperature, eliminative pressures, etc. Here they are treated, not in terms of motivation, but of representation of special forms of experience. To them should be added others rarely considered, such as dermal irritations or itches, losses of balance, sweet and bitter tastes and smells, very loud noise, very bright light, and others whose survival value is direct in the sense of impairing or potentially impairing or restoring or potentially restoring physiological functioning of the body. The directness of significance for survival of these experiences means that it is not mediated by the other forms of experience represented in the space, time, or social dimensions. These survival-related forms of significance have the property of capturing attention except under very special conditions.

The second type of significance is far more complex and characteristic of humans because it is derived from the development of the other flexible capacities. In contrast to the survival type which is innate, that is, occurring directly upon the existence of the specified conditions, this type is generated from learning.[8] It has evolved along with the great cortical development of the human brain and comprises a set of types of events or processes that occur as a result of it. These types of events have indirect significance for survival. Their significance is mediated by learning, yet they register significance immediately in the sense of producing a special quality of experience that also innately captures attention. These events are the emotions, and they are significant because they signify various forms of the relationship between the learning of the individual and the current conditions of his environment. Basically, they signify forms of concordant and discordant interaction with the environment.[9]

The emotional type of significance experience has evolved because the other flexible capacities of humans permit the development of very complex planning which regulates the relationship of the person to his environment over time. There are many ways in which this planning can be discordant or become discordant with environmental conditions. When they are, the individual's survival is potentially endangered. When the implementation of his planning is concordant with the environment, it usually is not. He must, therefore, also be able to represent the existence, or the restoral, or the elaboration of concordance. The emotions, then, signify a variety of ways in which the individual is and is not functioning with his ecological system, including, of course, members of his group and of neighboring groups. The limits for survival of the emotional type of significance are discussed in the section below on motivation.

Different emotions signify different kinds of variations of the relationship of the individual to his current environment. For example, the emotion of anger occurs when the environmental conditions interfere with the implementation of plans. This interference commonly is called frustration and should be understood as referring to the relationship between plans and conditions. The emotion of anger captures the individual's attention to the interfering conditions, permitting learning about them. The more important the goals of the plan and the more complete the interference, the greater is the intensity of the anger, in other words, the more significant is the situation. The emotion of anxiety signifies a different variation of the relationship between plans and environmental conditions. This variation signifies uncertainty about planning. It is based on the capacity of the individual to anticipate different sequences of experiences and the probabilities of each. The more important the anticipated sequences are for the person and the more equal the probabilities of each, the greater the anxiety. For example, playing Russian roulette with a two-barreled gun produces more anxiety than doing so with a six-gun. The emotion of terror signifies the inability to organize any interaction with the environment.

These variations are not matters of intellectual understanding of conditions.[10] They are automatic states that occur under the conditions stated. The individual does not necessarily know why he is experiencing the particular emotion. He just experiences it under the defined conditions. However, the emotion captures his attention, permitting learning about them, although it is clear that the learning resulting may have no relationship to the relevant conditions producing the emotion, for example, superstitious learning. This manifests the great flexibility in the capacities of the significance dimension. There are a great many possible conditions of the person's environment which might produce frustration of one or another plan, or uncertainty of which plan to implement. Yet each emotion is reliably evoked by the *type* of variation in the interaction between environmental conditions and individual plans for interaction with the environment. The emotions signify types of conditions to be avoided or sought in future planning. To do so, the individual, by attending to them, learns both in terms of the generalization-discrimination capacities and anticipation-postication-probability capacities. These provide new information which enters into the planning process.

It is not sufficient that significance be restricted to discord with the environment. Evolution has ensured that the individual has the capacities to signify states in which the environmental conditions and the individual's plans are coordinated. The emotion of contentment/joy is the primary one of this type. Contentment signifies that one's interactions with the environment are going, and promise to continue going, smoothly. It produces the "whistle while you work," "God's in His Heaven, all's right with the world," "on a roll" phenomena. Joy is the most intense form of this emotion, signifying the reinstatement of many potential but previously blocked plans such as those invoked by the news that one has just won the state lottery or inherited money from a rich relative. Curiosity also can be understood as an emotion. It commonly is experienced along a dimension from interest to fascination. Although it generally is regarded by psychologists as evoked by small discrepancies from expectations, which it is, it is important to note that instead of being disruptive or aversive, it leads to attraction and exploration. This is because the small discrepancy does not disrupt plans. Rather, it allows for elaboration of them, if only in anticipation. In contrast, great discrepancies from expectation produce fear because they represent the breakdown of organized interaction. A suggested list of primary emotions, conditions producing each, and the initial tendencies toward behavior is provided in Figure 6.2.

The great flexibility of the emotions is most evident in their conditionability. Primary emotion is what is evoked by the innate conditions such as those previously defined—frustration, uncertainty, small discrepancies, etc. Fundamental to the function of emotions is that those aspects of environmental conditions which are attended to when the emotion is evoked become capable of evoking the emotion when they are again encountered or anticipated. These conditions are represented by the space capacities. Whatever attention focuses upon at the time becomes automatically at-

Figure 6.2
Theory of Primary Emotions

Innate Evoking Conditions	Emotion	Behavioral Consequences[1]
General ongoing organization of mind; establishment and implementation of plans without anticipation of interruption	Joy	Continued implementation of plans
Breakdown of mental organization; large discrepancies from expectations	Fear	Disorganized behavior, paralysis, attempts to restore organization of some kind
Occurrence of two or more expectancies in a given situation; uncertainty	Anxiety	Vacillation, procrastination, seeking information to resolve uncertainty
Interference with the implementation of a plan; increasing probabilities of interruptive expectancies	Anger	Reorganization of the plan to escape, avoid, or overcome the interfering conditions
Small discrepancies from expectation	Curiosity	Exploration, familiarization
Decreasing probability of facilitative expectancies	Sadness	Nostalgic reminiscence, efforts to confirm old expectancies
Decreasing probability of interruptive expectancies	Relief	Repeated evocation of declining expectancy
Inability to establish more than very short-range or repetitive plans	Boredom	Restless movement from one brief activity to another; stereotyped behavior
Sudden unexpected substitution of one related organization for another; remote associations	Amusement/humor	Laughter and attempts to repeat the process
Increasing probability of facilitative expectancies	Hope	Repeated evocation of the increasing expectancies; dwelling on them

[1]These are only initial reactions, stated in general form. There are no specific behaviors inherently associated with any emotion beyond the autonomic.

tached to the emotion.[11] The recognition of that condition or the anticipation of it produces the emotion. This is the essence of attitude formation and occurs in the fashion psychologists call classical conditioning.
Classical conditioning is a useful concept, not because of its relevance to
conditioned reflexes such as eyeblinks, lifted fingers, or startle reactions,
but mainly because it helps to understand the experience of emotions in
conditions that do not innately produce them. Moreover, the attendant
phenomena to classical conditioning of stimulus generalization and higher
order conditioning increase the immense flexibility of this capacity. They
account for the astonishing variety of human attitudes. Consider, for example, the great variety of phobic objects. In addition, any recognizable
environmental condition can be conditioned to more than one emotion.
This helps to explain not only such phenomena as ambivalence in relationships but also the nature of changes in attitudes.[12]

The flexibility of the emotional capacity also is manifested in its relationship to behavior. No emotion is innately connected to any behavior
except, perhaps, for certain autonomic reflexes like blushing, blanching,
etc. This is a major way in which humans are distinct from almost all other
species. They can learn to respond in a vast variety of ways to conditions
that produce any emotion. The infant may reliably cry to almost any frustrating condition, but that is because he lacks the means to deal with it.
He quickly learns to inhibit his crying and to deal with the conditions in
any of a variety of ways. The types of conditions which innately produce
each emotion indicate the initial early childhood direction that behavior
will take. Frustration tends to produce behavior which overcomes the frustrating condition, allowing for continued implementation of the plan which
has been interfered with. The small child tries to remove obstacles, including parents, or to grasp for the desired object. However, he quickly learns
what such behavior signifies for his continued interaction with the environment and learns other means, which may include giving up the goal
altogether. Curiosity tends to produce exploration or information seeking,
but these can be replaced readily by repulsion or avoidance of information. In this process of learning how to deal with conditions innately producing emotions, the flexible capacities of the social dimension play the
major role.

Survival significance processes and their inflexible sources, given the long
dependency of the human infant, normatively produce child-rearing practices that introduce the child to highly reliable and immediately effective
learning of how to terminate them and thus restore organized interaction.[13] They are, therefore, forms of significance that very early serve to
regulate planning so that the more complex learning demanded by the
emotional form of significance tends to develop around it, even though it
is capable of fundamentally changing it. How and why this occurs will be
discussed in the upcoming section on motivation. It is important at this

point only to emphasize that emotions are primary sources of significance. They are presented here as capacities for representing experience.

The Social Dimension

The long period of dependency on others of human offspring ensures that they are social beings. Their flexible capacities, while giving them the equipment to learn how to deal with the complexity of social life, preclude the inherent behavioral responses to a simpler and more consistent environment available to most other species. Instead, human evolution has produced two other very flexible capacities adaptive to the complexity of human social life. They are the capacities for speech and for imitation.

The capacity for speech is immensely flexible. The child can learn whatever form of speech it consistently hears. There are many languages and dialects which humans speak. Linguistic competence permits the individual to generate an enormous range of utterances, including those never before generated by himself or others. In addition, speech can serve to extend vastly or to restrict the development of the person's other flexible capacities. In spoken or written form, it can open windows on the world, close them, or prevent their ever being opened. Inevitably, it always both extends in some ways and restricts in others. For example, speech is the basis of the development of the reflexive capacity discussed in Chapter 4. It allows the person to recapture and reflect on the inner world of his thoughts, feelings, and imagery. Even more importantly, it opens to him the inner world of the thoughts, feelings, and imagery of others. Yet, at the same time, it always provides a highly restricted form of exploration of these realms via its role in the development of his worldview and mode of thought. It also can elaborate his recognition and anticipation or posticipation of space and time into intricate systems of immense scope, for example, infinity, eternity, the number of angels which can dance on the head of a pin, and the existence of subatomic particles that have a life of billionths of a second. Yet the system learned excludes the possibility of the learning of any other system. Speech extends the potential of the human being so that he can learn the complexity of life in the social group in which he lives or some variant of it, but restricts his learning to only very limited extensions of that system.[14]

The other very flexible capacity that appears to have evolved out of the social nature of the human being is imitation. Imitation only recently has garnered the interest of psychologists. Its implications have hardly begun to be appreciated. It provides a major avenue to the solution of the long neglected questions of the origins of the vast repertory of behaviors of which humans are capable. Response repertories have been taken largely for granted in learning theory and very weakly conceived in developmental theory. What seems clear is that imitation suggests the development of a vast pool of possible combinations of patterns of behavior. More importantly, this pool appears to be drawn on by nothing more than the one-time observation of a pattern of behavior in another person. Even the small child, on seeing Mother sweep the floor, can then grasp the broom and attempt sweeping behavior, albeit crudely. Or he can sit on a chair, pick up a telephone, and jabber into it, although he hasn't the slightest idea what a telephone is. Any adult can model even the most bizarre position of the body, including facial expression, and a child or other adult can give an imitative approximation of it.

Imitation appears a similar process, whether of speech or nonspeech behavior. The child rapidly becomes adept at imitations of heard speech as if he were capable of combining speech sounds in almost any order. This combinatory property of imitation seems most obvious in play with sounds such as children's "pig-Latin" and alliteration. According to anthropologists and linguists, such play apparently is found in all human groups. It seems very likely that imitation is the primary basis on which both verbal and nonverbal behavior develops. Not only is the developing child introduced to behavioral skills by imitation, but by combining this capacity with speech and modeling, these skills become refined to a high degree. Think of a parent instructing a child on throwing a baseball accurately or repeating words so that the child can imitate them ever more precisely. In addition, it is on the basis of the experience of imitating behavior that the child often is introduced to its meaning in his group. For example, when the small child imitates his mother's sweeping behavior, he quickly discovers that it has a purpose which is made significant to him.

Summary

In the conceptualization of human nature, the highly flexible capacities that have been grouped into those of the space, time, significance, and social dimensions are central. They allow the individual to represent his environment in multiple and intricate ways.[15] They provide the raw material, so to speak, that is woven into the complex plans of the person for interaction with the environment. They are the stuff of personality, which is, perhaps, best defined as the organization of learning. They are what most distinguishes humans from other creatures and accounts for their ability to manipulate their environments via the use of tools. They also account for the remarkable paradox of the evolution of capacities to deal very effectively with the environment and, at the same time, to develop patterns of group life which can serve neither the survival of the individual nor the reproduction of his genes.

HEDONIC MOTIVATION

The conceptualization of motivation has plagued psychologists from the beginnings of their science. Under the influence of the theory of evolution, psychologists began to understand it in terms previously applied by individualists to other species. It was thought that if humans evolved through a process similar to that of other species, then their behavior also should be attributed to instincts, that is, nonvoluntary reactions. The concept of instinct eventually was translated into that of drive, which served to separate the motivational component from the behavioral. In the drive view, the individual is motivated to act when one or more of his inherent sources of drive reaches some threshold. These inherent sources are conceived in terms of what is necessary for the individual to survive, such as food, water, oxygen, rest, escape from pain, etc. They constitute a differentiation of the old idea of the instinct for self-preservation into distinct assumed physiological processes, each of which operates to instigate a drive to behavior. The behavior elicited by the drive state, with the exception of a few innate responses, is that which had resulted in past experience in reducing the source of the drive, for example, seeking and drinking water if the source were thirst, finding and eating food if it were hunger, etc.

This commendable effort to preserve consistency between evolutionary and psychological theory has proved far from useful outside the highly contrived and restricted conditions of animal laboratories. Most fundamentally, it puts an intolerable strain on the explanation of the vast bulk of human behavior that has no obvious relationship to the stipulated sources of drive. This has necessitated the addition of the idea of learned drives, which has proved very difficult to integrate into drive theory. In addition, other research required assimilation of new sources of drive called positive drives, such as curiosity/exploration, because they lacked the aversive qualities of the original set. These, too, placed a severe strain on the consistency of drive theory. More recently, the basic assumption of drive theory—that motivation functions to activate or energize the individual—has been questioned on the ground that it implies that, without operation of some source of drive, the person is quiescent. This view doesn't fit well with the recognition that the individual is a living organism whose bodily processes are constantly functioning. If resting and sleeping are understood as forms of behavior, then the individual is constantly behaving and there is no need for any explanation of activation. Rather, what is needed is an explanation for changes from one pattern of behavior to another. For example, why does a person reading a book at one moment arise and answer the telephone when it rings and a few moments later ignore the phone and continue reading? In addition, drive theory has no place for clinical views of the importance of emotions in motivation, such as anger, love, guilt, anxiety, jealousy, depression, etc. These considerable problems for drive theory have led increasingly toward its abandonment and the introduction of the idea of incentive motivation—a so far rather hazy notion that behavior results not so much from inner pushes (drives) but from outer pulls (incentives) such as being drawn into a candy store by the sight of the candy in the window. Conceptualizing these incentives has proven at least as difficult as has learned drives.

A new conceptualization of human motivation is urgently needed, one which has the richness and power to help to explain the great variety of forms of the direction and alteration of behavior that are observed. It also must have the capacity to account for why individuals engage in behaviors that are, or potentially are, inconsistent with their survival or with the reproduction of their genes. The following is an attempt to suggest the broad outlines of such a view. It addresses some of the most fundamental issues in psychology and takes the following positions: (1) Human motivation is hedonic and incentive in nature; (2) human behavior is intentional; (3) emotions are adaptive; (4) consciousness is functional in the determination of behavior; (5) human motivation tends to, but does not ensure, either the survival of the individual or the reproduction of his genes.

The argument for this conceptualization of human motivation takes the following form:

1. Human behavior is organized to attain anticipated goals through implementing plans and is regulated by a feedback process relating the goal and the plan to current environmental conditions.

2. Goal setting is regulated by a complex hedonic process of maximizing anticipated pleasure and minimizing anticipated unpleasure.

3. Pleasures and unpleasures are innate integral properties of survival and emotional significance capacities.

4. Hedonic processes serve to regulate attention to environmental conditions at the time of their occurrence, allowing the person to learn the relationship between the two by the process of classical conditioning.

5. Hedonic conditioning to attended aspects of environmental conditions results in the occurrence of hedonics when these aspects are all or part of anticipated experiences.

6. The hedonic process occurring to anticipated experiences regulates planning for the attainment of environmental conditions which maximize pleasure or minimize unpleasure or, most often, a combination of the two.

7. The ability to plan to maximize pleasure—that is, to restore organized interaction with the environment—and to minimize unpleasure—plan to escape or avoid disruption of organized interaction—is the basis of the capacity to survive, and therefore to reproduce both the individual and the species.

8. The great flexibility of the capacities involved in this regulation of human behavior carry the potentials for humans to be motivated in ways which may not

serve either their survival or their reproduction; yet, at the same time, as they develop this way for some individuals, they carry the potentials for others to recognize these possibilities (vicarious learning), to plan to avoid them for themselves, and to influence others in a similar way.

The Hedonic Process

The hedonic process is an innate, integral property of the significance capacities of the individual. The survival significance capacities are recognizable experiences. One of their properties is the quality of either unpleasure or pleasure.[16] Each primary emotion is also a distinctly recognizable experience, and one of its properties is either the quality of pleasure or unpleasure.[17] These are qualities in the same sense as those of color in vision. They are part of events in the central nervous system. Hedonic processes in the significance capacities have a dimension of intensity such that they can vary from weak to strong. The intensity of them varies directly with the intensity of the survival and emotional significance experience, for example, the greater the hunger the greater the unpleasure, the greater the anxiety the greater the unpleasure, or the greater the joy the greater the pleasure.

Both the discrete experiences identifying an emotion and its hedonic component are conditionable. For example, the memory of a frustrating experience, at least initially, redintegrates anger and unpleasure. However, only the hedonic component of survival significance experiences is conditionable. For example, memory of an experience of hunger, thirst, a bitter taste, or having one's tooth drilled evokes unpleasure but not hunger, thirst, bitter taste, or a pain in the tooth.[18]

The occurrence of the hedonic process regulates attention. That is, there is attention to the quality of pleasure or unpleasure and to some aspect or aspects of the current environmental conditions. Which aspect is a function of the current organization of the total person plus the influence of innate attention-regulating processes such as movement, large variations in stimulation, etc. The simultaneous occurrence of the hedonic process and the recognition of whatever is attended to produces the conditioning of the two such that the recognition of the object, setting, etc., or the occurrence of it in thought redintegrates the hedonic quality experienced.[19] This constitutes attitude formation. An attitude is defined, usually, as a predisposition to respond positively or negatively to the object. However, it is more useful to conceive of the attitude as a conditioned feeling rather than as a predisposition to respond, because there is no behavioral component to an attitude. An attitude toward something recognized or thought about is only one component of a complex process of organization that may be manifested in any of a great variety of behaviors.

The regulation of attention by hedonic processes entails that they are never unconscious per se. The object of the attitude is subject to defensive processes, but the hedonic component of the attitude is not. Thus, the person may experience anger, anxiety, or sadness and not know why or what it is connected with. The defensive process may result in thoughts which evoke other attitudes that replace the original hedonic component with another one, but the original hedonic component was experienced initially, albeit perhaps very briefly.[20] In fact, it regulated the initiation of the defensive process.

The Incentive Nature of Motivation

Humans are not usefully understood as driven by hedonic experience to behavior. Neither intense pain nor powerful emotion instigates behavior. That is because all behavior, with the exception of reflexes, is the manifestation of very complex states of organization of the total body. Hedonic experience always occurs in the context of such states and constitutes a change that interacts with the remainder of the state plus the information from the current environment to determine a new organization. The behavior of the person is the manifestation of this new state of organization. Moreover, the behavior always is based on the attainment of anticipated environmental conditions, because it is regulated by anticipated goals.

This incentive nature of motivation occurs because of the capacities of humans to represent sequencing in experience. After very early childhood, the possibilities of experiencing situations in which no expectations are evoked diminishes rapidly. By adulthood, at least, the individual is capable of forming possible expectations for any situation encountered. As a result, his behavior will be motivated by his assessment of the relative pleasure or unpleasure of his current situation and of those he can anticipate. For example, a solitary person hurt in a car accident who thinks he has a broken back or neck, even though in great pain, will not move except reflexively unless he anticipates either that not moving will produce even more pain or death or that by movement he can reduce the pain either immediately or eventually. When he does move, it will be in a particular fashion in accordance with his learning as reflected in his anticipations. Behavior always is regulated by anticipated hedonics relative to current hedonics. Continuing the same behavior, even if that means remaining "motionless," is motivated behavior based on anticipated hedonics.[21]

Goal Setting and Planning

A goal can be defined as an anticipated set of environmental conditions toward the attainment of which the individual is currently implementing a plan. A plan can be defined as an anticipated sequence of behaviors and environmental conditions leading to a goal. For example, a person is in one set of environmental conditions and experiencing pleasures and/or unpleasures due to either primary or conditioned hedonics. This setting inevitably evokes anticipations of possible behaviors and the attainment of new conditions, including possibly ending up in the same conditions. As the new conditions are anticipated, pleasures and unpleasures conditioned to all or components of them are evoked. Individualists experience these processes in terms of "I could do this, which will have some consequences I like and some I don't, or that, which I also have mixed feelings about. Which shall I choose?" All of the processes that result in the consciousness of particular anticipations may not be, and usually are not, conscious. From the naturalistic standpoint, what is occurring at this time is a complex process of weighting the anticipated conditions in terms of their hedonics. That set of anticipated conditions that carries the maximum conditioned pleasure or minimum conditioned unpleasure automatically becomes the goal situation. That is the essence of the idea of hedonic motivation. The conditions associated with the greatest organization or the least disruption of organization determine the goal. The goal is thus established as the regulator of behavior. The behavior will be that which is part of the anticipation of what behavior leads to that goal. In simple cases, a single goal sets the plan.

That a goal regulates behavior in accordance with a plan for its attainment is evidenced in many ways. A person seeking to attain a goal is almost always immediately aware of environmental conditions inconsistent with his plan. He is not merely aware that conditions are not what he anticipated but of their implications for his goal. For example, if a student read in the newspaper one morning that his college had burned down, he would think immediately not only that there was no building for him to attend class in but also that his goal of getting a degree was being interfered with. A person distracted from an activity may then ask himself, "Now, where was I?," and not only his activity but the goal toward which it is relevant will be recalled. Disruptions of plans to a goal immediately produce alterations of the plan, if possible, designed to attain the same goal. For example, if a person is driving to a particular location and finds a sign indicating his road is closed, he will immediately be thinking about what alternative route he can take *to his goal.* Many of these alterations occur with virtually no hesitation or time lost because the plan exists at a level of abstraction that readily encompasses substitutable alternative behaviors. Only these come into play because the goal is regulating the planning.

The vast bulk of human behavior is regulated by very complex and long-range plans designed to attain multiple goals. It would be too great a diversion here to discuss the establishment of long-range goals and the complex rounds of life by which individuals go about trying to attain them. These topics are discussed in the sections on value systems and the round of life in Chapter 9. However, it is important to emphasize that many factors enter into them. To begin with, humans are capable, particularly with the aid of speech, of formulating extremely extended sequences of anticipations. A simple example would be the plan of any individual for getting from his home to his place of work in another town. Important here is that each distinct set of anticipated conditions in the sequence may have hedonic conditionings, for example, that is a dangerous curve, that is an ugly section of town, the drive by the lake is beautiful. That is, the individual will be anticipating the experience of various pleasures and un-pleasures as the plan is implemented. This factor is responsible for the observations that a person will engage in behaviors or attain conditions that he finds very unpleasant and will do so with knowledge beforehand. This apparent contradiction of the principle of maximizing pleasure and minimizing unpleasure can be explained either in terms of the unpleasant conditions being less unpleasant than any other anticipated or as regulated by the greater pleasure of the long-range goal—"It will be worth it in the long run" or "Hard work pays off in the end."

Another complexity in human goal setting and planning comes from the capacity to represent probabilities of the occurrence of sequences. Some anticipations are more likely than others and, other things being equal, the establishment of the plan will be regulated by the sequence with the highest probability. Unless two or more sequences have certainty, a bird in the hand is worth two in the bush. Another factor is that the individual can represent time limits on the goal-setting and planning process. That is, he can learn that the goal and plan must be formulated within a certain time or that some plans or parts of them require that particular behaviors or conditions occur within a given time. There is also the possibility of the attainment of subgoals during implementation of a plan toward a more important goal. For example, one can take the scenic or the dull route to a location, or take a section of a required college course that does or does not include a friend or has a pleasant or unpleasant professor. Both plans and goals can change as a result of new learning during the course of implementation of a plan. The process is immensely complex but can be understood in terms of the interaction of a limited set of factors.

It follows from the previous discussions of incentive motivation and goal setting and planning that human behavior is intentional. All behavior is regulated by the future as it is represented in anticipations based on past experience. The present is regulated by the future based on the past. There is no implication here that the individual has only conscious intentions, that is, goals. He almost always has some conscious way of thinking about what he is doing and why, but it may be, and often is, a defensive derivative of another intention of which he is not conscious. In either case, his behavior is intentional in the sense that it is goal-oriented, purposive, and regulated by anticipation.

It also follows that, contrary to conventional thinking, the emotions serve adaptive, not maladaptive, functions. They serve to signal maladaptive and adaptive relationships to the environment. Moreover, through their conditionability, they serve to permit the individual to anticipate maladaptiveness or adaptiveness and to plan to avoid the former and to attain the latter. Thus their primary function is to preserve organized interaction with the environment. Perhaps the main reason why the emotions have been regarded for so long as maladaptive is the observation that sometimes individuals act impulsively, or rather plan poorly, when conditions producing strong emotions occur. For example, out of strong anger or jealousy, people may kill; or out of depression, commit suicide; or out of fear, run away from conditions that must be dealt with. However, it is important to recognize that, while such behaviors occur, they are not normative after childhood. In fact, they usually are regarded as immature behaviors. This means that the individual has not learned a normative way to resolve or deal with the underlying conflict, not that the emotion is irrational or maladaptive. The vast majority of members of a group, even though they experience strong emotions, tend to respond adaptively. This has required a great deal of learning during development. There is no doubt that for a period of perhaps twelve to fourteen years, or even a little longer, strong emotions in children may produce behaviors poorly adapted to conditions. Normatively, in any human group the child is protected from the more serious consequences of these reactions by the supervision of older members until he has sufficient learning to use his emotions adaptively. Thus, it appears human evolution has made the emotional capacities and a long period of dependency in childhood interdependent in human nature.

The hedonic approach to human motivation also emphasizes the functional properties of consciousness, where consciousness is understood as attentional process. Far from being epiphenomenal, consciousness serves the key purpose of selectively identifying, in most cases, the information relevant to learning about what serves the maintenance of organized interaction with the environment. It serves to select from all that is going on around the individual those conditions related to disruption of organization or restoral of organization and feeds them into ongoing total bodily organization, that is, relates them to the proper context of previous learning operant at the time.[22]

The Evolutionary Paradox

The flexible capacities of humans provide the solution to the riddle of how a species can evolve to become the most adaptive and able to manipulate its environment and at the same time develop group ways of life that do not serve either the survival or the reproduction of the genes of substantial proportions of members. Among these capacities, that of speech plays the principal role. It permits the conditioning of strong emotions to abstract concepts that, under many circumstances, can dominate goal setting and, therefore, behavior.

The capacities to generalize and to discriminate are largely regulated by the speech that the young child hears. The words of the language spoken by the significant others in his stratum of his group direct the process of generalization and discrimination to provide their definitions in terms of the core of conditions consistently correlated with their usage. The development of linguistic competence, however, is not simply an intellectual exercise. A great deal of it is systematically related to what is significant to the group life. As a result, some concepts become strongly conditioned to particular emotions or combinations of them with their hedonic components. The most important of these constitute a limited set which comprise the shared value system of the group or stratum. An explanation of the development and functions of value systems is offered in Chapter 9. Here it will be emphasized only that these value concepts become the primary motivational bases for individual behavior.

Value concepts probably always are products of the development of the reflexive capacity. That is, they emerge from speech-directed reflection on behavior. They constitute for the individual the most important ways of thinking about behavior and experience. They are, as some psychologists have noted, the most inclusive attitudes.

Values associated with the self-system are the primary sources of self-esteem or its opposite. The individual inevitably will be strongly motivated toward maintaining or attaining high self-esteem. It should not be surprising, then, that in some groups males will engage in considerable risk taking or in martial practices which evidence their masculinity. Nor should it be surprising that various forms of martyrdom occur in the fulfillment of moral values. It is important to note that these behaviors that are inconsistent with the survival of the individual are normative behaviors at least for members of particular strata in a group. Many other practices potentially inconsistent with survival or with the reproduction of genes constitute nonnormative but not uncommon goal setting based on more severe degrees of common conflicts occurring in development in a particular group. Thus, among twentieth-century Americans, common conflicts in the learning of masculinity and femininity in childhood may result in strong hedonics conditioned to the concept of self as the opposite of what is normative for sexual identity—homosexuality, or common conflicts over the learning of the moral place of sexuality in life may result in the avoidance of sexual behavior either on an idiosyncratic basis or in a socially channeled form such as celibacy in the priesthood. A value for the unconditional love of some other may become so difficult to attain that the individual may decide that the promise of love by a god or some other after death will provide more pleasure than any further attempts to attain love in current life (suicide). The metaphorical meaning of freedom may be such that the individual comes to prefer death to tyranny, for example, "better dead than red." Even physical torture for the masochist can be less unpleasant, because of its meanings in the relationship to the sadist, than the anxieties or guilts that it allays.

These may be considered by products or side effects of the evolution of a set of very flexible capacities which give humankind its particular niche in the ecology of this planet. These capacities permit humans to adapt to an astonishing array of environmental conditions, including adaptation by altering the conditions substantially, such as with electricity, submarines, air conditioning, dams, clearing of land, etc. At least equally important is that the social dimension of these capacities provides the basis for learning from the observation of the behaviors of others. Consequently, although whole human groups may develop ways of life that may prove inconsistent with their survival, and perhaps those of their neighbors, others can learn about the relationships of these ways of life to survival or to reproduction. This learning becomes part of the process of further goal setting. Thus human evolution has produced a self-correcting process which serves to preserve the species even though it does not serve to preserve many of its individual members.

FIELD-ORGANIZATION OF BEHAVIOR

Having a set of very flexible capacities means that the organization of behavior is complex. There exists what will be called here a field-organization of behavior. The field is the total person. However, the focus of this view will be on the nature of learning about the environment to the neglect of its relationship to the organization of functioning of the whole body.

The idea of field-organization of behavior is based on the recognition of the complex interrelationships among all aspects of human learning which are generated by the order in the environment. For social anthropologists this order is called "the culture," but it includes the order in the nonhuman environment. Thus, it is equivalent to the sophisticated form of the idea of an ecological system where the members of a human group are regarded as integral parts. The developing child is introduced to this ecological system simply by daily living in it. From the moment of his awakening in the morning, his environment is influencing him in many ways. Increasingly, as he develops, almost any stimulation evokes related processes in a fashion which rapidly establishes whole-brain activity. The brain as a field is organized and functioning. This view is the very opposite of the behavioristic notion of chains of stimulus-response habits. As the individual behaves and encounters changes in his environment, the feedback stimulation enters an already organized field which processes it.

All behavior occurs in space and time and in the pursuit of goals. These three dimensions, discussed earlier, become increasingly integrated during development into complex patterns of behavior that flow relatively smoothly from one to another. This is due to the order in the developing person's environment. Patterns of group life constitute the main part of the context in which the child is learning, and the child's experiences inevitably will reflect these patterns. One need only consider the close parallel between the daily life of a school-aged child and that of workers in the occupational realm in the United States today. The child has to orient to daily life in a very similar, if general, way. He arises in the morning and his behavior is governed by whether it is a school (work) day or a weekend day. He must dress accordingly and think in terms of readiness for school and its time scheduling. When he gets to school, he has his assigned area and place within it, much as does a worker on the production line of a factory or in an office. He then is engaged in tasks assigned by his teacher (boss) and learns that he not only has standards of performance but is competing with others for the scarce rewards of good grades (pay and promotion). His day has the same general schedule of work, lunch break, work, termination of work, and return to home. The transition from high school to the workplace in these general terms is very facile.[23] There seems little reason to doubt that something similar occurs to children in all human groups, although the patterns vary immensely across groups and, to some extent, among the strata of a group.

This general pattern of life establishes for each individual the space and time frames for all behavior. For recent Americans, the time frame is the workweek, consisting of five variations—workdays, Saturdays, Sundays, holidays (including vacation periods), and sick days. Every day is one of these and has its general organization. In agricultural groups the time frame may be that of the main crop cycle. For nomadic groups it may be seasonal or based on cycles of flora or fauna. Near the magnetic poles of the earth, it may be organized around periods of light and darkness. The space frame of life is that bounded by the areas in which regular activities take place, although these will be supplemented by some recognition of a wider space rarely visited or occupied only before or after death. This supplementary space is normatively very much secondary to that of daily activities. Once this space frame is learned, it takes on the character of a boundary for activity. It is differentiated into locations in which particular kinds of activities occur.

The two dimensions of space and time become steadily integrated into sequences of time, locations, and activities. These are the primary scripts of life. A script in its simplest form can be understood as a sequence of behaviors in interaction with components of a location. Examples of this might be cooking a meal, eating at a restaurant, a visit to the doctor's office, getting dressed in the morning, playing bridge with friends, planting a particular crop or harvesting it, a typical day at the office, etc. Scripts then become organized in more complex forms of sequences of simpler scripts. For the average American in recent years, daily life on a weekday (workday) is a very stable and complex script of dressing for work, having breakfast, getting to work, work, lunch, work, getting home, having dinner, and then, usually, some regular evening script before retiring. Saturdays, Sundays, holidays, and sick days are different complex scripts. All other activities tend to be interpolated into these scripts or to be systematic variations of them.

The scripts, of course, are intimately related to the goals which the individual seeks in life. In fact, the child learns his primary goals (values) as he performs in and learns life's major scripts. Thus, script performances are the primary means by which goals are attained in life. Once the individual has learned his system of values and his space and time frames, his life is organized into quite stable repetitions of complex scripts. Very important in this learning is that, through the capacities for generalization and discrimination, the individual learns scripts at various levels of abstraction. This is because, through discrimination learning, he comes to identify a number of possible variations of general scripts. For example, most of the tasks of the school day have the same general script of sitting at one's desk, studying from some book, listening to the teacher lecture, and trying to answer the teacher's questions. This is the same whether it is spelling, or history, or composition, or geography. Similarly, in the work world of the adult, one can take any of many jobs, and they do not vary with respect to the general daily script of the workday. Playing cards at X's home or eating at X restaurant has variations from the same activities in other homes or restaurants but within the same general script. The generality of scripts can vary. For example, the general script of a game of golf is the same for all golf, but there are systematic variations for full courses and executive courses. Within any full or short course, there are the variations that come with the terrain and layout of the course, playing in wind or rain, etc.

Central to the idea of the field-organization of behavior is the idea that the various levels of abstraction of any script are always *simultaneously* parts of the field. A game of golf at X course is simultaneously a game of executive golf and a game of golf. The individual processes the experience at all of these levels. It is not different with respect to goals. While winning the bridge game at X's house, one is simultaneously winning at cards and winning in competition in general. This particular Tuesday is a Tuesday as well as a workday in the week. Grabbing a quick lunch at the nearest McDonald's is a quick lunch and a lunch. The nearest McDonald's is also a McDonald's and a quick lunch place and an eating place. Thus, there is always a complex hierarchical organization to the field of behavior. It is fundamental in understanding behavior, because the feedback to the individual from his behavior in a particular time and place is monitored or regulated at all levels.

The field-organization of behavior should be understood in terms of "top-down" regulation. That is, the most abstract level is the primary regulator. For example, with respect to the subscript of having lunch, the abstract components of workday, eating place, and getting food are most important. Experiences inconsistent with this level of regulation have the greatest impact on organization. Tuesday, quick lunch place, hamburger, and a drink are at a more specific level. This particular Tuesday, the local McDonald's, a Big Mac, and a vanilla shake are at a more specific level. Feedback from such experiences as the McDonald's has gone out of business, it is out of vanilla milkshakes, or the wait will be so long I won't get back early enough for today's crucial department meeting, usually will require reorganization of the field at more specific levels, for example, go next door to Wendy's, have a chocolate shake, and eat the hamburger while walking back to the office.

The key to "top-down" field-organization of behavior is that what happens to the implementation of a plan toward a goal in time and place is potentially significant at any level of the hierarchy. The higher the level, the greater is the need for reorganization of the field. However, it is equally important to recognize that the field has a script organization which is also hierarchical. Having lunch is only part of the complex script of daily life, and daily life is only a variant of the general round of life by which the individual is attempting to realize and preserve the realization of all his values. Thus, to be driving to work and to have an accident in which one is seriously injured affects not only getting to work but the whole daily script and very likely the individual's round of life. It will have implications, not only for his job, but for his family relationships and other non-work related activities and relationships. One cannot explain the behavior of a person without a conceptualization of the total field of which it is only the observable manifestation.

At the most specific level of script organization, the individual is interacting directly with his environment. Take, for example, the daily workday script. For most Americans it has the sequence described earlier. The first part is to get dressed for work. That is an abstract level. The individual will have his personal script for getting dressed. He may first put on underwear, then shoes and socks, then shirt, then pants. At the most specific level, it requires picking up particular items from particular locations. This requires interaction with his environment. It entails that attention be fine-tuned to space and sequence. To put on his shoe at this level requires that there be a shoe to pick up. His specific script may be to reach under the end of his bed for a shoe because his getting-undressed script includes putting his shoes there. He anticipates that when he reaches under the bed his hand will touch a shoe. He requires this feedback from the environment to continue to perform the script.[24] If his wife has moved his shoes in order to vacuum, let us say, and not replaced them, then his script implementation is interrupted at this very specific point. It is very unlikely that such experience will entail reorganization of the field at any higher level of abstraction. He will simply implement his expectation of the next most probable location of his shoes, as it is likely that similar events have occurred before. However, if in reaching for the shoe, he cuts his hand severely on the corner of the bed frame, there may be reorganization of the field at the level of daily script. He may have to reorganize for the too-sick-to-go-to-work script and start implementing his dress-for-the-doctor's-office-visit script, and so on. If a man is having lunch on a workday and, looking out the window of the restaurant, sees his wife hit by a car, his field will be reorganized, perhaps, at the very highest level. He will not only reorganize for getting his wife to the hospital, abandoning his usual workday script, but will be reorganizing at the level of his round of life in terms of the implications of his wife's injury or death. It is important to recognize that such reorganizations, whether specific or very abstract, begin extremely quickly on the feedback from the environment and can be organized and implemented without any, or only very minimal, conscious planning. This is because the total field is operant at the moment, and the feedback is monitored at every level.

Also central to the total person field-organization view of behavior is the recognition that the field includes the total body of the person. Learning during development is not confined to the brain. As the nervous system is constantly interacting with the other organ systems of the body, there is an integral relationship between the brain-states or processes and the manner in which the other systems are functioning. The disposition among psychologists to dichotomize body functioning into healthy, normal, optimal versus unhealthy, abnormal, less than optimal states masks a great deal of variation in body functioning which is necessary to understand behavior. Particular feedback from the environment may interact with any of a variety of states of functioning in ways which influence reorganization of the field. These interactions can have a cumulative effect over time. Consequently, the psychology of human nature, consonant with the naturalistic view, must include terminology and principles for the conceptualization of total body functioning. This does not confound psychological science with biological science. As explained earlier, it is a matter of conceptualization at the most abstract levels.

A final consideration in this topic is the relationship between the conceptualization of the personality and of the field-organization of behavior. Here it is important to maintain a focus on a conceptualization of personality that serves to explain the full range of patterns of behavior observable across time and space. It follows that the scripts and goals the person learns and has are aspects of personality. However, these are too specific for the explanation of the broad ranges and patterns of behavior of the individual that personality theory serves. As this topic occurs prior to the conceptualization of personality, which will be presented in Chapter 8, only the most general sort of indication of the relationship between personality and field-organization of behavior is possible.

Personality is manifest in the selection of scripts that the individual performs. There seems little doubt that the extent of individual selection of scripts is a major variable in group ways of life. In some groups the major script repertories of individuals are ascribed rather than achieved. Perhaps comparing upper-middle-class modern American life with that on the medieval manor suggests this distinction. Yet there always will be some room for selection such as friendships and leisure-time activities. Included here must be those less common and briefer scripts which the individual interpolates into the normative general script performances of his group or stratum, for example, hobbies. A second way in which personality is related to field-organization of behavior is in the manner or expressive style in which script performances occur. This is what is indicated in current trait psychology where such terms as aggressive-assertive, dependent-independent, rigid-flexible, extroverted-introverted are employed. The third way—probably most important and very complex—is in the ways in which feedback from the environment are reflected upon. Most obvious here, perhaps, is reflection on the self-system, that is, what the experience means to the individual about himself. In addition, reflection in terms of worldview and ideology are important. Finally, the form that this reflection takes as mode of thought also must be recognized. All of these are central to the explanation of reorganization of the field of behavior generated by the feedback from the environment in the performance of scripts.

CONCLUSION

The approach to human nature through the idea of flexible capacities, hedonic motivation, and field-organization of behavior provides the conceptual power necessary to resolve the "anthropologist's dilemma." It does so by recognizing that the order in environmental influences shapes the development of these capacities. It preserves a consistency with evolutionary theory but avoids the narrower and more teleological forms of that theory. Its emphasis on environmental influences avoids the long-standing pitfalls entailed in the assumption of the inheritance of personality traits and behavioral dispositions, of which sociobiology is only the latest form. In their place, it focuses attention on individual variations in the flexible capacities. Such variations lack the constriction of trait and dispositional views because, whatever they are, they too are shaped by the order in environmental influences. This approach favors such ideas as variation in the heredity of attention span, frustration tolerance, some forms of memory, sensory thresholds, etc., none of which can be tied directly to behavior or to stable personality traits. At the same time, it permits explanation of very diverse behaviors in those who may have very similar forms of flexible capacities.[25]

This approach obviously requires a great deal of fleshing out, particularly with respect to memory processes, conflict management, complex emotions, and the roles of speech and imagery. Some important aspects of human nature not included in the foregoing have to do with development through the life span. Some of these are addressed in Chapter 9 on personality development. Before that topic can be adequately conceptualized, it is necessary to deal with the most neglected aspect of the general model of psychology—a conceptualization of environmental influences.

Environmental Influences through the Life Span

Every person, with rare exceptions, is born into a human group consisting of three or four interacting generations. Members of the older generations have been strongly influenced during their lives by now deceased generations. Many of the artifacts of the group were produced by members of long-deceased generations. Over many generations this group has developed a complex and dynamic relationship with its nonhuman environment. In addition, the group has long-worked-out relationships to the other human groups in its environment. The group, its nonhuman environment, and neighboring groups all have their dynamic processes of change that are interdependent. The dynamic processes have rates of change that, at any period of time, can be located on a dimension from very slow to very rapid.

The pattern of interactions of members of a group with one another, with their artifacts, with members of other groups, and with the nonhuman environment constitutes the life of the group. It is the total environment for members of the group.[1] However, no individual member ever experiences it totally. No member ever interacts with all other members of his group in all the patterns of interaction, nor with all the group's artifacts, in all its settings, or with neighboring groups. This is why the socioanthropological idea of a culture that socializes its members generation after generation has not proved useful. It is too gross, too rigid, to explain how environmental influences interact with individuals to determine the broad ranges of behavior that constitute the group life. A reified culture or social system is both inconsistent with a naturalistic view of human science and unnecessary. Environmental influences are far more individualized.

The more recent redefinition of culture in terms of webs of meaning, conceptual structures, and symbol systems only partially overcomes the reification problem. There remains to be explained the ontological status of these webs, structures, and systems. Meanings, concepts, or symbols must be understood as properties or characteristics of individuals and, therefore, as psychological in nature. However, cultural anthropologists are properly opposed to the psychologizing of the concept, because it fails to account for the bases of the individual's acquisition of these characteristics. They insist that something outside the individual must be responsible for the bases.[2] Unfortunately, the ways in which they refer to this something frequently retains the quality of a reification.[3] One consequence of this disposition is to give to culture a monolithic quality too rigid to account for the variations of meanings among the members of a group. A second consequence is the resultant necessity to account for the dynamics of culture over time.

The usefulness of the concept of culture can be preserved without its undesirable implications by recognizing that webs of meaning must be recreated in the individuals comprising each new generation. Such webs cannot be handed down or passed on except as they provide the conditions of life that recreate the learning of the individual. Learning is a complex process which goes on in the person. However, the person is born with only a set of very flexible capacities for learning. Therefore, it must be the conditions of his life that are responsible for his recreation of webs of meaning. That is, the culture is outside the individual in the very complex arrangements and sequences of experiences that produce the learning of them. Apparently, one of the major problems which cultural anthropologists have created for themselves is the disposition to think in terms of a trichotomy of the precultured individual, culture, and the natural (nonhuman) environment. In this they seem to adhere to the individualistic disposition, discussed in Chapter 3, to separate the social from the nonsocial environment. It must be recognized that, from the standpoint of the newborn member of the group, the environment is a very complex mixture of the two. Moreover, the properties of each are interdependent. They constitute an environmental matrix within which the new member learns. This matrix is what is referred to herein as environmental influences or conditions of life. It must be understood as sequentially encountered through the life span.

The concept of culture is preserved by the recognition that many of the conditions of life for each member of the group are similar enough that, at the abstract level of learning, they produce a significant body of shared learning, in other words, shared webs of meaning or conceptual structures. At the same time, this approach leaves plenty of room for variations of conditions specific to the different strata of the group and still other variations specific to individuals. The concept of culture is preserved, but without its monolithic and rigid qualities. Equally importantly, the approach provides the bases for the understanding of the dynamics of cul ture via all things which contribute to changes in shared environmental influences, for example, technological developments, cultural diffusion, natural catastrophes, the dynamic stresses within the shared learning itself. If the shared conditions of life are very similar for several subsequent generations, culture only appears to be handed down or passed on. If they change significantly, so does the culture. Culture is not psychologized. Its ontological status is the shared pattern of environmental influences to which individuals are subject as they live from birth to death. To be more precise, it is the pattern of shared patterns of environmental influences that comprises the experiences of members of all the strata of the group. That is, culture comprises a set of shared patterns. This set itself includes a portion that is part of each subset. This overlapping portion is what makes each individual a member of his group, but it is only part of culture. Members of each stratum have a larger shared pattern of conditions which produce variants of a web of meaning. Membership in a stratum entails differences in webs of meaning from that of other strata, yet each stratum has its sense of the meaning for them of members of the other strata. These variants of a web of meaning for all strata taken together are the psychological product or expression of the culture.

Perhaps the greatest difficulty with the concept of culture stems from the fact that the speech and behavior of other members of the group are central aspects of the conditions of life for each member, and this speech and behavior reflect the webs of meaning that these others have learned. However, it is essential to bear in mind that webs of meaning per se are never part of the environmental influences on any individual. The influences of other humans always are their speech and behavior that express the webs of meaning they have learned but which, themselves, cannot be experienced by another.

In summary, culture is an important and useful concept if it is not reified or psychologized. It exists outside of each member of a group in the form of the pattern of life conditions to which each individual is exposed through his life span. It is not all of these conditions, but only those shared by all members *and* those widely shared by members of each stratum. These conditions include the speech and behaviors of other members of the group. The effect of the exposure of each member to the set of conditions widely shared among members of his stratum and of all strata is his learning of a web of meaning that is a variant of a prototypical web of meaning in his group. In this sense, these webs of meaning are the psychological product or expression of the culture.[4]

Human science cannot make the mistake of going to the other extreme from monolithic culture represented by realist psychology, by regarding environmental influences as utterly fragmented. It cannot treat environment as nothing more than the conditions of the experimental lab and its independent variables with no concern for environment in natural settings

(Bronfenbrenner 1979). It cannot treat environment as nothing more than isolated trauma that produce abnormal behaviors, nor as unrelated experiences producing this or that particular bit of learning. There is order, pattern, and system in the environmental influences on every individual throughout his life span. It exists in the personalities of the others he relates to and how they perceive his relationship to them in the ways in which he is introduced to common activities, in the arrangements of artifacts and natural phenomena, in the processes of nonhuman things, animate and inanimate, and in the functioning of his own body.

The failure of psychologists to attend to order in the environmental influences on the individual and the manner in which this order is encountered through the life span is primarily responsible for their inability to make significant contributions to social problem solving. There simply is no psychology of normative behavior. Nothing whatever has been contributed to the understanding of what individuals share as members of their group or of their stratum in the group. While most socioanthropologists have been attributing the vast bulk of behavior to the influence of a reified culture or social system, psychologists ignore the pattern of group life. Instead, being strongly attracted to genetic and chemical accounts, they seek explanations within the individual. While the latter certainly have their roles to play in psychological science, they must be recognized as secondary factors which help to understand variations from the normative behaviors which give cohesion to group life and distinguish it from that of other groups.

There is order in environmental influences. The key concern for a theory of environmental influences lies in how to conceptualize the ways in which they are organized so that they re-create the webs of meaning during the life span of each individual. This chapter presents the approach of relativistic naturalism to this topic. It is based on the social anthropological concept of age-grading systems as modified by considerations from life-span developmental psychology.

AGE-GRADING SYSTEMS IN INDIVIDUAL DEVELOPMENT

In social anthropology an age-grading system is comprised of sets of expectations held by members of the group concerning the behavior of other members for particular periods of time through the life span.[5] That is, the life span is divided into periods during which particular behaviors are regarded as appropriate and inappropriate. These expectations are understood as social pressures on the individual to conform to group norms during each period. Different expectations are held for various groupings of members. Most members do conform. Those who do not are considered deviants. In this way the culture, or way of life, is passed down from generation to generation. Thus, age-grading systems are one way of conceiving of environmental influences on individual development.

Age-grading systems have been discovered in all groups studied.[6] This is something that human science can scarcely ignore. However, the anthropological conception of them is of little use in its present form. It fails to account for why members of a group hold the particular expectations for particular periods. It treats the individual as little more than one who conforms to the expectations of others. This ignores the relationship between earlier and later learning in individual development. By focusing only on social expectations, it neglects all other influences. Finally, it does not account for why some members fail to conform. Clearly, a more psychologically sophisticated conception of age-grading systems is required.

Unfortunately, little help with this task is provided by developmental psychology. At first glance, it appears that the prominent idea of stages of development is similar to age-grading. Although whether or not human development proceeds in stages has long been an issue in psychology, it appears that most developmental psychologists think it does. The agreement, however, stops there. There is little agreement on which and how many stages there are and little conceptualization of what determines initiation and termination of a stage. The views presented differ significantly from the age-grading idea in regarding all stages as fixed and universal and in usually ending with adolescence.[7] None of them in any way can be regarded as proposing a conceptualization of environmental influences through the life span or any part of it. However, there are useful suggestions concerning the nature of some stages sprinkled through the psychological literature. The following account draws on these and many other sources in attempting to make the age-grading system idea serviceable in human science as a conceptualization of environmental influences.

A revised definition of an age-grade is: a period of the life span during which the individual encounters a set of conditions that is not encountered normatively at other periods of the life span and that requires extensive new learning and a reorganization of his round of life. An age-grading system is the particular sequence of age-grades which the individual encounters through his life span. An age-grade, then, is a stage of human development during which the individual adjusts to, copes with, or learns within a particular set of conditions, given what he brings with him from his variant of human nature and from his learning in previous age-grades. The key terms of the definition are "set of conditions" and "period of the life span." These require considerable elaboration. It has to take a form consistent with the general model of psychology. Human nature has been conceived in terms of flexible learning capacities, hedonic motivation, and field-organization of behavior. It follows that environmental influences must be conceptualized in a specific enough form to translate their effects on the individual into these terms.

Sets of Conditions

The major distinction between the definition proposed for age-grades and that of the social anthropologists is the substitution of the term "sets of conditions" for "sets of expectations." This is done to deal with the key question of where the expectations come from. It takes the position that the set of conditions of the age-grade, interacting with the individual's personality as it has developed to the time of encountering them, determines the further development of his flexible capacities and, therefore, of his behavior. Over time in a human group, at least during periods of slow rates of change, members of the group become familiar with normative and abnormative behaviors during the various age-grades of their system. Hence, they come to expect those kinds of behavior and to judge them accordingly. Their expectations do become environmental influences on the individual, but these are very much secondary to the influence of the rest of the conditions being encountered. They are secondary in the sense that the acceptable normative adjustments are not produced by group expectations. They normatively occur and are accepted. Only the abnormative adjustments are subject to group pressure as unacceptable. Coping with the set of conditions is what dominates the life of the individual during the age-grade.

Before elaborating on the term "set of conditions," it may be useful to cite some general examples to illustrate the idea. One set of conditions marking the onset of an age-grade for older generations of Americans was entrance to public school. This was required by law. At about the child's sixth birthday, he started first grade. Prior to that time, the child in the middle class, normatively, had remained at home each day with occasional visits to the home of friends primarily playing in unsupervised and informal ways or doing small chores. Thus, the beginning of school marked a great change in his life. From then on, on weekdays, he spent the bulk of his daylight hours at school, under new authority figures, doing new activities with a largely new group of peers. He learned that his parents were very interested in his behavior and performances in these new circumstances.

A vastly different set of conditions was encountered by the same generations of Americans in the age-grade called "middle age." These conditions included the "empty nest," that is, the last stages and completion of the movement of the children out of the family home, usually as a result of marriage and the setting up of their own domiciles; the consequent restriction of home life to the marital couple only for the first time in eighteen or more years; the menopause of the wife, which had significant consequences for the husband; the encountering of many young adults of their children's age in adult work and social settings; the death or dependency—emotional, material, or financial—of aged parents; and the largely negative stereotype of middle age in many forms.[8] Middle-age was a stage in which the individual had to adjust to these markedly new conditions of life. Normatively, the age-grading system for these generations of middle-class Americans had eight age-grades—infancy, toddlerhood, preschool, grammar school, adolescence, young adulthood, middle age, and old age.[9]

The examples given illustrate two key aspects of the age-grading approach to environmental influences. One is that an age-grade constitutes a stage of development in which the whole pattern of life undergoes significant change. New or changed relationships, activities, and settings occur. Extensive adjustment is required. It may be positively or negatively anticipated, smoothly accomplished or beset with difficulties, relished by the individual or bitterly regretted. Normatively, it will be a very mixed experience. The second aspect is that age-grading systems are systems in that the sets of conditions in succeeding age-grades are not independent of those in preceding ones and not just for proximal age-grades. The impact of any age-grade is a function of what the individual brings with him as personality development from the integrated influence of all previous age-grades.

There is a high degree of order in age-grading systems because of the necessity, in all human groups, to recognize and assimilate the life-span development of each member into the ongoing pattern of group life and because of the generational structure determined by the human reproductive system. Infants are born into the group, but there are severe limits to the functions they can serve in group life. There must be arrangements for their care. As their capacities develop through both maturation and learning, they can be assimilated in new ways. Particular relationships are developed and have important consequences for what happens in later age-grades. Children go through the changes of puberty and become adult in size and physical and reproductive power. These capacities have to be managed by socialization to the group life. The new generation begins to produce offspring, but at about the same time their grandparental generation begins to die off. The dying generation constitutes the parent generation of the generation that produced the generation now producing offspring. There can be no doubt that the members of all human groups recognize in important ways this generational structure of both the human life span and the group's way of life. The ways in which each generation functions in group life and the relationships developed vary greatly across human groups, but there inevitably are important continuities in them because human learning is an integrative process. The sets of conditions which comprise age-grades always are largely experienced in terms of changes from previous conditions which are heavy with significance.

The analysis of environmental influences by age-grades logically starts with the first one because what comes first determines how what comes later is processed, and what comes later must be integrated with what is already learned. The infant begins life with his variant of human nature that consists mainly of a set of very flexible capacities. The order in his environment, then, determines how they develop. There is a great deal of order, because the infant is born into a group way of life. It has its forms of assimilating the infant to it. There are many different ways of life and therefore many different forms in which the infant is introduced to them. Ethnocentric views such as that in American psychology about the mother-child relationship and the importance of love cannot serve as a starting point for this analysis.[10] A neutral approach can be made in terms of three components of an age-grade—the significant others related to, the activities engaged in, and the settings in which relationships and activities occur.[11] The patterning of these determine the child's learning of space frames, time frames, significance, and the primary scripts of group life.

Significant others refers to those persons who either interact on a regular basis with the individual or are regularly observed although not interacted with, or, although they do not interact frequently, do so in contexts of particular importance to the individual, for example, the principal of his grammar school, a grandparent, or a "bully" on the school ground. This dimension must include fictional others such as gods or spirits and figures heard or read about but not directly interacted with, such as heroes, past or present, and fictional persons in books or myths.[12] Important aspects of this dimension are the number of significant others, the dropping out of significant others from the previous age-grade, and the frequency of interaction compared to that in the previous age-grade. For example, in the middle-age age-grade referred to above, the "empty nest" refers to a marked decrease of interaction with the children; being thrown back on the marital relationship means a marked increase of husband-wife interaction; the death of a parent means the dropping out of a significant other. In the example given of the age-grade when public school begins, the teacher and classmates represent new significant others, while a peer friend may go to a different school and be seen much less often, as is also the child's mother. Specification of this dimension of an age-grade is made independently of the dimension of activities engaged in.

Activities engaged in must be defined in the broadest possible fashion to include the formal and the informal and those participated in or only observed. They can be as brief as playing "this little piggy," or having a race from the car to the home, or taking away a forbidden cookie and applying a few whacks on the posterior. They can be as long as taking a college course, daily close care of a dying parent, fasting, etc. There are important methodological problems of specifying activities having to do with both identifying what constitutes a unit of activity and deciding on the level of abstraction to be employed. They must be based on observation, not inference, concerning intentions. These problems are not insurmountable but clearly require far more extensive observation over time than is conventional in realist research. The extended observation serves to specify repetitiveness of activities and interactions that identify their initiation and termination.

In specifying activities engaged in, it is necessary to include whether they are solitary or dyadic or involve multiple others, the nature of artifacts used, and their time duration. Also important are the frequency of engagement in each activity and its relationship to that in the previous age-grade, including identification of activities no longer engaged in. Finally, sequencing of particular activities with relative frequencies should be identified.

Examples of activities can be drawn from the middle-age and public-school age-grades mentioned earlier. Six-year-olds have to travel to school, engage in various types of studies, take tests, cooperate on class projects, take gym class, stay after school, etc. At home, they usually are discouraged from certain activities now regarded by their parents, and sometimes by themselves, as appropriate only for younger children. In addition, they often compete with siblings at home in displaying new knowledge and in comparing their performances with respect to grades and academic skills, sometimes encouraged by parents. They are introduced to new activities through peers they meet or observe at school. On the other hand, middle-aged mothers engage markedly less often in many common child-rearing activities such as cooking meals, laundering, shopping, providing emotional support and advice, and disciplining. Fathers are no longer providing, protecting, and disciplining children. Many games, sports, and informal activities previously done with the children occur rarely or never. Activities with dependent aged parents increase, such as helping with maintenance in the parental home, taking them shopping or to the doctor's, informal visiting, planning budgets to include financial aid for them, etc. The marital couple usually now have more funds available to spend on themselves. With the "empty nest" and the wife's menopause, sexual relations may increase or decrease. A dependent parent may move in with a middle-aged child and spouse, introducing considerable change in activities.

The specification of settings also must be broadly conceived to include both the natural and the artifactual. The frequency with which a setting is experienced and its relativeness to that of the previous age-grade are important. Settings no longer lived in should be indicated. The sequencing of settings and the relative frequencies of each sequence need to be identified. Settings may be as restricted as confinement to a wheelchair or menstrual hut or as expansive as a tourist resort or a college campus. School-aged children begin to live in the school building, the classroom, the playground, the school bus or route they walk to school, and the homes of new friends. They spend much less time in their homes and yards and, during the week, only at certain periods of the day. Middle-aged people may spend more time in doctors' offices and restaurants, the homes of their aged parents or of their departed children, or in travel. They spend less time in settings watching their children perform or where they did things with or for their children.

A very important fourth dimension of sets of conditions has to do with the combinations of the first three. Activities always are engaged in within some setting and usually with some other persons. Moreover, daily life involves repetitive patterns of these. These combinations of activities with and without others in sequential settings are the bases of script learning, planning, and reflective understanding.

All environmental influences on the person can be encompassed in specifying the sets of conditions which define the age-grades of a person's life. This often will require that the dynamic course of certain conditions during an age-grade be identified. For example, during middle age the individual's aged parent may first be only emotionally dependent, then materially dependent, and then die. During the grammar-school age-grade, the child interacts with a series of teachers and engages in a curriculum of subjects. The age-grade cannot be understood in its impact unless these aspects of it are taken into account.

The task of specifying these components of each age-grade in an age-grading system appears overwhelming if the order in group life is not kept in mind. This order is best approached, not from the analysis of the age-grade of the individual, but from the opposite end—the role structure of the group. (Role definition and analysis is addressed in Chapter 10 and the general methodological approach of human science in Chapter 11.) The role structure reveals the system of social stratification of the group. Each member can be placed in it in terms of the set of roles or role variants he performs. Age-grade analysis starts by stratum, looking at the general pattern of change in conditions through the life span. Common variants such as those associated with urban, suburban, and rural areas quickly emerge. These are only variants of a common pattern. For example, individualistic middle-class life began with birth into a conjugal family in its own domicile and a division of labor between husband and wife who were married because of a deep emotional commitment; then changed in the child's relationship during toddlerhood as parents regarded the child as big enough to begin to learn to stand on his own two feet; changed again as the child became ready for peer social play, a wider range of settings, and the learning of femininity or masculinity and the rest of the value system; then again in the elementary school years; then via puberty, high school, and the emphasis on preparation for adult life and heterosexual relationships; then in marriage, family, the division of labor, and participation in adult community life; then the "empty nest," dependency of aged parents, the climacterium, etc.; and finally the set of conditions defining old age. Within this general pattern, the components of each age-grade can be specified at various levels of abstraction down to the very specific for an individual. Individual personality can be seen to be only a variation around shared character among members of a stratum. It must be remembered that the human scientist is not so much trying to construct the personality of the individual as he is trying to specify the particular form of the universal components of personality defined in his psychological theory (see Chapter 8).

A better perspective on the age-grading approach is gained when the variety of conditions of the first age-grade in group life across human groups is considered. For example, in some groups children are born into extended families, polygamous or polyandrous ones, families in which the blood father lives in another village and does not play a major parental role. In some groups marriages are arranged rather than based on deep emotional commitments. In others there are vastly different forms of the division of labor in the family and vastly different forms of domiciles for the child. In most there is no formal schooling. Technologies and artifacts, geology, climates, and flora and fauna differ radically. These are the essence of the conditions of life which make up age-grades. They occur in interdependent sets in an age-grading system. It would not be difficult for a resident social anthropologist to identify the combinations of common relationships, activities, and settings for various age-groups in his subject community by daily observation of the group way of life once he learned their basic space and time frames. For this it is not necessary to understand anything about the meanings. This is an approach to the environmental influences that, in interaction with human nature, determine meanings.

Period of the Life Span

The other key term in the definition of an age-grade is "period of the life span." A period is a division of the life span, usually a matter of years, during which the individual is adjusting to, or learning within, a particular set of conditions. It is a stage concept entailing extensive qualitative changes in the person resulting from the interaction of the set of conditions encountered and his personality at the time. The onset of the period coincides with the occurrence of the conditions. This onset can be relatively brief in its initial form, a matter of days or weeks, or it can develop as a set over a period of up to a few years. It is not meaningful to regard it as occurring abruptly in association with an event. Even quite concentrated initiation ceremonies do not constitute the set of conditions marking an age-grade. Rather, they serve to identify dramatically for the initiate the time at which he should attend closely to the coming conditions. The conditions are never mere information conveyed in speech or writing. They are changes of the sort just elaborated. For example, knowledge that a significant other has died does not represent a condition or set of conditions. It signals the coming conditions to be encountered, for example, when X, Y, and Z activities are sought, the deceased is not available to participate, observe, respond, etc. The individual only encounters the conditions when he is ready for the activities.

One key to understanding the stage idea is that it requires extensive new learning and reorganization of the round of life. Individuals often make minor adjustments to their round of life, for example, when changing jobs or their form of travel to work, or when a member leaves or joins their work group, or when bowling league is rescheduled, etc. Age-grades entail sets of related conditions which normatively emerge together over a short period of time. Consequently, they require considerable change in the pattern of ways in which a person goes about achieving his goals. These adjustments are not quickly made, because the individual's round of life is an interdependent pattern of relationships, activities, and settings. There are many ramifications of attempted changes. The person has to learn about the consequences and meanings of them and work them through, not merely contemplate them.

This does not imply that a stage ends when the person makes an adjustment or rearranges his round of life.[13] A new age-grade may begin while the person is still adjusting. The individual has a very limited control over only some of the age-grades in his life. For example, a person may be able to avoid retirement entirely late in life. Yet he does not control his spouse's physical condition or most of what determines his own, nor the virulent negative stereotype of old age, or the sense that his own death is likely to occur within the next few years. Age-grades are not teleological. They have no implied or predetermined end. The individual lives within the conditions of an age-grade and his adjustments to them until the next set of conditions is encountered.

Given the human capacity for anticipation and long-range planning, adjustments of a limited nature can be started before an age-grade starts. For example, many children have attempted to prepare themselves for what school will be like before starting, sometimes aided by parents, or a person can now participate in fairly elaborate preretirement programs. However, these adjustments are quite limited because of the complexity of a new age-grade, the need to develop new skills, and the inevitable role of the reactions of others involved in it. If such preparation for an age-grade becomes normative, it is part of the conditions of the age-grade in which the preparation occurs.

Perhaps the key question about age-grades concerns what determines the occurrence of the changes in significant others, activities, and settings. The examples already cited reveal many possible conditions. One basic determinant is the significance to others of physical maturation in the individual. For example, older generations of Americans regarded the development of the child's capacities to walk and talk, around age one, as important aspects of the readiness of the child to learn to "stand on his own two feet," that is, take responsibility for his actions. This, plus other developments, initiated a new age-grade. In all human groups the maturation of a female's capacity to reproduce or to menstruate has great significance for other members of the group, and, along with other developments, produces new conditions for the pubertal individual.

Allied to this determinant are initiation ceremonies and legal obligations or privileges attached to age and sex combined. These are institutionalized significances for others, for example, pubertal rites, compulsory schooling, or compulsory retirement. All of these significances are relative to the group, or stratum of a group, and are relative historically within the group.

A more prominent determinant of many age-grades is the significance to others of the behavior manifested by the individual as a result of his learning. For example, older generations of Americans understood manifestations of the assimilation of a worldview and of the formation of a consistent identity as qualifications for taking on adult responsibilities and privileges, such as marriage, family, and career. They called it "maturity," "settling down," or "becoming realistic."

A third major determinant of the conditions of an age-grade is alteration in established relationships due to changes in the lives of others. Almost all humans, at any point in life, have developed a round of life which involves continuing alliances and affiliations. Long-range planning and strong emotional attachments ensure that these alterations will require significant adjustments by the individual. Examples already cited are the moving of children from the parental home in the parents' middle years or the serious debilitation or death of aged parents. The relationships may include many besides the familial.

Very important in the determinants of age-grades is the inevitable generational cycle. Relationships to others of different generations guarantee significant changes at particular periods of the individual's life span. This has been particularly the case in American life. Attachments to grandparents and parents, and later to one's children and grandchildren, produce systematic generational alterations of relationships. This is also the case in many other groups, while still other groups may have quite different forms of generational relationships.

In summary, the overwhelming majority, if not all, of the determinants of age-grades comprise some combination of (a) the significance for others of maturational developments of the individual, (b) the significance for others of particular forms of learning achieved by the individual, and (c) alterations in the relationships with others caused by developments in their lives. There can be many combinations of these determinants. However, an age-grade is initiated by a set of conditions engendered by them.

AGE-GRADING SYSTEMS AND SOCIAL STRATIFICATION

Particularly important in human science is the usefulness of age-grading systems for determining the social stratification within a group. A stratum is a subgroup of persons who have developed through very similar age-grading systems.[14] This follows directly from the general model of psychology. Since human nature is a constant in the formula for most individuals, changes in environmental influences account for differences in personality and behavior. Since the vast bulk of variations in human nature across individuals is minor in nature, compared to what is shared by members of the species, the contribution of variances to differences in behavior and personality is peripheral. If a subgroup experiences a similar sequence of environmental influences, it will be similar in basic, but not peripheral, personality and behavior.

One should not be misled by the conventional American obsession with individual differences which has been dominant among both laymen and psychologists. This disposition can occur only at the cost of ignoring the many similarities among subgroups. That there is some, but neglected, recognition of similarities is revealed by laypeople's propensity to think in terms of social class, of "our kind" when choosing where to live and whom their children should marry, and by psychologists' pragmatic, nonconceptual use of social variables in their research. The disciplines of sociology, anthropology, and political science have long placed primary emphasis on shared characteristics.

The emphasis here on similarity of age-grading systems introduces a vagueness that must be addressed. The key to the definition of "similarity" lies in the human capacity for classification of experience. This is a capacity to represent the common elements in a number of experiences. It ignores the noncommon elements. For example, small children may play quite different table games or variants of sports and still abstract the same idea of what a game or that sport is. People in the United States can observe a great variety of selfish behavior in others and all learn that humans are selfish by nature. Children can observe the clothing of many males and females and learn that men and women dress differently. Therefore, it is not necessary for two or more people to have exactly the same experiences for them to share a great deal of learning.

It follows that subgroups of people who experience similar sequences of relationships, activities, and settings will share very substantially in their learning. Characterization of this learning in socioanthropology tends to focus on such terms as norms, roles, social values, expectations, etc. This topic is addressed in the following chapter. Here it will suffice to emphasize that, given similar learning and a particular situation, people will behave similarly. Thus, by observing the conditions of age-grading systems, it is possible to group people on the basis of their similarity. Individual differences in personality can be understood as variations around normative stratum-personality because they are determined by variations around normative age-grading conditions.[15]

It is useful to keep in mind that the age-grades in a system are not independent of one another. There are inherent dynamics or courses of development in the system. In addition, the development of human learning from the general to the specific gives it coherence through the life span. For these reasons, the collective personality characterizing members of a stratum constitutes something in the nature of a personality type among related types which comprise the total population. This gives social stratification a fundamental place in human science which will be explained further in the closing chapter.

AGE-GRADING SYSTEMS AND SOCIAL CHANGE

The age-grading approach to environmental influences also is useful in the conceptualization of social change. Essentially, social change is change in age-grading systems across generations in a group. If there were no social change, each stratum of a group would experience the same age-grading system generation after generation.

There are several general sources of social change or, to put it more usefully, changes in the total matrix of the group. They often are interdependent. One is technological development producing new artifacts that, in turn, alter the interactions among members of the group. A second is the dynamic inherent in the relationships among the strata of the group. These produce such phenomena as civil wars, revolts, class conflict, discrimination against scapegoat groups, etc. A third source is individual initiatives. They result from competition, rivalry, commitment, inspiration, necessity, and conflict. They probably are rarely more than precipitating contributions to already prepared potentials for significant change. A fourth is particular forms of interaction with neighboring groups. These include war, occupation, alliances, emigration, immigration, diffusion of technology or ideas, etc. A fifth source is the dynamic of the nonhuman environment of the group. This includes changes of ecological balances of flora and fauna, geological restructurings, climatic alterations, etc. Many important changes result from interactions of these sources. For example, strata dynamics can produce emigration that produces conflict with neighboring groups, or agricultural practices can produce ecological imbalances, or technological diffusion can aggravate class conflict, etc. These phenomena have their proximate effects on the group by changing the conditions of various age-grades for various strata or individuals. Which age-grades are changed for which groups or individuals determines the nature of the change process generated. This is because the effect of a change in any given age-grade is mediated by what those in that age-grade bring with them from previous development. Given the characteristic of human nature that learning proceeds from the general to the differentiated, the earlier the age-grade in which a change is experienced, the greater the difference in those affected. This difference is then manifested through all later age-grades. Because significant others are a basic part of all age-grades, changes for some individuals inevitably effect changes in the age-grades of others. It follows that the more members of a group affected by a source of change, the greater the likelihood of the ramifications of change.

If one knows the structure of a group, either sociologically in terms of its role and institutional structure or psychologically in terms of shared personality in each stratum for each age-grade, then the impact of any change can be predicted, within the limits of the theory employed.

ENVIRONMENTAL INFLUENCES AND REIFICATION IN SOCIAL SCIENCE

Reification here is defined as the attribution of existence in the universe of things which cannot be perceived by the human senses, including their technological extensions. It is useful to distinguish two types of reification. The first is attributing existence to things regarded as unobservable parts of observable things, such as subatomic particles. The second is reification of things in addition to what is observable. Here the concern is only with the second type. It also is useful to distinguish between reification and apparent reification, which actually constitutes a way of talking about real things. Many social scientists engage in apparent reification, often explicitly. Unfortunately, many others claim to do this but end up attributing characteristics to these entities that make them serve the function of true reifications. Current social science rests very heavily on these types of reifications. Among them are cultures, social systems, roles, institutions, economies, polities, languages, and living ideas. Relativistic naturalism rejects all these reifications. They are unnecessary for the explanation of human phenomena.[16]

The ideas of roles and institutions are useful in conceptualizing the total matrix of a group. They have no existence apart from human behaviors. When behavior changes, roles and institutions change. These terms, as used here, then, are only apparent reifications and do not imply that roles and institutions do anything or have any influence on people. Individuals do not play roles. They behave in particular ways. The ways in which these behaviors are repetitive and/or similar to the behaviors of others is the definition of a role. The role and the institution based on role analysis are conceptualizations of behaviors, not things distinct from them.

Neither are there economies nor polities. In an earlier chapter it was explained how the disciplines of economics and political science were derived from the individualistic worldview. This produced the ideas of economic behavior and political behavior. These are totally illusory. Neither economists nor political scientists have ever been able to define their disciplines in a way which distinguishes their domain of behavior to be explained from any other (Samuelson 1981, 6; Lipset 1969, viii; Dalton 1973, 454–64; Easton 1965).[17] The common view among social scientists that each discipline constitutes a set of variables which can be studied separately or in relation to one another is a fiction. What they study are arbitrary, conventionalized, operational measures, not any definable realm of behaviors distinct from the realms of other disciplines. There is no fashion in which the full range of human behavior can be divided into the economic, the political, or any other such categories which can be studied, explained, and added together to account for the total range.

This is why these two disciplines have remained primarily policy sciences. They are problem-solving disciplines using the conventions of decision-making agencies and individuals for particular purposes. This is also why the more recent trends in both disciplines toward behavioral science have revealed their basic reliance on psychology. The individualistic ideas of "rational man" and "selfish man" on which economics and political science are founded are being abandoned without any clear and agreed-upon views to replace them.

Closely related to the idea of culture is that of language. Cultures are said to include a language. Each generation participating in the culture is said to learn the language. The language is passed down from generation to generation. Whether language directs thought or vice versa is a major issue. Such views reify language. What is referred to by the term is actually an idealization of speech created by linguists. A great deal of the speech of people said to use the language does not conform to this idealization. Speech is behavior. It is based, like all behaviors, on the interaction between learning and momentary conditions. What is called "the language" is, like the role, an abstraction from similarities in the speech of members of a group. It is a conceptualization of behavior, not something distinct from it. As an idealized conceptualization, it represents a selection from among the speech utterances of members of a group of one form used, perhaps, by a few members.

Acceptance of the idea of a language-acquisition device (Chomsky 1972) in human nature does not justify reification of language, although it does place this reification in the class of those representing unobserved things as parts of observed things. At best, it can only refer to shared, learned forms of development of an inherent speech capacity. This shared learning has only a rough correspondence with the idealizations linguists call a language. The most obvious evidence comes from the vastly different ranges of vocabularies among members of a group, including different connotations and even denotations of the same words. Even with respect to syntax, there are many variations and inconsistencies across members of a group, although a shared basic core determines many speech utterances.[18]

CONCLUSION

The conceptualization of environmental influences through the life span in a systematic form and with a cross-cultural perspective has important implications for human science. It provides a basis not only for extending psychological science to members of all human groups (thus, assimilating psychological anthropology and psychohistory), but also for bridging the long-standing gap between the socioanthropology of social stratification and the weakly conceived social control variables of psychological research, such as social class, educational level, religion, sex, race, etc. Further, it provides a useful counter to the current strong trend toward genetic explanations of abnormative behaviors and social problems as reflected in much work in psychology, the new "halfway-house" disciplines between psychology and biology, and in sociobiology. This trend has been prominent in trying to understand violent crime, homosexuality, schizophrenia, manic-depression, hyperactivity in children, and the changing roles of the sexes and races. Via the virtual obsession with the concept of intelligence, it also is used to understand success and failure in the area of achievement.[19]

This trend toward the heredity side of the long-standing issue of nature versus nurture is readily understood as a compromise in the transition from the individualistic idea of free will to that of naturalistic determinism. Abandoning the explanation of behavior in terms of the exercise of free will, it maintains the disposition to search for explanations within the individual rather than in the environment. This reflects the individualistic view that environment plays only a selective and sporadic role rather than providing the order and pattern in experience through which the individual learns the normative ways of his group and his stratum and the variations from this order that produce abnormative behavior.

It is worth noting that this *Zeitgeist* of search for genetic explanations carries a potential for grave social danger and individual injustice (Graham 1990). If behavior is regarded primarily as due to genetic endowment, there are very limited ways of dealing with it. If it is regarded as undesirable behavior, the individual can be isolated from others, treated by surgery, placed on a lifelong drug-control schedule, or prevented from propagating his genes by genetic engineering. At the same time, the environmental influences that may be producing the behaviors of concern remain. The possibility here of value influences in human science are obvious. The trend toward genetic explanation carries on the interest present from the start of experimental psychology in the control and manipulation of, rather than in the understanding, of human behavior. At present, it appears to promise to replace radical behaviorism as the ultimate form of such control.

Advancement of the environmental side of the nature versus nurture issue recently has received its major impetus from outside the social sciences in the areas of changing racial and sexual identities and roles. The individualistic worldview attributed the behaviors of these groups to their nature as men, women, and races. As the society changed, regenerating the struggle for equality, controversies erupted centering on these individualistic beliefs. To counter them, minorities, the aged, and females have been forced to explicate how their behaviors have been determined by their socialization in the society and not by their inherent nature.[20] It has been a tough struggle, gradually supported by many social scientists. Unfortunately, other groups, such as violent criminals, manic-depressives, etc., are not represented by such political-action organizations. However, human scientists could extrapolate from the recognition of the role of environmental influences in determining the behaviors of the genders, the aged, and the races and, using the systematic conceptualization of these influences presented here, avoid the dangers inherent in the genetic approach. At least, they could insist that the search for environmental influences be undertaken before any conclusions about genetic determination are drawn.

Finally, and perhaps most important of all, systematic study of environmental influences through the life span provides an avenue through which the serious limitations of realist science can be revealed. Such study, if taken within a cross-cultural perspective, will reveal the order and pattern in the group way of life and its variations by strata. These patterns, in turn, will strongly suggest the usefulness of the concepts of shared learning, worldview, and mode of thought in explaining human behavior and lead to the recognition of the relativism of knowledge.

8

Universal Components of Personality

Personality development is the third dimension of the general model of psychology. It is a conceptualization of the results of the interaction of the individual's particular variant of human nature and the particular environmental influences during his life span. Environmental matrices have been conceived in terms of age-grading systems that require new and reorganized learning during each age-grade. This periodic learning and reorganization are personality development. Personality is defined as the organization of learning during each age-grade in the individual's life span. The flexible capacities of human nature begin to be shaped at birth, if not prenatally. The essence of these capacities is representation of the order in the environment and within the body. However, the individual is constantly having new or changed experiences with others and activities in settings. All of this experience occurs to the continuing human organism. Psychology must have terms and principles for explaining how it is organized and its continuities and discontinuities in order to explain the behaviors of the person throughout his life span.

Central to this conceptualization is the recognition that the behaviors of an individual for the vast bulk of time constitute an orderly pattern of activities, not spasmodic response to first one then another stimulus. Individual life is largely a repetitive series of script performances with variations and with identifiable types of interpolated briefer scripts. The scripts may change at various levels of abstraction, such as when an individual is temporarily unemployed or takes a new job, or a child is born, or new activities are essayed. Yet the subjective experience of the individual is largely one of meaningful continuity that he can report in a reasonably orderly manner even for what is anticipated over considerable periods of time. Moreover, he can report his understandings or explanations for past behaviors and experiences in a manner that has considerable order and cohesion. Both in the behaviors and in the reports of understanding and explanation of them there are continuities and discontinuities across age-grades.

At the same time, there is a great variety of script repertories and of forms of understandings and explanations of experience across human groups. Psychological theory must provide ways of conceiving personality development that have universal application. Scholars who have devoted themselves to the study of groups other than their own inevitably have developed terms that they find useful for communicating about diverse groups. Among these are worldviews, cosmologies, religious belief systems, modes of thought, styles, norms, values, genres, periods of expressive forms (for example, early, middle, and late periods of famous writers, artists, musicians), types of languages, and so on. Some even suggest characterizations of forms of group life such as Appollonian and Dionysian (Benedict 1934); inner-, outer-, and tradition-directed (Riesman, Denney and Glazer 1950); or the quality of national character such as paranoid, compulsive, or depressive. Unfortunately, none of these terms have precise definitions or embeddedness in any larger theory, save the implicit worldview of the scholar. Yet they point out useful directions for the task of human science.

Most efforts are addressed to some implied adult range of the life span. More recently in history and social anthropology there has been a keen interest in childhood but nothing approaching a systematic conception of personality development has been suggested with the exception of those by psychoanalyts. The recently emerging disciplines of psychohistory and psychological anthropology have had to rely on psychoanalytic theory as the only one rich enough and sufficiently integrated to help to organize their material. However, they have become keenly aware of its limitations, long recognized in psychology, such as the vagueness of its concepts of sexual and aggressive instincts, the lack of an explicit theory of learning, the neglect of adult development and its Western ethnocentrism. Consequently, human science today is faced with the tasks both of formulating terms and principles of personality theory for cross-cultural use and of conceiving personality development through the life span. Drawing on the clues provided by scholars of our own and other human groups and on various sources addressing life-span development, a conceptualization is offered below of a set of universal components of personality and, in the next chapter, of their development through a sequence of universal age-grades. It is proposed that the behavior of any person, past or present, in any human group can be usefully explained in terms of these components and the age-grade at which his behavior is being explained. No pretense is made that this is more than a very general initial framework which will require considerable elaboration and/or modification by a concerted effort of scholars from many disciplines.

One of the difficulties presented by the terms used by various scholars in talking about diverse human groups is that the imprecision of their definitions gives many of them overlapping meanings. The terms used here represent a sort of theoretical factoring of extant terms. The universal components of personality proposed are: worldview, ideology, mode of thought, identity, expressive style, practical knowledge, perceptual-motor skills, and unconscious dynamics. These are the components which develop during stable periods in the history of a group. Personality in transitional periods is addressed in Chapter 9.

WORLDVIEW

Worldview is defined as the beliefs that constitute for the individual (1) the overarching sense of meaning in life and death and (2) the general system of classification of persons, things, and processes which he uses to categorize experience. These may be implicit or explicit. They constitute the individual's understanding of the nature of reality. Worldview is the way in which the person has learned to reflect on experience. It provides the tools for understanding all experience. In this sense it constitutes a view of the reality behind appearances. All that is actually observed are forms in which reality is being expressed. There are other forms in which it could be expressed. Worldview defines the limits of the possible and, therefore, distinguishes reality from fantasy.

The sense of meaning in life and death has four components. They are: (1) the number of significant figures that determine the conditions of life; (2) the attributes of each of these figures; (3) the dominant emotional qualities in the relationship of the individual to each of the figures; and (4) the role of the person in the relationship(s).

There are probably two primary reasons why an overarching sense of meaning in life and death occur. One is that the flexible capacities of humans are designed to permit long-range planning. Humans are by nature anticipating, goal-striving beings. The recognition of human mortality and birth will require understanding in these terms. A life of understanding order and planning accordingly can hardly be expected to entertain such arbitrary limits. To do so would be equivalent to considering the end of meaning. A person would be in the position of asking himself, "What can it mean that there is no meaning?" Human flexible capacities are capacities for understanding. They will inevitably provide meaning for all experience.[1]

The second reason is based on the capacity to represent significance in experience. The human being is subject to powerful feelings which become conditioned to aspects and categories of experience. When these are combined in the process of planning, the individual is susceptible to profound hope and elation and equally profound disappointment and regret.

He must have, and inevitably will project meaning on, these experiences. These projections are the beliefs of worldview generally called "religious." They cannot come out of whole cloth. They are metaphors for the basic orientation to life established in very early childhood, as explained in Chapter 2. Consequently, they are largely implicit and rarely critically examined.

Worldview also includes the higher levels of the person's system of classification of experience, including a system of abstract beliefs about the characteristics of each category. The system of classification is probably never articulated systematically by more than a few members of a group. However, some subsystems may be highly articulated. Judicious questioning can reveal the whole system.

From consideration of the four components of the worldview beliefs in the meaning of life and death, it is possible to suggest a typology of worldviews.[2] An initial list might include the proselytizing, the propitiatory, the superstitious, the power-coalition, the paranoid, the hierarchical, and the polarized types. Central to these types is the individual's relationship or relationships to the figure or figures in his early life structure.

A proselytizing worldview is based on the belief that the individual himself determines the nature of the relationship. There is the sense of internal locus of control of one's destiny. Consequently, the individual must constantly assess life in terms of his own responsibilities, strengths, and weaknesses. He will assess the lives of others in the same terms. Thus, life becomes a matter of proselytizing the self and/or others to determine one's current and ultimate fate.

A propitiatory worldview is based on the belief that the figures are capricious in their relationship to the individual. The only possibility of influencing the relationships is to attempt to gain the favorable attention of these figures. This will most likely be accomplished by a combination of propitiatory offerings of gifts or bribes, in any of many forms, and of divining their likes and dislikes so as to cause them as little trouble as possible.

The superstitious world view is based on the child's learning of a fatalistic relationship to the figures. He has no influence on his fate. What will happen will happen, and he must make the best of it. Without actual influence, the individual, in order to have any sense of an ability to anticipate and plan, must deceive himself into thinking he can have influence. As there is no such basis, he must develop a superstitious understanding. This will take the form of magical acts and rituals. As these are superstitious behaviors, they will have no systematic relationship to events. Hence the individual must, like a paranoiac trying to maintain his delusional system of beliefs, invent other explanations. Common among these will be the belief that the acts or rituals were not properly carried out, were not carried out with the proper fervor or motivation, or that countervailing acts or rituals of others have interfered.[3]

A power-coalition type of worldview is based on the beliefs that the figures reward those who serve them well and that the figures vie among themselves for their own self-interests. The individual, then, is faced with assessing which figure or coalition of figures has the greatest or, at best, some power to reward him and then finding ways to serve it. As the coalitions may change over time, the individual has to be prepared to switch allegiance but be careful lest they change in the future.

The paranoid worldview is based on the belief that the figure or figures are deceptive and sinister. They cannot be trusted. They can have evil intentions with respect to the individual. The only recourse of the individual is to be constantly on his guard, to be skeptical of any expectations of help or kindness, and to be secretive about those aspects of his life that he deems of importance so that the figures cannot deprive him of them or use them against him.

The hierarchical type of worldview is based on the child's learning that there is a hierarchy of figures in which power over him increases toward the top. Figures lower in the hierarchy can help him in more limited ways. Often they can be most helpful as intermediaries to those higher in the hierarchy. His task is to find out in what ways any figure in the hierarchy can be of help, which figures have more intermediary influence, and how he can enlist their support.

The polarized worldview is based on the learning that one or more figures are interested in the individual and can be influenced to provide support but that there are one or more other figures who are sinister and whose interests bode ill for him. The individual, then, must find out how to influence the positive figures and how to avoid the power of the negative ones.

This typology may be used to identify other types of worldviews comprising combinations of the basic types, for example, polarized-proselytizing or hierarchical-propitiatory. It may also prove useful to order these types on one or more dimensions, for example, internal-external locus of control from proselytizing to superstitious.

IDEOLOGY

If worldview is the individual's understanding of the nature of the reality behind appearances, ideology is his understanding of the appearances themselves.[4] However, it is more than this understanding. It also includes attitudes toward the apperances, attitudes toward changes in them, and beliefs about how preserving or changing them can be accomplished. Thus, ideology is the individual's view of what conditions of life are and ought to be—his idea of the good life. Unlike worldview, ideology includes attitudes and therefore is fundamental to human motivation. It relates the individual to his group in terms of what he wants to preserve and change in group life and how he goes about these goals.

Ideology must start with the understanding of appearances. The individual constructs a view of the nature of the life of his group and how it is significant for him. Only from this vantage point can he decide what and how he would like it preserved or altered. Ideology, too, has a developmental course, because the appearances experienced at different periods of the life span are not the same.

It follows from the definition of worldview and of ideology that ideology is dependent on worldview. Not only is the individual's understanding of experiences based on the application of his worldview, but he cannot decide how appearances can be preserved or changed until he has an understanding of the reality behind them. Effective action must be within the realm of the possible. Humans can dream of impossible changes, but such dreams do not become part of their ideologies. This does not mean, of course, that if people share a worldview, they also share an ideology. That is because ideologies are based on the understanding of appearances, and worldviews always allow for reality to take many forms. It also is because ideologies are partly based on how the individual understands that group life is affecting him. It was emphasized in Chapter 6 that the person's system of values becomes the dominant form of what is significant to him. (Values are treated more fully in Chapter 9.)

Ideologies, then, are primarily determined by how group life, as the individual understands it, is related to the realization of his values. If he is consistently getting and expecting to get out of life what is important to him, then his ideology will be a conservative one. He will want little or no change in group life. If he is having great difficulty in realizing his values, then he will have a radical ideology which demands substantial change in group life. This is one dimension of ideologies—the conservative-radical one. However, it implies nothing about how preservation or change is to occur. Means are determined by how group life is understood and by the possible as defined in worldview. The individual's ideology, then, includes his system of values in the sense that one can identify them by an analysis of his ideology. It may prove useful to separate the value system from ideology and add it as a ninth universal component of personality. However, its embeddedness in ideology would seem to make this unnecessary.

Another dimension of ideology is from inarticulate to articulate.[5] Individuals will know what they like and don't like, but they may devote little effort to relating such experiences to the understanding of group life. This is far more likely to be the case for conservatives than for radicals, because those who desire change most often will employ means which affect the fortunes of others. If the others are less radical, they will oppose many efforts at change. The radical finds himself forced to persuade others to his view and therefore must be prepared to answer their objections.[6]

Even among the adult members of a group, there may be many who do not and cannot, without considerable effort, articulate their ideologies except in fragments on particular occasions. This does not mean that they do not have an ideology. It means only that they have not developed skill or interest in articulating it precisely and systematically. Their ideologies constantly are manifested in their relationships to the group. They are implicit and could become articulate in a short time if the individuals become so motivated.

It seems very likely that a typology of ideologies would start along the same lines as the typology of worldviews. This is because the young child's initial sense of how life is working out for him, what he likes and doesn't like about it, and how change in it can be effected is based on the use of his inchoate worldview. If that worldview is that his behavior determines his fate in life, then to improve his fate, he will have to proselytize himself and others. If it is that the performance of specific rituals at specific times and places determines his fate, then he must perform or participate in these rituals. However, as the developing child is exposed in subsequent age-grades to wider ranges of experience in the life of his group, there is much room for variations of interpretations of how his society is functioning and who or what should be preserved or changed. Thus, within the general type of ideology, there can be various subtypes. It also is very likely that these subtypes will be highly correlated with the various strata of the group.

IDENTITY

Identity is defined as the system of beliefs and attitudes toward the physical organism which is the individual being who has this system. The individual is a physical organism. He has many capacities to experience this organism. He has exteroceptors for seeing at least large parts of it and for hearing, smelling, and tasting it. He has touch receptors which register doubly when parts of the organism come into contact—an experience which does not occur on contact with any other object. He has interoceptors for registering balance, muscle action, muscle fatigue, nausea, etc. He is capable of turning his attention to his thoughts, feelings, and imagery.[7] His speech capacity permits him to learn that others experience him as an organism in many ways. Their experiences of him play a major role in conditioning his attention to this organism. He can distinguish this organism from other organisms and objects by registering the difference between contact with himself and with other things, and by registering the relationship between the feedback from his own behavior as it is correlated with the observation of other things. These capacities permit the individual to represent himself as an object among objects.

The individual inevitably is an object of significance to others in his group. As a result, they will draw and condition his attention to himself at those times in which it is important for them to do so. They will give him a linguistic label and use it to refer to him in speech with others as well as with him. In these ways the individual becomes a significant object in his own experience. In what ways and how elaborate are these ways, there is great room for variation across groups and individuals.

Significant others will provide him with the bases for reflection on himself and on his characteristics and for reflection on the meanings of them. These are the beliefs of his identity. At the same time, because his behavior and other characteristics are made to have significance to him, he will develop attitudes toward them. This occurs, as does all attitude learning, in the form of classical conditioning where the neutral stimulus is the characteristic of the self which becomes conditioned to an evoked emotion. For example, when the American child misbehaves in some way and his mother exclaims "bad boy" and spanks him, he learns a negative attitude toward his badness. The beliefs about what characteristics he has comprise his self-concept. The attitudes he learns toward his characteristics comprise his self-esteem. Together they constitute his identity.

The possibilities for learning about the self suggest that it may be useful to consider distinct types of identities. Three possibilities are individualized, compartmentalized, and group types. Individualized identity is the type of identity most familiar to recent Western civilization and that specified in the current psychological literature based on the work of Erikson (1963, 1959). However, it seems likely that in different human groups there is the possibility of considerable variation in the differentiation or complexity of individualized identity. That is, this discrete self may come to be reflected on in few or many ways. It may have very limited or very extensive attributes. In terms of early reflective learning, the child may have this self invoked very frequently and characterized in many ways in the explanation of experience, as is the case with individualists. On the other hand, the discrete self may be invoked but its experiences attributed most often not to its characteristics but to things and processes external to it. It may have been the case, at least among the peasantry, in the early Middle Ages in Europe, that more than a simple differentiation of self was precluded by the explanation of experience in terms of the influence of myriad demons and angelic spirits, which were not only responsible for many circumstances of life but could take possession of the person's body and cause his actions. A small range of characteristics of the self were significant for warding off the demons and for receptivity to the angelic spirits. Otherwise, the individuality of the person had little development. The disposition to refer to persons in terms of their occupations, such as miller, carpenter, or smith, or to that of their father, or to their place of residence or origin suggests this impoverishment of self-concept.

A second possible type of identity is the compartmentalized. In this type there is the learning of a discrete physical object, but characterizations of it are separated into sets limited to particular relationships or sets of roles performed.[8] The attributes of self are grouped in terms of what is necessary, desirable, or undesirable in each relationship. The child experiences little or no reference to the self as a common element across relationships. This type of identity is implicit in Erikson's (1963) concept of ego diffusion and explicit in Lifton's (1971) idea of Protean Man. The individual does not develop any sense of self-sameness and continuity across time and situations. Instead, he reflects on himself in different ways at various times in accordance with whom and what he is doing. The attributes of self in each compartment of identity may be few or many.

A third possibility is a group identity. It is not based on development of a discrete body image but on a field-type image of interactions among a number of persons.[9] These persons are not perceived in discrete terms. It is the interactions that are the focus of attention and are characterized and reflected upon. Perhaps the idea is partially represented by the ideas of a team and teamwork, although these terms as currently used in this society are infused with much individualized thinking. From the standpoint of the child's development, he rarely, if ever, has his attention drawn to himself and his actions independently of others and theirs. The group is characterized or differentiated by attributes. The self concept is "we" rather than "I," where the "we" is not understood as an aggregate of discrete persons but as a corporate person. This identity seems more likely to occur in groups in which life is organized into collective enterprises, whether based on vertical and extended family groups, or on participation of individuals in particular cooperative functions. In the latter case, there is the possibility of another type of identity: group-compartmentalized. The individual may participate in multiple groups without ever having his attention drawn to characteristics applying across groups. It also seems possible that group identity may have a hierarchical organization such that the individual reflects on the characteristics of subgroups in which he participates and on groups of groups, possibly topped by the total social group. For example, in a highly centralized bureaucratic society, the individual's identity might include the shipping and receiving group, the corporate group, and the national group. Whatever the groupings, the individual never learns to reflect on himself as a discrete entity. Even an illness or injury is understood in terms of group functioning as in the expressions "the team is weakened by injuries," or "the team is not at full strength."[10]

MODE OF THOUGHT

This component of personality as explained in Chapter 2 is the characteristic form in which experience is processed and in which ideas are manipulated. It is learned on the bases of the orders in both linguistic and nonlinguistic experience. It appears to be established by about the age of four when most children display learning of the basic syntax of the language of their group. However, the course of speech development strongly suggests the basis of it is there by age three. It, too, has a developmental course. It sets the criteria of logical reasoning in the group, although the learning of shared premises is necessary to meet a group's criteria of rationality.

Mode of thought is fundamental to the individual's identification of events and facts and his approach to problem solving and planning. A typology of modes of thought is important for psychological theory. Some possibilities exist in typologies of languages. Analysis of the units of experiences in terms of how the child's attention is regulated in the early years in different groups will be required. The typology probably will have to develop out of the application of human science to diverse groups.[11]

EXPRESSIVE STYLE

This is the characteristic variant of behaviors by which the individual performs the scripts of life in his group. It is a consistent repetitive variant of the forms of behaviors observable among members of his group. Here consistency and repetitiveness do not entail that script performance is always similar. The expressive style may be one of inconsistency, but it is consistent in its inconsistency or flexibility. This component is the equivalent of most of what the current psychology of personality traits encompasses, because trait psychology always has reflected the individualistic interest in individual variation, such as aggressive, introspective, dependent, rigid, ambitious, selfish. However, psychological theory must deal with variation across all known groups. There is no reason not to expect that important aspects of expressive style may be widely shared within a group. It is useful for explaining genres in art, music, dance, literature (including myth making and telling), self-decoration, clothing, architecture, and other practices long neglected in psychology. It sometimes is used to describe group ways of life. Within a group, expressive styles can be expected to vary across social strata and across individuals within strata. It, too, has a developmental course through the universal age-grades. An approach to a typology of expressive styles is suggested in Chapter 9.

PRACTICAL KNOWLEDGE

Practical knowledge is the body of specific learning that results from daily interaction with artifacts, places, and particular others. It is to be distinguished from reflective learning. However, it does include those aspects of formal knowledge—what is learned secondhand by verbal exchange—that are "factual" in the sense that they are the practical knowledge of others or things or processes which he learns from them without direct experience.

Practical knowledge is the basis on which the individual implements his goal planning through actual behaviors based on recognitions and anticipations. Thus it is the component of personality that provides, along with perceptual-motor skills, the interface between the person and his environment. It should not be confused with plans, because planning is influenced by all components of personality. However, in order to carry out a plan, the individual must interact with the environment, and this must be done through practical knowledge. Practical knowledge is learned at various lower levels of abstraction, because the capacities for generalization and discrimination permit the learning of recognitions and anticipations of types or classes of experiences. The recognition that linguistic experience plays a significant role in the learning of practical knowledge does not confound it with reflective learning because it is limited to the concrete content of what is experienced, including verbal labels, not explanations and interpretations. For example, it would be practical knowledge that the familiar form of address should not be used with certain other members of the group, but reflective knowledge that they are different sorts of beings, such as royalty.

Practical knowledge is distinguished from worldview in being restricted to the lowest levels of the system of classification. It consists mainly of very specific knowledge of persons, things, and settings, such as that A is an eggbeater, B is a coati-mundi, C is a mandala, D is a holy place, or that you need a key or hot-wiring to start a car, that section of river X holds piranha, women walk behind their husbands, poisonous toadstools can be mistaken for edible mushrooms, curare-tipped arrows kill game, etc. However, it seems useful to include in practical knowledge a knowledge of *types* of ordinary things and settings, because it is the basis on which the individual can interact with never-before-encountered instances of things or settings. For example, in using the bathroom of a house entered for the first time, the person may try to turn the water faucet clockwise or counterclockwise because his practical knowledge is that faucets turn on either clockwise or perhaps in one of four different ways. Practical knowledge is that knowledge needed at a particular point in the implementation of a plan in order to carry it out. Plans always are implemented in settings and have time components. The basic knowledge of time and space, that is, units of measurement of them, is therefore part of practical knowledge. A typology of practical knowledge should emerge from a consideration of the forms of nonhuman environments, technologies, and social stratification across human groups.

PERCEPTUAL-MOTOR SKILLS

Perceptual-motor skills are complex patterns of interaction with persons, artifacts, or natural objects. They include patterns that require one or more others to perform. Examples include the behavioral patterns involved in the fashioning of artifacts, dancing, swimming, playing musical instruments, tree climbing, shooting weapons, spearing fish, physical combat, sewing, skinning, calligraphy, etc. They do not include the practical knowledge that usually accompanies these skills. The skills per se are the patterns and sequences of patterns of behaviors requiring coordination, speed, strength, sensory acuity, and various complex sensory-muscular combinations of these. Thus, for example, very rapid but intelligible speech or sustained production of properly pitched high (for the person's voice register) musical notes are perceptual-motor skills, while myth telling and musical interpretation of a song include other forms of learning.[12] Even the ability to explain how one performs these skills is not a skill per se.

Almost all behavioral interaction with the environment requires complex organization of behavior. However, perceptual-motor skills should not be understood to include only those of high precision and reliability. Rather, they can be scaled on a dimension of deftness, accuracy, or effectiveness. In this way, groups and individuals can be compared with respect to their learning of particular skills and types of skills. Any individual can be partly described in terms of his relative development of them, including no development at all, for example, persons who cannot swim. A typology of perceptual-motor skills probably would be based on forms of nonhuman environments and technologies across human groups.

UNCONSCIOUS DYNAMICS

Unconscious dynamics refers to the unresolved conflicts, the defensive processes by which they are managed, and their developmental history which play central roles for the individual in the interpretation of experience and, therefore, in the determination of the field-organization of behavior. A conflict is defined as an interference with goal attainment, where interference refers to the occurrence of conditions requiring restructuring of the plan for the attainment of the goal. Defensive processes are defined as specific and systematically used forms of variation from normative logic that attentional processes are conditioned to in order to escape disorganization of thought. These dynamics can be divided into two categories: the normative and the abnormative. Normative dynamics are comprised of those conflicts and defensive processes that are shared by almost all members of the group or a stratum of a group. Abnormative dynamics refers to those which occur to only a very small proportion of the members of a stratum. The normative dynamics are so widely shared that the behaviors and experiences they influence are not perceived by the members of the group as odd or inappropriate. They are chronic. Their consequences are assimilated both to other shared components of personality and to legitimated scripts and combinations of scripts. Abnormative dynamics, being not widely shared, produce behaviors and experiences that are perceived as problematical and as requiring, at least potentially, some form of special attention from the group. They may be chronic or acute.

Normative unconscious dynamics result from the inevitability of conflict engendered in the child by the necessity to assimilate to the group way of life. This will be the case particularly in early childhood when there are strong pressures on the child to adapt in particular ways, sometimes by discontinuities in child-rearing practices, sometimes by requirements of the child to adapt rapidly, and almost always by limitations of the understanding by adult members of the capacities of the child. This failure to understand the capacities of the child is due to the selective manner in which reflection on experience has been learned in childhood by the older members of his group. Those aspects on which they have not learned to reflect are lost forever. Other normative unconscious dynamics can be generated by serious conflicts in later periods of the life span. These are probably always of the discontinuity type (Benedict, 1938).

An example of an early childhood discontinuity conflict is the individualistic practice of moving the basis of the child's relationship to the parent figure from almost unconditional love to a strict conditional love at around age one. This engendered a fundamental insecurity of the child in the relationship, setting the stage for a lifelong struggle to establish and maintain self-esteem. An example of a discontinuity conflict in later life was the individualistic experience of middle-class, middle-age mothers of the "empty nest" after twenty to thirty years in which child-nurturance was their central preoccupation and basis of self-worth.

An example of conflict based on too rapid expectation of adaptation was the individualistic pressure at about age three for boys to learn masculinity at the same time that they were expected to give up much of their dependence on their mothers and for girls to learn feminity at the same time that femininity was devalued implicitly vis-a-vis masculinity.[13]

Another type of conflict not uncommon to human groups stems from rigid expectations of conformity to demands beyond the child's capacity to comprehend, resulting in anxious compulsion to have and abide by systems of strictly enforced rules. This probably occurs mainly in the years between one and three when the child has not developed sufficient linguistic competence to understand or clarify instructions.[14]

Abnormative unconscious dynamics result from conflicts that are atypical for the group or stratum. These can be subdivided into those for which the group provides legitimated forms of assimilation and those for which it does not. Examples of the former are the *berdache* among the Sioux Indians (Erikson, 1963, 151–52) and the priesthood and monastic or convent life for some individualistic Catholics. Nonlegitimated unconscious dynamics can result in tolerated marginality, banishment, incarceration, or other punitive measures, or the group's form of psychotherapy. Some abnormative dynamics result from atypical experience at so early an age that they become chronic, for example, most psychoses in individualistic America. Others are acute and temporary but play key roles in the personality of the individual while operant, such as many neuroses of individualists treated successfully by psychotherapy or dissolved by circumstances of the person's life (spontaneous cures).

Once established, unconscious dynamics go through a developmental history as the individual continually attempts to manage his conflicts as they are evoked in new circumstances which block old but offer new forms of expression without resolution of the conflicts. Central to this history of the dynamics is the age-grading system with its sequence of new conditions of life. At each age-grade, some forms of behavior are regarded as no longer appropriate, but new forms are. For example, so important was physical prowess in the establishment of masculine identity that individualistic boys not only spent much time playing sports but were highly sensitive to any perceived insults. They were ready to, and frequently did, fight in defense of their masculinity, although always being careful to avoid those fights they thought they would lose. However, during the adolescent age-grade, they gradually learned that fighting was not an appropriate adult form of conflict resolution. In fact, it was unlawful. In addition, they learned that, except for the very few who could make a living from their athletic prowess, sports would have to play a minor role in adult life. They lost their primary means for establishing security in their masculinity. It had to be translated into economic competition and dominance over females, both very difficult endeavors. Consequently, they developed an intense interest in following professional and amateur sports. They made heroes out of John L. Sullivan, Jack Dempsey, and Rocky Marciano as well as football and baseball players. These men represented the masculine ideal to which they aspired but never attained.

Through the flexible learning capacities of generalization and discrimination in the context of a vastly increasing knowledge, the individual becomes capable of an impressive array of symbols and metaphors conditioned to his conflicts and their defensive management. At the same time, the interrelatedness of the age-grades in his age-grading system ensures that the conflicts can be evoked in an ever-increasing number of circumstances. All of these processes are related. The result is that, in the interpretation of experience and in planning for goal attainment, the unconscious dynamics have much work to do. Due to the defensive processes, the individual is not aware of most of this work. Much of what flashes into his consciousness appears strange to him. However, he is very much aware of the resultant goals, plans, and his reflections on them.

Although unconscious dynamics may well be the most central component of personality, it is listed last here in order to address its relationship to the other components. It plays significant roles in their development. It does so by contributing to the experiences and behaviors of the individual, the organization of which constitutes his personality during each age-grade. Thus, individualitic men struggled defensively to establish and maintain their masculine identities in the comparative mode of thought and, therefore, selectively observed themselves and females in ways which helped them in their quest. Eventually, the feminine nature of females became part of their worldview. Women were feminine by nature, not by environmental influence. At the same time, their defenses ensured that they would not become aware of the less masculine aspects of their behavior or thoughts and feelings, helping them to a more secure masculine identity. Difficulties with their masculinity influenced their ideology toward the desire for a society that helped them realize or de-emphasize their masculine values, although the nature of the ideal society could vary markedly among men. The conflict over adequate masculinity influenced expressive style as well. The small male's compensatory cockiness or humor, the large but unconfident male's slouching unassertiveness, the bully's aggressiveness, and most males' exaggerated independence in relationship to females were common forms of expressive style among individualistic men. Male emphasis on a strong distinction between their logical rationality and the illogical emotionality of women contributed to the development of their mode of thought. Male-type practical knowledge and perceptual-motor skills skewed the development of these aspects of their personalities, partly due to defensive selection of what made them feel masculine and distinguished them most clearly from females.

Although unconscious dynamics have been very influential in the development of the other seven universal components of personality, one cannot understand any meaningful domain of observations of an individual from only these other components. They will not suffice to account for many inconsistencies in his behavior, particularly those of which he manifests no knowledge, many temporary strong anxieties, or the selectively illogical reasoning he uses in certain circumstances, as assessed by his own group's criteria of logical reasoning. Nor will they account, in conjunction with new circumstances, for some of the alterations in his round of life, particularly significant ones such as changing jobs, divorce, or giving up old friends and activities. Neither will they account for most of his dreams and some of his fantasies, nor slips of the tongue, jokes or reactions to jokes, nor much of his creative endeavors and many attitudes toward particular persons, objects, and activities. Unconscious dynamics are mainly responsible for the differences between the individual's identity and the identities attributed to him by others who know him well.

CONCLUSIONS

It is proposed that the behaviors of any member of any human group, past or present, can be explained comprehensively in terms of these eight universal components of personality: worldview, ideology, identity, mode of thought, expressive style, practical knowledge, perceptual-motor skills, and unconscious dynamics. The individual is always behaving and, therefore, always engaged in the implementation of some plan or plans. Therefore, he is using some part of his practical knowledge and often some perceptual-motor skills. In the formation and changing of plans, except perhaps at the lowest level of their "top-down" organization, his unconscious dynamics have played substantial roles. The conscious content emerging during this planning process has been and continues to be reflected upon in terms of his worldview, ideology, and identity employing his mode of thought. He carries out his plans using his expressive style.

As the person behaves in his environment and with longer-range anticipations in his plan, feedback from the environment and his body is processed by the reflective components. This is the essence of field organization. If the feedback is totally consistent with the ongoing organization in both its current and planned dimensions, there is no reorganization of the field beyond the sequencing already incipient. If, however, the feedback is not consistent, there is reorganization, beginning at the highest level of the hierarchy at which the inconsistency is significant. In a sense, the meaning of experience for the total field always is assessed. For example, when the individual interacts with another, he is expecting the other to respond in a particular way and in a type of way. Let us say that, for reasons peculiar to the other person's personality at the time, he responds differently than expected. The individual must then process this negative feedback. In this processing, done in his mode of thought, his worldview, ideology, and identity all will be operative. That is, what the feedback in the circumstances means for his understanding of reality, of his understanding of his group way of life and what he wants to preserve and change in it, and of his understanding and evaluating of himself will be assessed. Various possibilities, with various degrees of probability, will occur. Depending on the nature of this assessment, unconscious conflicts and defensive operations may come into play. The field will be reorganized at whatever level there is disruption of the plan in such a way as to maximize organized interaction with the environment *as regulated by the whole plan.* For example, an individualistic employee, talking to his boss about a raise, when refused may quit his job or speak in a manner which gets him fired. This may seem to be behavior increasing disruption of organization, but it is not necessarily. Quitting his job or standing up to his boss may be less disruptive for his identity and/or ideology and/or worldview than accepting the situation and returning to his work. The boss's refusal of the raise could be interpreted reflectively, in terms of worldview, as a manifestation of human nature of yielding to the temptation of greed by denying a deserved raise. In terms of ideology, this could be interpreted as another example of management exploiting the worker, which must be opposed. In terms of identity, it could be interpreted as a personal rejection of a loyal employee, with deeper roots in feelings of parental rejection generating a counterdependent defensiveness.

It must be kept in mind that, in relativistic naturalism, what is to be explained are domains of observations, not specific behaviors individually. The description of a person is that which explains the domain. A domain is defined by an age-grade or subdivision of an age-grade. It is a period of time in which the individual behaves in all his scripts and settings. The description of his personality must include all eight of these components of personality in order to account for the whole set of behaviors observed. If the cross-cultural perspective of relativistic naturalism is maintained, the usefulness and necessity of this approach will be appreciated.

The inclusion of unconscious dynamics as one of the universal components of personality has the most profound implications for methodology in human science. The explanation of the personality of the individual requires that his unconscious conflicts, his defensive processes, and the history of the two be understood. For normative unconscious dynamics, which are the most central to the understanding of the behaviors of members of a group, this requires either the study of the individual's development until the age-grade he is currently living in or the application of a psychological theory sufficient to identify conflicts and defenses and their developments for individuals in any human group from the careful analysis of broad domains of their current behavior. The latter simply is not available and will not be until some universal theory of personality types emerges from and is programmatically used in the study of a broad range of human groups. Only by becoming familiar with the age-grading systems of many societies can psychological theory be elaborated to include types of conflicts and defenses generated during the development of the individual from birth to death and types of courses of their development.

Another major implication for human science emerges from the recognition of the size of the task. It is the questioning of the usefulness of comprehensively explaining the personalities of individuals. Such an orientation is an anachronistic legacy of the individualitic way of life. It stems from the individualistic focus on the responsibility of each individual for his actions and the proselytizing worldview and "great man theory" of history which follows from it. If the implicit belief in human free will is abandoned for the view of the flexible capacities of human nature and for the role of environmental influences in the determination of human behavior, the focus of human science turns to the nature of the group way of life and its system of social stratification that produce the shared characteristics of members of the group. For this approach, another science is needed—the science of sociology which, by identifying the role and institutional structure of the society and the ways in which members with particular demographic characteristics are related to this structure, can reveal the system of stratification and thereby the age-grading systems for each stratum. On this base, psychological science can proceed to identify the shared characteristics (collective psychology) of the group and its variations by strata. This analysis will explain, at the psychological level, the overwhelming proportion of the variance of behavior across human groups. In turn, from this base, understanding of selected individual personalities for special purposes can proceed. This approach to human science is the topic of the final two chapters.

—— 9 ——

Development of Personality through Universal Age-Grades

The eight components of personality are all established in their earliest form in the first few years of life. They have a developmental course through the life span. The understanding of the individual's personality must take into account where the person is in this course. The course is determined by the age-grading system through which he develops. There can be no doubt that age-grading systems vary across human groups, historically within each group, and for the various strata within each group. Within the age-grading system of a stratum of any group there will be individual variations of the sets of conditions around the normative conditions. In this sense, the personality of an individual can be recognized as partially shared with members of his group, even more shared with members of his stratum, and in some respects unique. Variations in the inherent capacities of human nature interacting with the particular conditions of the individual's age-grading system will contribute to the nature of his personality at each period of the life span. However, it is important not to neglect consideration of the shared aspects of personality in favor of preoccupation with the unique. Such an approach is based on taking for granted the shared and on unfamiliarity with the patterns of behavior in the many human groups known to social anthropologists and historians.

Age-grading systems vary in two ways. One is the number of age-grades in the system and the periods of the life span they cover. The other is the particular sets of conditions in an age-grade. Thus, there may be an age-grade for a particular period of the life span in more than one human group, but it will be defined by different sets of conditions for each group. Moreover, roughly the same period of years may constitute an age-grade for one group but be divided into two or more age-grades for another. Although age-grading systems vary across human groups and among the strata of each group, there are sound reasons for assuming that there is a general order in them that is universal and around which there are local variations. This universal order consists of three age-grades prior to the attainment of fully adult status within a group and two thereafter. During these age-grades, personality has very distinct forms of organization, although all are intimately related. They are identified as primary personality structure, differentiated personality structure, integrated personality structure, midlife personality structure, and terminal personality structure. They are determined by the interaction of the normative maturational course of the human life span and the four-generational composition of the human group. Differences in age-grading systems in different groups and among the strata of each group serve only to regulate the general process of personality reorganization within the five universal age-grades. (See Figure 9.1.)

PRIMARY PERSONALITY STRUCTURE

The infant starts life with no learning, only his undeveloped flexible capacities. He is completely dependent on others for many years. However, his environment is ready for him. The group into which he is born has arrangements for his care that provide order in his experience. His learning of this order is unlike any learning which occurs later in life, in that it has nothing to build on. No experience is similar to something already familiar. No experience is just different enough from something known to permit discrimination. He has no system of classification of things or sequences. He has no linguistic skills that permit him to recapture and reflect on what has happened. He simply learns the order that is there.

This earliest learning is of a special kind. It is in the nature of the learning of a schema of life, a general scenario of what life is all about—what is regularly related to, the general approach to the relationships, the basic kinds of significance, and general space and time frames. It becomes the ground within which all later experience is embedded. Freud has suggested a very similar idea in that the child's earliest relationships are the prototypes for all later relationships. For example, relationships to all older men always are variations of the relationship to the father; to older women, of that to the mother; to peers, of that to the siblings. However, he placed an emphasis on these relationships during the phallic period when the Oedipal conflict develops. Here, the prototypical social learning is placed in the first three years of life and is even more general and schematic. It is more like the view of visual learning of recognition of human faces mentioned earlier. The child first learns a general schema of a human face, one that serves for all faces indiscriminately. Then he differentiates this schema into several types of faces, dependent on the extent of his exposure to different others, and finally fleshes out the types with the features

Figure 9.1
Tridimensional Model of Psychology for Relativistic Naturalism

ENVIRONMENTAL INFLUENCES

Age-Grading Systems

Universal Age-Grades:	birth-3/4[1]	3/4-11/15	11/15-40/50	40/50-60/70	60/70-death
			PERSONALITY DEVELOPMENT		
	primary personality structure	differentiated personality structure	integrative personality structure	midlife personality structure	terminal personality structure

Universal components of personality

worldview
mode of thought
identity
ideology (value system)
expressive style
practical knowledge
perceptual-motor skills
unconscious dynamics

HUMAN NATURE

Individual variant of:

flexible capacities:

  space
  time
  significance
  social

hedonic/incentive motivation

field-organization of behavior

physical characteristics[2]

---

[1] There is also a universal prenatal age-grade.

[2] Includes size, physiognomy, handicaps, maturational schedule. These are partly hereditary potentials and partly due to environmental influences. In their developed forms they combine with the other aspects of human nature and interact with environmental influences during each age-grade to determine personality.

of particular persons. Later experiences with new faces always entail their placement as faces, a type of face, and a particular face.

Linguistic development appears to be of a similar nature. The child first speaks one word at a time. However, these are properly identified as one-word sentences, because it is clear that the child is using them pragmatically. He may utter the sound "baw" (ball), but he may be communicating "There is a ball," "I want the ball," "Give me the ball," "Is that a ball?," etc. When he begins to utter two-word sentences, he has only increased the specificity of his communication by identifying his pragmatic intent, for example, "There ball," "Want ball," etc. Linguistic competence develops from the increasing elaboration and ordering of the elements of the pragmatic communication.[1]

It is proposed that human representation of order proceeds from the general to the specific. The earliest learning is of a general orientation to life which constitutes a framework within which all later learning is refinement and elaboration.[2] This basic orientation to life provides the foundation of all the universal components of personality. Later learning never escapes these foundations. It can only elaborate and refine them. It is established in the first three years of life, because it requires development of the reflective capacity in a very rudimentary form. By age four, most children construct grammatically correct sentences, although they are simple in form and lack the refinement of the irregular forms. However, by age three, they appear to have the rudiments that express their mode of thought. The reflective capacity accompanies development of a rudimentary type of identity, and with that comes the earliest form of ideology. The learning of speech constitutes one of the earliest and most important perceptual-motor skills. At the same time, the child is establishing practical knowledge and other skills involved in the common interactions with the environment to which he is exposed. In his performances his basic expressive style is manifested. The basic normative conflict or conflicts are established with their prototypical defensive processes. Suggestions regarding the nature of each personality component of primary personality structure follow. Lacking sufficient information about child development in other groups in a usable form, examples from the middle-class individualistic form of each component are suggested.

Primary Worldview

As discussed in Chapter 2, the overall nature of this earliest orientation to life itself is the first form of the individual's worldview. It provides the bases for what becomes an articulable and specific set of beliefs that constitute the person's view of the meaning and purpose of life and death. It also provides the first general and inchoate categories that become differentiated and then integrated into the system of classification into which all experience is divided. There are the godlike figures or essences with their powerful, mystical, and authoritative properties and the experiencing self in relationship to them. There are the dominant, intense emotional experiences regularly evoked by interaction with them. There is the sense of the role of the self (type of identity) in the determination of these interactions and the occurrence of these emotions. There is the sense of another realm in which the figures exist and from which they come and go in their periodic interactions with the self in the realm of the self with its basic properties. There are other things with which both the self and the figures interact independently or with which both the figures and the self interact at the same time and that affect the relationships. These constitute the framework of meaning within which all of the child's experiences are interpreted. He has no other basis on which to approach or understand new forms of experience.

Primary Identity

The patterned arrangement of the small child's life determines which type of identity is established. For the individualistic child, this was the individualized type, with the basis for a high degree of differentiation. In the first three years of life, the child learned that his relationship to the one significant figure in his life was largely determined by his behavior. Much time was spent in making the child aware of his physical body as an entity and its causal relationships to events around it, and especially of his role in determining parental approval and disapproval. However, differentiation of his self-concept was very rudimentary, as most judgments were made in a few terms such as good, bad, naughty, nice, dirty, and clean.

Primary Ideology

The earliest orientation to life includes the establishment of basic significance in experience. The survival types of experience almost certainly dominate through most of the first year, but the management of organized interaction with the environment for this type of significance is quickly and reliably established as the child learns what do when when in pain, hungry, thirsty, tired, etc. Other learning becomes organized around the pattern of this learning. For example, the eating and sleeping arrangements characteristic of his group or his stratum in the group are established for him. In this process, the conditioning of hedonic experience to particular persons, artifacts, and settings occurs. When the child is awake and not engaged in the management of survival types of significance, his flexible capacities are being developed in terms of other aspects of the order in experience. His need for the presence of significant others, which becomes important for his management of organized interaction, and his great curiosity and growing ability to imitate what he observes make him an active member of the group. Others will utilize these characteristics in relating to him and introduce him to various age-appropriate activities, artifacts, and settings in which group life is centered. As a new member of the group, he will have important meanings to at least some others. As his behavior accords with what they expect of him or the reverse, they will visit upon him emotional and survival types of hedonic experiences around which he learns. Pleasurable interaction with and avoidance of unpleasant interactions with these figures constitute his prototypic value system. What he is learning is what he does and doesn't like about his experience, what he wishes experience were like, and rudimentary learning about how to experience what he likes and avoid what he dislikes. This is the foundation of his ideology.

For individualistic children, primary ideology was based on enjoying parental love and attention and avoiding rejection and punishment. The child learned that love and rejection were usually based on his behavior, which he learned to reflect on in terms of his free choice. Hence, how to enjoy the good life became a matter of regulating his own behavior so that he was always good and never bad. This was the basis for a proselytizing ideology, in which the person most often proselytized is the self.

Primary Mode of Thought

The combination of the orders in linguistic and nonlinguistic experience establishes the child's primary mode of thought. His daily experience is organized, both consciously and unconsciously, by others in ways that establish units of experience and the important aspects of order within those units. The mode of thought henceforth divides experience into this type of unit and its variants of internal order. For example, the individualistic primary mode of thought was developed by the fragmentation of experience into short-term units of the child's and others' behaviors and their immediate effects, which were then approved or disapproved. Moreover, each of these units was discrete, because they were perceived in terms of discrete acts of free will. The various characteristics of the self invoked also were discrete in the sense that each could be changed independently of the others. The order in the unit of experience, as reflected in his language, was subject-behavior/predicate-object, placing the emphasis on the person and his behavior. The mode became something like "Z did X to Y . . . bad; C did A to B . . . good."

Primary Expressive Style

All members of a group or stratum share the main elements of the earliest orientation to life. This orientation will define the basic level of expressive style. Within each stratum there will be individual variations around the stratum style. Characterizing such styles across diverse groups must await much observation designed to understand the range of orientations to life which occur. For individualists, perhaps, the essence of expressive style can be called manic-depressive. These terms are used here to refer to a dimension of mood-swing range. It is based on the dominance in the child's experience of love and rejection by one significant figure. The child learned to judge himself and all others in terms of these forms of approval and disapproval. When he felt loved, life was good, he liked himself, and he entered into activities with confidence and enthusiasm. When he felt rejected, life was no good. He didn't like himself and approached activities with a lack of self-confidence and with apprehensiveness. Since his self-concept was central to his management of this relationship to his parents, he came to judge himself in terms of his goodness or badness as his increasing self-reflectiveness directed his attention inward. Individualists think in terms of ups and downs, high and low self-esteem, strengths and weaknesses, and of the importance of changing those attributes of self which produce the negative feelings. The average individualist experiences frequent ups and downs but within a narrow range of intensity most of the time. Some individualists are characterized as moody, meaning their ups and downs have both greater intensity and duration. The persons diagnosed as manic-depressive by professionals are those atypically subject to the greatest intensity and duration of mood swings and of characteristics that develop out of them.

Primary Practical Knowledge and Perceptual-Motor Skills

Most of the practical knowledge in this age-grade probably is the learning of basic scripts such as feeding oneself, dressing oneself, bathing oneself, and the conventions of communication in the group such as taking turns in conversation in our society. Other aspects concern the learning of the common settings in which activities occur. Probably also basic is learning ways to attract the attention of significant others when desired. The development of a basic vocabulary must be included.

The most important perceptual-motor skills are the development of linguistic competence and large motor coordination. Also prominent are learning to concentrate attention for a brief period of time and how to inhibit verbal and motoric response when necessary. Accompanying the learning of basic scripts are particular skills in their implementation, such as eating with chopsticks, tying shoelaces, managing different-sized drinking cups, and perhaps performing certain dances, chants, or songs.

All of this learning can be regarded as generic, setting the stage for the learning of many variations for new activities, relationships, and settings.

Primary Unconscious Dynamics

In this age-grade the basic conflict or conflicts and the prototypical defensive operations are established. It is extremely unlikely that there will be no conflicts, because the child with his basic hedonic motivation will have to be prepared for the learning of the social form of motivation in his group, that is, its value system. In addition, his caretakers will have to arrange for him to learn the ways in which his undisciplined curiosity and boundless energy are inimical to his health. This means that there will be considerable frustration visited upon him. The anger it engenders in him will then have to be directed in socially appropriate ways. There can be little doubt that in every human group this anger will not be permitted to be directed in any significant amounts toward those who are doing the frustrating. This would be the natural inclination of the child because he first attempts to persevere in his little goal striving and only gradually learns new means of overcoming obstacles.

For individualists, the fundamental conflict was over the preservation of their relationship to the mother as they explored their world and depended on her for many goal attainments. This became a conflict because, at around age one, a new age-grade began based on the parental assessment that the child was capable of becoming responsible for his freely chosen actions. No longer was he an essentially passive infant dominated by needs beyond his capacity to meet. Rather, he was perceived as actively engaging his environment and motivated more by wants than by needs.[3] Thus began the struggle variously identified as "the battle of wills" and "the terrible twos" (actually, the second and third years of life). The mother/child relationship changed from one of largely unconditional love to one of overwhelmingly conditional love. He found himself subject to disapprovals which he experienced as rejection and punishment in a variety of forms. As a result, he became deeply concerned to secure love and avoid rejection. The means to this end was to inhibit disapproved behavior before it occurred and to disapprove of it as part of his budding identity. This was the psychological foundation of individualism. It was the very gradual transference of his primary concern for the love of his mother to one of love for himself, in other words, self-esteem. He had to learn to love himself and reject himself on the same bases as did his mother. This was the basis of a distinction between his real self in the sense of how he experienced his behaviors and thoughts and his ideal self in the sense of how he would like to behave and think. The struggle to be the ideal self would dominate the rest of his life.

The predominant defense he learned was to turn against himself the anger he felt at his frustrating mother. He was developing the capacity to feel guilt. At the same time, his many attempts to behave in parentally approved ways sometimes led to success and sometimes to failure. This was co-opted by his main task of sitting in judgment on himself in the form of self-disgust and pride. He learned to turn the frustrations of failure into ambition to be more successful in these first simple enterprises. This basic conflict and this defensive process could not be conscious. He had to defend against his disapproved impulses, his anger at his parent figure, and his anxiety about rejection. Defensively, he had to understand the relationship in terms of the goodness and badness, and efficiency and inefficiency of the exercise of his own free will. For his fate in life, he had no one to blame or praise but himself.

DIFFERENTIATED PERSONALITY STRUCTURE

In the first few years of life, the child cannot be assimilated in an active way into the common activities of his society. He only slowly comes under verbal control. His physical body comes under his control at about the same pace. However, by about age three the child has a rapidly increasing vocabulary and understands much more than he can express. At the same time, he becomes well coordinated in large muscle activities. This large muscle control permits the child to imitate an extensive range of modeled behaviors. It seems very likely that in all societies the child with these new capacities will enter upon a new age-grade, which means he will encounter a new set of situations with which to cope or in which to learn. This is because older members of the society will perceive him as ready for, or capable of, not to mention actively seeking to enter into, whole new sets of the activities of his society. His behavior is readily controlled by others, mostly verbally. He can be instructed easily in simple activities. He can imitate complex modeled actions. He is highly motivated to imitate and explore what others are doing.

The child of three or four will be regarded as old enough to contribute at least to his microgroup's life by taking over small chores or helping with adult activities in a secondary role. He cannot be left on his own much because his behavior can easily disrupt various aspects of group life, for example, by making noise at the wrong times, by misuse of property, by relating inappropriately to others with different forms of status, etc. His behavior will have to be regulated in some fashion, and that will always be in a fashion meaningful to his significant others.

However, it is highly misleading to give the impression that the regulation by others of the child's life constitutes a direct and conscious determination of what he learns. He will learn, normatively, to be a constructive and typical member of his group or stratum, but how the regulation of his early life produces this learning will have only a partial relationship to what the significant others do and believe they are accomplishing. This is because the child's learning capacities are very complex. He is learning in many contexts and in ways of which his elders are unaware. For example, he learns from their modeling of behavior even when they are not aware that they are modeling. He learns from observations of other children. He learns from aspects of storybooks or myths that others do not consider salient. He learns from discrepancies, of which elders are unaware, between what they say and what they do. He learns from complex combinations of these experiences that are not under any adult's control. Nevertheless, all his learning emerges from the actual nature of group life as it occurs around him and with him.

There is very great order in it. The child is introduced to a particular set of activities which are systematically related to various settings. Thus, basically, he learns the scripts of everyday life. There is order in the activities themselves. For example, all the games to which individualistic children are exposed are of the nature of a competition for scarce rewards under a set of rules. Parents may think of the game as a diversion that the child inherently enjoys but, in fact, they are introducing the child to the competitive nature of their group. In cooperative societies most of the activities provided for the child will have a cooperative structure. In all groups girls will be systematically introduced to sets of conditions distinct from those of boys.

In this second universal age-grade, all of the child's experiences represent variations of the components of primary personality structure. It could not be otherwise because primary personality structure is all the child has to orient him to experience. However, many of these new experiences will not be the same in all respects to his past experiences. For example, other adults of different status or in different roles will relate to him somewhat differently but not entirely. He will notice variations in their attributes. Yet he will be concerned about the emotional consequences for him of these relationships. These emotional experiences also will vary systematically from those established in primary personality structure. The child will experience variations of how his behavior affects his relationship to new figures because they have different status and he encounters them in different kinds of activities and possibly in different settings.

For individualists, the differentiations of primary personality structure can be suggested. To begin with, around the age of three the father entered their lives in a new, more intense fashion. Never before confident of how to relate to his small children except briefly or superficially, he now regarded them with their new verbal and motoric skills as ready for his major contribution as a father. This contribution was distinctly different for sons and daughters. He was still perceived by his children as an authority bestowing love or rejection conditionally upon their behavior but now in ways which varied significantly from their relationship to their mother. His daughter found that the ways in which her behavior influenced her relationship to him were of particular kinds. They were systematically different in many ways from those of her brother. This turned out to be the case for almost all relationships to adult males as compared to those with adult females. Other relationships had generally the same structure but with particular variations. In school the teacher was definitely a parent figure but concerned with somewhat different kinds of performances with less power to affect them emotionally and somewhat different attributes. The case was similar with the parents of their friends when visiting in their homes.

Generally individualistic children found a number of variations in the figures they related to: There were mothers, fathers, teachers, other parents, store owners, various relatives, and friends of their parents. They varied from sitting in judgment on the child in ways very similar to the original figure to making virtually no judgments at all. They were very nice, nice, uninterested, mean, and very mean—all of which constituted variations of experiences of love and rejection in relating to them. Consequently, the child's attitudes were systematically differentiated into loving, liking, indifferent, disliking, and hating these new figures. At the same time, he was learning to attribute a whole range of characteristics to himself based on how particular behaviors influenced particular figures.[4]

Differentiated Worldview

In general, each of the four dimensions or components of primary worldview become differentiated by the kinds of variations suggested. However, these new experiences occur in the context of the rapidly increasing linguistic competence of the child. The inchoate primary worldview remains as ground, and the consciousness of the child is increasingly directed and conditioned by speech. Thus, the mysteriousness of much early experience is not preserved. For example, the unknown realm from which the early figures appear and into which they disappear vanishes as the child becomes familiar with the larger context of the life of the adults around him. At the same time, however, new mysteries are introduced in the form of discrete rituals interposed into his usual routines and words enter his vocabulary that refer to beings, things, and places that he does not experience directly or does so only on special occasions. That is, the child becomes aware of the religious aspects of the life of his group. This awareness occurs in systematic fashion in terms of the relationships of the rituals and words to particular events and behaviors. A major task for the child is to grasp their meaning, to infuse the behaviors and words with content. This is the basic fashion in which the general properties of primary worldview become shaped into the form of a particular religion or variation of it. To describe this process briefly and much oversimplified, the religious mysteries are infused with the meanings of primary worldview while assuming an articulable form. Among individualists, for example, the Christian God is at first some strange physically absent loving but judging parent figure. Christ, as the son of this parent figure whom all adult figures greatly praise, can only be the model for the ideal self.[5] The child has many experiences and words to infuse with meaning, and thus the process is lengthy and complex. This process surely is always made more distinct and complex by the special manner in which adults talk about their religion and in which they act during religious practices, not to mention their unwillingness or inability to provide specific and clear explanations for the child because their own capacity to articulate is limited by having gone through the same process in their childhood. That is to say, religious concepts and beliefs constitute a metaphoric code for the translation of inchoate primary worldview into articulated integrated worldview. But what is being encoded is not articulable. Differentiated worldview is partially the learning of the code words and coded ritual behaviors element by element.

At the same time, the other major aspect of worldview—a system of classification—is developing. The variations on the theme of primary worldview in all its dimensions are providing the categories of experience at all levels of the system simultaneously. The child has to infuse them with meaning, including the relationships among them. That is to say, the child is learning object identifications, concept formations, and class inclusion and exclusion in an ever-elaborating manner as he is introduced to larger segments of the total environmental matrix and new forms of its activities, relationships, and artifacts.

Differentiated Identity

Primary identity becomes vastly differentiated by the ways in which its basic attributes are divided into subattributes. For individualistic children in various new activities, relationships, and settings, lovability became differentiated into smartness, carefulness, honesty, strength, beauty, perseverance, neatness, etc. Unlovability was differentiated into stupidity, sloppiness, dishonesty, weakness, ugliness, laziness, being a sissy, etc. These concepts had to be developed through understanding how particular behaviors in particular activities, relationships, and settings were related to them.

A major aspect of the differentiation of primary identity always concerns biological gender. What attributes are approved or disapproved in boys are always systematically distinguished from at least some set for girls. This whole process is complicated by the other components of social stratification in the group. Some types of behaviors are appropriate for members of one status but not others. In this fashion the social stratification of members of a group is recreated each generation. In differentiated identity the child thinks about himself in these proliferating terms but in a fragmented fashion based on the activities and relationships of the moment.

Differentiated Ideology

Primary ideology differentiates by variations of what determines the relationship to primary figures. As these determine the child's emotional states, they constitute what is most important to him. Thus they signify what can be good or bad about life and how the good is to be preserved and the bad changed toward good. Such learning always will be a direct reflection of what is important generally in the life of the group. Socioanthropologists and some historians have long used terms like values and norms for this aspect of group life, although the terms never have been given very clear psychological definition.

Values have been usefully defined by some social psychologists as the most inclusive attitudes (Newcomb et al. 1965). Attitudes were defined earlier as emotion conditioned to any representation. Since values are the most inclusive attitudes, they refer to very abstract concepts with emotional conditioning. They are the concepts which define what *kinds of representations* are most important. Thus, they differentiate the prototypical values of primary ideology. Value learning, then, involves two processes—very abstract concept formation and emotional conditioning to these concepts.[6]

The concept formation part of value learning, then, occurs because there are certain patterns of common elements included in a wide variety of the child's experiences. For example, what is systematically different for boys and girls will define the concepts of masculinity and femininity. For individualists, the little boy began to have such experiences as being asked to show his muscle, or whether he was strong enough to lift or open something. He was told he would grow big and strong like his father. He observed his father do the things that required the most strength. He was encouraged into activities which required strength. He read or was read stories in which men did these kinds of things and women did not. He observed his father's reactions to feats of strength. He found his peers thinking in terms of strength as well as his elders. From such experiences he could and did abstract the concepts of strength and weakness. Similar accounts could be given for experiences resulting in the concepts of winning and losing, of clean and dirty, honest and dishonest, etc. Through all the experiences of the child after age three, there is systematic variation around a limited set of concepts.

The child will not only abstract these concepts. His emotions will be conditioned to them. The child has his emotions evoked in all or most of the specific situations that involve the pattern of elements defining the concept. This is a very complex process of learning in which both unlearned and previously conditioned emotions play roles. The child can learn through experience with several different emotions, unlearned and conditioned, that certain kinds of situations are accompanied by unpleasures (disruptive emotions) and others by pleasures (organizing emotions). For example, when the child has learned that punishment accompanies disobedience to parents, he has abstracted the aversive aspect of several different disruptive emotions in many concrete situations, for example, no dessert for not eating his spinach, a spanking for taking a cookie between meals, or sitting in a corner for hitting a sibling. He has learned the value for obedience to parents.

The significance of the concept of values for psychology can hardly be exaggerated. In determining what set of conditions is of greatest importance in maintaining organized interaction with the environment, they orient the young group member to daily life. They select from among possible activities and relationships those to be emphasized. They provide the ends of action for which all else is means. They identify that level of abstraction of goals which reveals the foundations and continuity of action throughout the individual's life.[7]

Once the child learns values, his motivation is to realize them. That is, he behaves in order to attain the conditions that have their meanings. He seeks the experiences of the pleasure evoked by the conditioning of positive emotions that accompanies the evocation of the value concept. For example, the individualistic child, once he has learned the value for achievement, is attracted to conditions that represent it. He enters competitions in which he has learned to expect he can win in order to have the experience of winning. He also avoids, if he can, competitions he anticipates losing. The little girl takes on the activities of grooming herself in order to have the experience of either seeing how attractive she is or obtaining evidence of it from others. Life becomes oriented toward attaining value experiences and learning how to do so. Conversely, it also is oriented toward avoiding value-negating experiences and learning how to do so.

The learning of values is at most only partly a conscious process. It is doubtful that those responsible for children's development in any group think in terms of the child's learning of a value system.[8] Rather, they think about the appropriateness or inappropriateness of the child's behavior in particular settings, activities, and relationships. Their language almost certainly has words which correspond to the values, but they are not consistently used to identify the common elements in the great variety of experiences through which values are learned. In many of these experiences, very different persons are involved—in some cases, only the child's peers, and in others, no persons.

Values help provide the answer to Geertz's (1973) dilemma—to account for the great natural variation of cultural form given the biological unity of mankind. They do so by revealing how that biological unity, that is, human nature of hedonic motivation, flexible representation, and planning and intentionality, becomes translated into social motivation relative to each human group.⁹ The motivation to realize values is social motivation in the sense that the conditions of life which produce pleasure and un-pleasure become defined by experience in the group. In a competitive group, the child will learn the values for successful competition with oth-ers. In a cooperative group he will learn the values for effective coopera-tion with others. In one group the member will learn a set of standards of femininity or masculinity different from that of another. He does so by having his innate hedonic capacities for pleasure and unpleasure *condi-tioned* to particular types of situations.¹⁰ The incorporation of this condi-tioning into expectations concerning what behaviors will produce what new conditions permit him to *anticipate* various pleasures and unpleasures and so to plan to maximize pleasure and minimize unpleasure. In this fashion he maximizes organized interaction with his particular environment.

The learning of a value system is the heart of differentiated ideology because value realizations and problems with value realization become the bases of what is good and bad about life. Ideology is about how to attain the good life. It follows that every ideology is fundamentally about how the group life can be arranged so that the individual or group maximizes value realization.¹¹ It also follows that it will be formulated in a way which takes into account the ways to get from the current arrangement to the ideal one.

Differentiated ideology, then, is the form which the good life takes as the child is translating primary ideology into one based on value realiza-tion where the value system is largely implicit and the focus is on more specific goals and conditions. There certainly are important phases of this process based on the gradual learning of the values and then learning the ways to realize each of them and then ever more complex combinations of them. However, the key to differentiated ideology is the structure of activities and relationships of the age-grade or age-grades between ages three and four and the major changes of puberty.¹² The child is engrossed in learning in these conditions and basically concerned with problems of value realization in these forms. For example, at first, individualistic chil-dren express their ideology in wishes and fantasies concerning the teacher not being so mean, or there being no bully up the street, or the new baby being given back to the stork. The ideology is fragmented and situation-oriented. The more experience he has with new activities and relation-ships, the more understanding he develops of why his life is the way it is and the less does his ideology have a fantastic quality. For example, the individualistic child stops wishing the teacher wasn't so mean and starts thinking that his parents should see to it the teacher is fired, that the bully should be arrested by the police, and that the new baby be given to child-less Aunt Maggie. He is learning how his society functions with respect to what is important to him.

DIFFERENTIATED MODE OF THOUGHT

It is difficult to conceive differentiated mode of thought without a clear perspective on types of modes. However, one clue to it is the developmental course of linguistic competence. The very general basic structure of syntax for the three-year-old does differentiate substantially in many ways without losing its general structure. The basic fragmented and analytic cause-effect nature of the individualistic mode of thought was differentiated in several ways. One is that the ideas of cause and effect were divided into accidental, intentional, and "act of God" forms and into single and multiple forms. Another is that its judgmental property became comparative. That is, the causes and effects were not only either good or bad, but better or worse than others. This was based on the learning of status systems primarily in the elementary school years. Among these status systems were the academic, in terms of letter grades; sports and games, in terms of first, second, third, also-ran, and last; and boys' pecking orders, in terms of toughness and weakness. A third form of differentiation may have been in terms of the temporal dimension of cause-effect sequences. That is, the child learned to think in terms of shorter-and longer-range sequences.

Differentiated Expressive Style

It is equally difficult to consider this aspect of universal personality without a basic terminology.[13] However, it seems very likely that it will be directly related to the nature of the value system learned. The kinds of values will infuse behavior with particular qualities—for example, those related to the differences between competitive and cooperative activities, individualistic and collective performances, and active and contemplative ways of life. In addition, expressive style will be differentiated within a value system by the various common forms of dealing with value realization and problems of value realization. In all groups the differentiation of values by biological gender will produce expressive styles also related to biological gender. The occurrence in all human groups of values for masculinity and femininity and for morality suggest that expressive style will differentiate along these lines. Consequently, in characterizing whole groups, there will very likely be a typology of value systems and subtypologies of gender and moral value systems.[14] Within each type, expressive style will be differentiated with respect to common variations of response to attainment and lack of attainment of value realizations of these kinds.

Differentiated Practical Knowledge and Perceptual-Motor Skills

During this age-grade practical knowledge proliferates enormously. The child is introduced to many new common scripts and variants of them. He is brought into contact with an increasing array of persons, artifacts, and settings. For example, the individualistic child learned virtually a whole new world when he went to school. Also important in this age-grade is practical knowledge about fellow members of society, both of the child's own generation and of older generations. Individualistic children learned about various types of authorities through their succession of teachers. They learned the various ways other children dealt with common situations and their consequences. Important to this learning is the beginning of the correlation of elements of these experiences that tend to accompany each other, for example, teachers who are tough but fair or tough and unfair, boys who are strong but nice versus strong but bullies, etc. This is the first level of patterns of experience that are to become integrated at the highest levels in the next universal age-grade.

Perceptual-motor skills also proliferate as the child is introduced to interaction with new objects in new settings. A great deal of this learning is the elaboration and refinement of skills. At the same time, it can be expected that children from different strata have more experience with certain skills and less with others than those from other strata. The most pronounced strata difference will probably be by sex. Some of it will be regulated by value realization as children discover they are more likely to be successful where particular skills are required. However, this will be very much a function of the extent of choice of activities permitted by the system of social stratification. Even the amount of skill development will be regulated by the nature of group life. The more contemplative the ways of life, the less emphasis there will be on the development of perceptual-motor skills. In all groups a major differentiation of linguistic skills will occur in this age-grade as the child learns the intricacies of syntax and the expression of irregular words.

Differentiated Unconscious Dynamics

The basic conflict or conflicts and the defensive processes also will become differentiated. Because the conflict(s) can never be resolved as the individual matures physically and moves into new conditions of life in the age-grading system of his group, it can only be channeled into new forms.[15] Conflicts in the realization of values will provide the major new forms in which the basic conflict is evoked. The defenses will take new forms as the premises of the worldview elaborate.

For individualists, this process was made very difficult by the development of the comparative mode of thought and its accompaniment by various status systems. The individual found himself constantly having to ground his self-esteem in comparisons to both his own previous self-assessments and to assessments relative to the value realizations of others. Self-esteem became measurable in terms of a potentially endless self-improvement, as reflected in such maxims as "every day in every way I get better and better" and "never be a quitter" and in terms of competitive, comparative status vis-a-vis others. Most prominent of these new forms of the conflict were, for males, those around masculinity and dependency and achievement and morality. Their strong feelings of dependency generated by early childhood were defined by their values as inconsistent with masculinity. Any dependent behavior or feelings were defined as effeminate. Yet the increasing comparativeness and competitiveness of life constantly generated such feelings. Achievement in legitimated tasks (and even some non-legitimated tasks in the peer group) was constantly hampered by the necessity of conforming to such moral values as honesty, obedience to the authority of the rules of the game, and loyalty to others. There began for males a life-long struggle with lying, cheating, and disloyalty in the pursuit of success.

For females, the major new forms of conflict lay in the acceptance of femininity as the devalued status of femaleness in her group became manifest, although not consciously fostered by others, and in the contradiction between competing with others for the scarce rewards of grades in school and some games and being a nurturant, empathic person.

The defensive processes of both sexes were differentiated mainly by the possibilities afforded by the comparative mode of thought. If one was not high enough in a status system of athletic prowess, academics, or beauty, one could always try to draw attention to those with even less and to have some of the higher status of others rub off on the self. Scapegoating and status-borrowing became the dominant forms of defense, particularly for boys. For girls, there was no defense in this age-grade for their devaluation, once they had to abandon efforts to be "tomboys," except intensified turning of anger against the self. Scapegoating required a projection of one's inadequacies to others and a displacement of the self-disgust or guilt to them. Status borrowing required introjection of the adequacies of others and reversal from self-disgust or guilt to pride or virtuousness. These defenses were inescapable, given the paradox of the belief that one was responsible for one's status, but the impossibility in a competitive way of life of everyone being number one.

INTEGRATED PERSONALITY STRUCTURE

During the few years following the main changes of puberty, the fragmented variations of primary personality structure which constitute differ-

entiated personality structure become integrated in a systematic and coherent form, which marks the transition to adult status or its equivalent in
non-Western societies. This integrated personality structure is based on
the development, through the capacities for classification, of the sets of
most abstract beliefs. The reasons for its development at this period of the
life span are twofold. First, the child's learning in the previous stage has
progressed to the point at which he begins to be able to deal with the
interrelationships within it. This is partly due to having learned the relevant representations sufficiently that classifying experience becomes more
facile. It is probably due more to the development of metacognitive capacities for organizing and manipulating multiple representations. The second reason is that the changes of puberty produce an individual with full
adult physical stature and powers. It is most unlikely that the members of
any human group will or can ignore these developments in the younger
generation. They can no longer be related to, either physically or mentally, as they were before. They are capable of fulfilling a whole new set
of roles, both constructive and disruptive. Recognition of these changes is
widely evidenced among human groups by pubertal ceremonies of change
of status, admission to adult groups, and extensive exchange of knowledge
previously regarded as inappropriate for children.

Given the changes in the child and the interest of older members of his
group in assimilating him as a full-fledged adult participant, or its equivalent in other age-grading systems, a complex process is initiated by which
the younger member integrates his previous learning by assimilating it to
the ways in which older generations present to him their forms of reflecting on experience. The older generations provide the generalizations from
experience which constitute their worldview, the main ideologies extant,
and the identity they attribute to him, relating it to others. The young
person either critically assesses its meaningfulness in terms of his learning
or uncritically conforms to it while working out the relationship privately.
Normatively, in periods of slow rates of change in the total environmental
matrix, the elders' ways of interpreting experience reflect well the order
in the young person's previous learning. They are meaningful generalizations of it. He appreciates their wisdom. He consolidates his ways of understanding reality, attributing identity, and assessing group life. His capacity to do this identifies him as finally qualified for adult status or its
equivalent in the eyes of his elders.

The systematically integrated belief systems comprising worldview,
identity, and ideology constitute the articulated or articulable form of the
individual's learning. There is much learning that is excluded from it, such
as his mode of thought, his defensive procedures, the unique elements of
experience, and those not regarded as significant by other group members.
Although mode of thought is excluded from these belief systems, it is not
excluded from experience. Older generations present to the budding adult

through speech the full range of normative organization of the components of thought or, rather, the full system available normatively for the
expressing of the content of thought. He can now interpret speech within
this system, convey his thought using this system, and carry on systematic
thought in its form. All the normatively used rules have been learned,
although no one may be able to articulate most of them, and this is recognized both by the individual and those with whom he interacts. He is
capable of sophisticated logical reasoning, given the content of his knowledge.

Much of the individual's expressive style to this point in development
will be articulated in his identity. However, the integrative process itself
is a form of reorientation to life which introduces new aspects of expressive style. In fact, the articulation of previous aspects is inevitably a determinant of subsequent style as the individual attempts to preserve desired
and alter undesired forms. What he does expresses the new aspects.

Integrated Worldview

Integrated worldview was discussed in Chapter 2. Only a brief summary
is necessary here. It is a system of beliefs about the nature of the reality
behind appearances. There are two major aspects of worldview. One is a
set of overarching beliefs concerning the meaning and purpose of life and
death. This is based on an externalization of primary worldview as it has
been shaped by intervening experience. Experiences between ages three
and four and the years following puberty select one form. This form normatively will be that of the dominant religion in the individual's group or
stratum.

The other development of integrated worldview is the abstraction of the
highest levels of the system of classification by which the individual cate-
gorizes his experience. Most prominent will be those concerning people,
both in the individual's group and outside it, that is, classes of human
nature such as male and female, fox clan and bear clan. It reflects primarily
the system of social stratification of the group. Important to this process
is that it is based on experiences with others whose behavior is motivated
by the pursuit of value realization, where the values are widely shared
among members of the group but with important variations by stratum.
Moreover, a significant amount of this behavior will be determined by
defensive processes that also are widely shared because the major conflicts
are widely shared. Thus, the generalizations about people or categories of
people will include the defensive processes without recognition of them.
For example, to discriminated-against minority groups such as slaves, and
members of neighboring groups with whom there is conflict, will be attributed inherent characteristics produced by the shared (socially legitimated) defensive operations of the dominant group.

The resultant of the shaped externalization of primary worldview and consolidation of the highest levels of the system of classification is a perspective on life both longitudinal and cross-sectional which has a stability and finality that is profound. The individual is equipped to understand in a general but clear way all subsequent and past experience. Because worldview is a summary of the actual order in group life as it is understood by members, it is a sound framework for mastery of present experience and anticipation of future experience. Because it is very widely shared, both with the peer group and older generations, it provides a strong basis for group cohesion.

Integrated Identity

In the integrative stage of development, the attributes of differentiated identity become organized into a coherent pattern. This pattern will be one recognizable pattern among a set by which members of the group classify individuals or subgroups. Integrated identity is assimilated in the same sense as worldview. That is, older members provide the abstract level of characterization of qualities and groups of qualities by using these terms selectively to describe others. The implications of these characterizations concerning actual or expected behaviors in various conditions are matched by the individual with his previous learning and perceived current dispositions. As these abstract attributes used by older generations are generalizations from the behaviors of others who have developed through substantially the same age-grading system, they help the individual to crystallize his identity meaningfully. The most significant attributes of identity will be those relevant to values and their realization. For individualists, for example, they included honest/dishonest, ambitious/lazy, attractive/ugly, smart/dumb, industrious/careless, etc. In more castelike societies, the attributes would be more likely to refer to the subgroups and roles performed, such as fox clan, turtle clan, shaman, apprentice, carpenter, smith, and so on. As a result, the individual understands himself as this kind of personality among the set of kinds identified.

This assimilation of integrated identity occurs for all of the types of identities suggested earlier. Those with the individualized type form a single identity encompassing, in more abstract terms, all their learned attributes. Those with compartmentalized identities will consolidate multiple identities without any identity that encompasses them all. Those with group identities will learn a coherent pattern of attributes that characterizes the group rather than the individual.

The stability of the identities so formed will vary with the forms of group life. In general, the less the castelike quality and the greater the social mobility in the group, the less stable will be the identity. However, it is important to recognize that identity is partially provided by integrated worldview. For example, among individualists, the properties of human nature are basic to all identities. One is always a human being and one of a subset of categories of humans—for example, for individualists male-female, child-adult, sane-insane, and member of a race. The believed inherent characteristics of these categories are inevitably basic to identity. However, in groups in which caste stratification is dominant, more of the attributes of identity will be given in the worldview.

Integrated Ideology

The postpubertal individual with his new metacognitive capacities becomes able to grasp the larger picture of the nature of the life of his group and why it is so organized. This encompasses all its major institutions. For example, fragmented experiences of individualistic children about the work world—seller-buyer relations, presidents and mayors, laws, the police, jails, the army, courts, private property, friendship, education, sports, museums, libraries, travel, allowances, banks, clothing, etc.—came to have meaning in a generally coherent scheme of democratic government, free enterprise economics, private property, the conjugal family, impartial laws and innocence until proven guilty, the weekly unit of workdays and weekends, etc. At the same time, their particular problems with value realizations, consistently interpreted for them in terms of their own attributes and willpower, was generalized to the understanding of the behaviors and life circumstances of others. In this way, they came to think about change in their society in terms of the yieldings and resistances to temptations to self-interest and immorality within the institutional structure. The major variations of individualistic ideologies were based on assessments of which individuals or groups were yielding to or resisting temptations and what should be done about them.

Again, integrated worldview plays a major role. The bulk of understanding, both of why group life has its particular form and how it could be functioning in a particular way, is logical derivations from integrated worldview. For example, for individualists, after about eighteen years of competing with others for scarce rewards in activities with specified rules, it seemed appropriate that their society had a democratic form of government. As it is human nature for people to be tempted to immorality for selfish reasons, the control of power is potentially corrupting. It follows that there should be arrangements for removing from power those who yield to its temptations. As everyone is tempted to corruption by his own interests, the closest humans can come to good government is to have each member (who is qualified) vote his own interest and let the majority elect its representatives for a limited period of time in which they can demonstrate their capacity or incapacity to resist the temptations of power.

The prepubertal child will have learned a variety of approaches fragmented by limited interests to change in specific areas of life. Integrated ideology combines and systematizes them into one of, or a variant of, the spectrum of ideologies extant in the group. In the few years following the major changes of puberty, the individual will assimilate the extant form of ideology that most closely matches his experience of what is right and wrong with group life and what changes would most likely improve it. What is wrong will be fundamentally a matter of problems in the realization of one or more values. The integrative period of development is one in which the individual must translate childhood forms of value realization into adult forms. This task is essentially one of constructing a round of life that maximizes value realization given the beliefs and attitudes with which the person currently has to work. If this round of life produces a high degree of value realization, the individual will develop a conservative integrated ideology designed to maintain it. If the round of life includes low degrees of value realization, much change will be regarded as desirable and the integrated ideology will be radical.

Integrated Mode of Thought

The new variations of primary mode of thought learned in differentiated mode of thought are consolidated and synthesized in integrated mode of thought. Experience is now processed in a consistent and sophisticated form that integrates all the components of mode of thought. Thus, the individual has mastered the logic inherent in the way of life of his group. At the same time, he has mastered the common varieties of illogic employed to handle his conflicts. This illogic can be understood as the operation of the particular defenses characteristic of the individual and his group. There will be a systematic relationship between the logical and the illogical aspects of integrated mode of thought. That is, particular defenses or combinations of defenses will be characteristic of particular forms of logic because the major threats are widely shared and foster shared defenses that legitimate the illogic—for example, rationalizations.

Integrated Expressive Style

Expressive style will be integrated in the sense that, within the limits of primary expressive style, the major aspects of differentiated expressive style will be consolidated into a consistent pattern. This occurs because the child's most serious difficulties with value realizations and his most successful ways of attaining value realization are the main focus of his attention. Those difficulties are unlikely to be overcome just because he enters the integrative phase. As a result, he will tend to maintain his ways of managing them, incorporating such awareness of them as he has into his identity.

On the other hand, it seems likely that the most significant aspects of expressive style recognized by the group or the individual's stratum will be those associated with variations of the new forms of worldview, ideology, and mode of thought. In general, the individual will be characterized as a group member in some such terms as stable/unstable, mature/immature, leader/follower, etc. With respect to worldview, it will be the individual's approach to his variant of the religion that looms largest. It may be that in all human groups a basic component of integrated expressive style will be a dimension something like devout, typical, casual, or deviant. With respect to ideology, it will be conservative, radical, or deviant and intense, normative, or apathetic. With respect to mode of thought, it will be something like logical, fuzzy, defensive, or crazy. These will be the most important ways of characterizing individuals because they have the greatest implications for the group. All other aspects of integrated expressive style will tend to be variations within the broad normative range of these basic aspects. That is, they will be variations of the typical worldview, of the conservative and normative in ideology, and of the logical in mode of thought. It will be within these categories that the aspects of expressive style noted above will be significant. However, there probably are considerable differences in the degree of variation and importance in the group of these aspects. In groups in which external locus of control of experience is dominant, individual differences in style will be either attributed to inherent nature or largely ignored as of no moment. In groups in which group identity prevails, there can be expected to be a limited set of group styles. Only in the differentiated individualistic type of identity will expressive style within the normative range play a major role in characterizing personality. Humans, in general, will attend to and make discriminations only with respect to differences which make a difference in experience.

Integrated Practical Knowledge and Perceptual-Motor Skills

By this age-grade the individual has amassed an extensive amount of practical knowledge. It encompasses all the common artifacts and settings of his group or stratum. He knows his way around in considerable detail. This includes familiarity with all the variants of how things work, so that whatever he has to interact with, he knows it either is dealt with in this way or that way (including consulting experts). In addition, he will very likely have developed special areas of practical knowledge related to particular roles he will be performing in the role structure of his group and in idiosyncratic areas such as hobbies. All of this knowledge constitutes the most specific levels of understanding in the ideology of how his society functions. The integration of this knowledge consists primarily in the development of the more specific levels of script performances and in the making of transitions from one script to another.

The basic perceptual-motor skills involved in everyday group life will, by this stage, be considerably refined and overlearned, such as in speech, utilization of common artifacts in oft-repeated routines, swimming, tree climbing, pottery making, cooking, sewing, archery, spear throwing, dancing and chanting, inhibition of dispositions to behavior, etc. These skills will be integrated in the sense of being combined into more complex performances or into role performances requiring intricate integration along with practical knowledge. Certain skills will be more highly refined due to their significance for the particular set of roles the individual will be performing in adult life in the group or as part of idiosyncratic scripts.

Integrated Unconscious Dynamics

In the integrative stage, these dynamics will become integrated into the other components of personality. The basic conflict(s) and defensive processes will be manifested in the integrated worldview which, as has been pointed out, is largely an articulated externalization of primary worldview in a specific form. For example, individualists understood the meaning of life and death in terms of the main beliefs of the Christian faith. The basic conflict was externalized as an omniscient God sitting constantly in judgment on the individual. The judgment both during life and afterward was based on the individual's free choices of actions. The upshot of judgment was eternal love or rejection by God. Thus, the individual was ultimately responsible for his fate in death as in life. In addition, the scapegoating defenses, having resulted in self-fulfilling prophecies, became built into the worldview as aspects of human nature. White males were the superior, only fully complete humans. Women were incomplete beings due to their weakness and emotional instability and required men to look after them. Members of other races were either subhuman, lacking either morality or the "smarts" to succeed, or childlike humans, not yet having learned right from wrong, but capable if missionized by the white race.

Unconscious dynamics also were integrated in ideology. For individualists, how their society functioned was understood in terms of individuals striving to improve themselves, the meeting of bodily needs, and living morally, but was subject to failures of will. The successful were understood mainly as more industrious but sometimes less moral. Therefore what was good about group life reflected the triumph of moral will, and what was bad reflected the failure of it. To improve it required proselytization of the self or others to resolve to resist temptation in the future. It was an ideology of change the person and you change society. Most people were perceived as "only human" in occasionally yielding to temptation but readily repentant. Criminals and the poor were those particularly weak-willed, and to them were projected many now unconscious weaknesses in the self, as reflected in the severity of the penal code and the view that, except for the physically handicapped, charity for the poor only rewarded their weakness of will.

The defenses against loss of self-esteem were integrated in identity. The middle-class individualist came to see himself as a good masculine or feminine Christian, hard-working (in his chosen occupation), more so than most of those lower in socioeconomic status and less so than most of higher status. This was not by nature but by willpower. He saw himself as having some weaknesses on which he was diligently working. He was optimistic about liking himself even better in the future, for it was up to him and he could do it if he tried hard enough. In some abilities he saw himself as superior to most others, and he took pride in knowing that these were self-made. He was sensitive to the judgments of others, but where he disagreed with them, he felt a charge of pride that he was his own person. Thus, his conflicts and his defenses remained unconscious, but their products generally became smoothly integrated into his identity.

The essence of individualistic experience is comparison and therefore a focus on differences. Thus, with respect to identity, the focus was on relative strengths and weaknesses of individuals, while the shared characteristics went unremarked. In expressive style, differences were inevitable as individual styles reflected comparative success in the realization of the various values. The necessity to look to the self for this, given the scarce rewards of a competitive way of life, put a premium on self-confidence. Only the fairly consistently successful emerged confident. The fairly consistently unsuccessful emerged unconfident. The majority were insecure in their confidence and therefore defensive about it. The individualists' normative expressive style, therefore, was one of considerable sensitivity about self-worth, a ready affability designed to avoid threat, and quick defensiveness when threatened, which took the scapegoating—status borrowing form in men and more often a self-denigrating form in women.

Unconscious dynamics played its role in practical knowledge and perceptual-motor skill integration by influencing this development into an emphasis on areas where the individual could maintain self-worth, leading to selection of a script repertory where this expertise would be maximized.

What is most important about integrated personality structure is that its development marks the assimilation of the individual into the adult life of the group. His worldview provides a stable foundation within which all experience is readily and meaningfully classified. It sets the limits on what is possible in life and thus establishes the range of ideologies to be seriously entertained. His ideology orients him generally to the ways in which he wants to perform in the common scripts of group life, determining the variants of performances in accordance with his desire for change and his views of how his behaviors are related to change. His identity locates him in the spectrum of his group. Moreover, his identity regulates the ways in which he implements his ideology by identifying his capacities—both those that are fixed and those potentially alterable. Thus, the nondeviant member of the group is thoroughly oriented to life in his group. His orientation to the group, both current and anticipated, is recognized as an acceptable variant of the ways in which other normative members orient. Consequently, he can plan in as long-range a manner as his worldview permits for the future realization of his values and commence to implement his plans.

This integration of personality within the general structure established in primary personality structure and of the differentiation of that structure appears to be the culmination of a cycle of learning that makes the person a fully socialized member of his group. There is little reason to doubt that the great bulk of the variance in the behavior of an individual through his life can be accounted for in terms of development up to and including the occurrence of integrated personality structure. His view of reality, his value system, his mode of thought, and *core components* of his identity, ideology, and expressive style have been established and will not change.[16] Yet it is certain that a significant part of the variance of his behavior in the last fifty to sixty years of his life cannot be accounted for in these terms alone. There is adult development within a general structure of continuity of personality, and it is of very great significance to the individual. Conceptualizing this development in psychology is essential but is particularly susceptible to ethnocentric bias. What is important in group life can be so varied that any attempt to generalize about development during the adult years must be kept at a very abstract level. Two adult forms of personality structure are suggested for this purpose—midlife and terminal.

MIDLIFE PERSONALITY STRUCTURE

This term is chosen because it places emphasis on the significance of the generational cycle in human life. The generational cycle refers to the inevitable recognition, however it is understood, that the normative life span of members of any group encompasses something akin to four cohort groups. These are based on the female life cycle because birth occurs, literally, only through the female. The cycle, essentially, is that for about fifteen to twenty-plus years females of one's cohort group do not bear children, then they do for about twenty to thirty years; and then they no longer do until they die in about another twenty to thirty years. It seems highly unlikely that this cycle escapes the notice of the members of any human group. Thus, at about the time females of one's cohort group are close to death, a fourth generation is being born. The individual cannot help eventually, and usually quite early, reckoning his life span in these terms. Moreover, because males inevitably will become deeply involved in any of several ways with females and their offspring in their group, this female generational cycle will play a significant role in their lives.

In Chapter 7's discussion of age-grading systems, it was emphasized that the nature of later-age-grades is dependent on that of earlier ones. Attachments, alliances, forms of status with privileges and obligations both in the present and in the future are heavily reliant on various continuities in the life span. Therefore, it seems very likely that the period of life at which significant other females normatively lose their childbearing capacity will mark the onset of an age-grade in the group's and each stratum's age-grading system. This will tend to correspond to the entrance of a new generation into the adult life of the group, the occurrence of a new generation into the group, and the departure of the oldest generation from the group. Each of these events cannot fail to have profound significance for members entering the third generation. An example of this for individualists was given in Chapter 7 in terms of the "empty nest," menopause, birth of grandchildren, reversal of dependencies of parents or their deaths, entry of one's children's generation into the adult work world, etc. None of these can be expected to have universal meanings, and some, not even universal occurrence. That is why the focus in midlife personality structure is on the generational cycle itself rather than in particular events which may be related to it only in some groups. Whatever the local events correlated with this cycle, they will have great significance for most, if not all, members.

The significance will be manifest in all components of personality. For example, among middle-class individualists, there was an intensification of interest in religion, a replacement of the attainment of the dream of the good life and denial of death with a renewed recognition of one's mortality, with an attendant elaboration of worldview. Most commonly there was an increase in ideological conservatism. Very commonly women became more depressed and passive-aggressive—that is, demanding more attention from significant others via hypochondria and psychosomatic symptoms. The counterpart in most men was an increase in mellowness and tolerance, although many became bitter and irritable. All of these developments ensured a reassessment of identity. For some, the difficulties produced more defensiveness in mode of thought, and in others, less as the new conditions forced a reassessment of value realizations and their future possibilities. Again, none of these changes in personality are likely to be universal. However, in all groups it is likely that there will be personality reorganization at this period.

TERMINAL PERSONALITY STRUCTURE

Another reorganization of personality appears very likely in the few years preceding death in late life. At some point the individual in any group will arrive at the conclusion that life in its commonly recognized form will end for him within a few years. This will be based on the historical recognition of cohort demise as it is expressed by older generations and learned by each succeeding one. It will always carry the significance of whatever form of immortality characterizes the religion of the group. It may be life in another realm (comforting or painful), reincarnation, continued existence as a spirit with various powers, etc. These general beliefs inevitably will take on specific immediate significance for the individual. These, in turn, will require psychological preparation of a substantial nature. There also will be some form of dispensation of material possessions, not to mention possessions of a less tangible sort. Members of one's own and younger generations, too, will recognize the impending demise and begin to make material and psychological preparations, some of which will be recognized and have effects on the older person.

As with the midlife reorganization of personality, there will be an altered perspective on the life span. The significance of religion will intensify, most probably, this time with a less abstract and more personal focus. For those anticipating negative forms of immortality, defensive distortions will crystallize, often in socially legitimated forms. Ideological thinking will take either a retrospective form, if nothing can be done about group life from the hereafter, or a revision along the lines of what can be done from the hereafter. The more troublesome and comforting attributes of identity will dominate in contemplation of what the afterlife holds for the individual. Expressive style will reflect these adjustments. Some perceptual-motor skills will decline. A terminal personality structure will be established if death does not occur before the reorganization is complete.[17]

PERSONALITY STRUCTURE IN TRANSITIONAL PERIODS

The foregoing account of personality development is based on the assumption of a slow rate of change in group life across generations. It is this slow rate that provides both order in experience within a generation and assimilation from older generations in integrated personality structure. When the rate of change in group life increases markedly, human development is very different. To begin with, there are multiple forms of early relationships. But they lack any integrated coherent form because they include elements of previous types of relationships and elements of newly developing forms. For example, young children today who are moving daily from relationships to parents at home to relationships with staff at nursery schools or day-care centers or babysitters to periods with grandparents cannot construct a primary personality structure of multiple figures and compartmentalized identities. The latter can be expected when the multiple relationships are integrated into a stable form of group life. Today parents in the home are likely to reflect conflicts and fluctuations between old and new sexual identities. The staff of nursery schools reflect not only these instabilities but also much individualistic maternalism mixed with elements of deterministic training about child-rearing. The various elements may or may not be similar across the major settings of the child's life. Moreover, many young adults caring for children part of the time are not stable in their own personalities as they grope for identity and meaning over time. The child can construct from such experiences only the most general sense of instability and need to assess his circumstances in order to adapt his behavior accordingly to preserve organized interaction with his environment. It can be no more than a minimal kind of structure, but it does prepare the child for the constant instabilities of succeeding years.

In the years following this primary personality structure, the child has little possibility of learning a value system. Values require abstraction of common elements from a wide variety of experiences with consistent hedonic conditioning. In periods of rapid change, there will be no such consistency of elements or conditioning. At best, the child can learn some attitudes at intermediate levels of abstraction and perhaps nothing more than fleeting interests. In this case, the bases of motivation never take on a social form and so remain at the presocial hedonic level—sensory pleasures, primary emotions, novelty, stimulation, and variety. As members of his group organize their behavior around these simple hedonics with their changing forms of realization but older generations still reflect the previous value system in various degrees, there is little chance of constructing coherent systems of classification. There is little consistency in the demands and expectations of others. Attributes of self often are contradictory, yet older generations often demand consistency in terms they understand.[18] There is no orderly differentiation of the primary personality structure, which itself has minimal structure. The best the individual can do for an integrated personality structure is to abstract the belief that there is no meaning or purpose of life and death. Life is nothing but constant change. Human nature is almost infinitely malleable or adaptable. There are no clear guidelines for ideologies developed primarily around methods of survival.

It must be borne in mind that transitional periods have a course to run. Personality development in the early generations entering this period will be plagued mainly by trying to assimilate the integrated personality structure of older generations to a decreasing amount of order in their own experience. This probably produces a strong reactionary flavor to ideology, since the only order known is the old one. Some changes will be attractive to subgroups with particular problems in the old order but opposed by other subgroups not so affected. Generation gaps will expand. The younger will resist application of the old system of classification to them and generally reject all forms of categorization. Cultlike groups, providing temporary forms of meaning and identity, often borrowed from neighboring groups, will appear. New vocabularies will emerge and linguistic structure will begin to be modified. Breakdown of linguistic communication will produce increasing reliance on nonverbal forms of communication such as music and dancing. The need to escape unmasterable reality will result in increased use of the inevitable group drugs. Frustration will be extensive and, without moral values, will produce strong tendencies to physically violent expression, generating concern with and more rigid forms of group regulation. Preoccupation with death in various forms or defensive avoidance of the subject will occur.

For generations in the middle of transitional periods, the instability of life will not be leavened by the attempt of older generations to preserve or return to the old order. It will be replaced by an increasingly restrictive and primitive order imposed by groups who control power in their own interest. The majority of members of the group will have a strongly ambivalent attitude toward it, needing some basis for order but resenting its partiality to a minority. At the same time, the direction inherent in the processes of change in the group will begin to be discerned in part by some members. The early forms of some new worldviews and ideologies will emerge and stir lively controversy and probably heavy repression.

For the generations toward the end of the transitional period, these new worldviews and ideologies will narrow to a few with substantial supporters and probably some revolutionary movements. Gradually, order will return to the experience of new generations. Life history and the historical moment will produce a generally meaningful new worldview based on a new primary personality structure. There probably is a period of struggle among ideological variants of this worldview until one prevails, coinciding with a new period of slow rate of social change. Personality development then runs its course through the new set of universal age-grades.

CONCLUSION

Eight universal components of personality have been proposed—worldview, ideology, identity, mode of thought, expressive style, practical knowledge, perceptual-motor skills, and unconscious dynamics. They have a course of development through at least five forms during the life span. In each of these universal stages of personality development, these components taken together constitute a general form of personality structure. The five personality structures are primary, differentiated, integrated, midlife, and terminal. It is proposed that the personality of any individual can be described in terms of the eight components of each of the five stages. This description will account for the overwhelming majority of the variance in all human behavior.

A number of suggestions have been offered concerning typologies of the universal components. However, it is cautioned that typologies are more usefully developed from the analysis of personality in many diverse human groups, both historically and regionally. Such typologies will be correlated with types of groups based on what almost certainly will be a limited number of forms of total environmental matrices that are themselves based on inherent limits in both human nature and the nature of nonhuman environments as they interact.

— 10 —

The Science of Sociology

The biological and psychological levels of conceptualization of human behavior are not sufficient for a complete human science. A third, more
abstract, level is required. This is the sociological level. Sociology is the
science that describes and explains the total set of behaviors of all members of a society, changes in it over time, and the similarities and differences among such sets during and across periods of the history of human
existence.[1] This science is required because of the unfeasibility of psychological explanation for communication about such broad ranges of behavior. Psychological explanation is possible but much too complex and lengthy.
Potentially, sociological explanation can be reduced to the psychological.
In this sense, sociology is psychology at its most abstract levels of conceptualization, just as psychology is biology at its most abstract levels of explanation.[2] All three human sciences address the same subject matter—
the behaviors of human beings. They are alternative, not complementary,
ways of conceptualizing that subject matter. Each has its practical purposes. One or the other can be used to describe or explain all human
phenomena from the smallest physiological events in the human body to
the misnamed "philosophy of history."[3]

Each human science is defined by its theory. Sociology is distinct from
both biology and psychology in that it accounts for the repetitive behaviors of all members of a society taken together rather than the behaviors
of members taken one at a time. Its terminology is one of civilizations,
societies, social stratification, demography, institutions, roles, functions of
a society, etc. Eschewing biological or psychological terms, it describes and
explains the behaviors of members of a society in terms of reciprocal roles,
structures of institutions, the relationship between demographic characteristics of individuals and the roles they perform, division of the population
by roles performed not based on demographic characteristics, extent of

fulfillment of the functional prerequisites of a society, and changes in all of these over time.

Social anthropology in current social science, after a promising start as large-scale efforts to describe and explain the ways of life of diverse human groups in terms of statuses, roles, and institutions, has steadily moved toward the schism of realist versus relativist science. Some practitioners have emphasized the emic analysis of the webs of meanings constituting group life while deploring the inadequacy of psychological theory for the task. Others have translated the original emphasis on status, role, and institution into a host of variables and emphasized etic analysis via the correlations of subsets of these variables across groups.[4] Some of the exponents of emic analysis now tend to regard their science as interpretative in the nature of the humanities, while many of those interested in etic analysis have taken the realist view of progressive empirical development toward general theory. Socioanthropologists manifest the transitional period in which they work by the generation of various alternative paradigms such as the general theory of action, cultural materialism, ethnoscience, culturology, exchange theory, etc.—none of which has gained a consensus of agreement among them.

Both the emic and etic approaches must be reconsidered in the light of the relativism of knowledge and science. Each employs implicit metatheory but in different ways. What is needed now is a concerted effort toward the formulation of a general theory of sociology drawing on the contributions of extant paradigms but avoiding their limitations.

To establish an adequate theory of sociology, a number of issues must be resolved. One is whether or not it is meaningful to postulate the existence of cultures or social systems independent of the behaviors of their member populations, that is, the reification of these entities. In Chapter 7, it was emphasized that such reification is both indefensible and unnecessary. In this chapter an alternative approach is proposed that can account for everything intended by the terms culture and social system without the problems of reification.

A second problem concerns the assimilation of the nonhuman aspects of the ecological system in which the members of the group are participants. These include climate, flora and fauna, natural resources, and geological terrain in their intricate interactions. Variations in these often are considered to be primary determinants of change in the way of life of the group during a particular period. Here it is suggested that the ecological system and its changes are reflected in the roles, institutional structure, artifacts, and demography of the group.[5] What sociology describes and explains are the patterns of group interaction and changes in it. Changes in the nonhuman aspects of the local ecological system of any significance to the group will be reflected in changes in the interactions. While it generally is useful in an introductory way in the sociological explanation of the life of any group to describe major features of the nonhuman ecological system, the nature of that system will be manifest in the complete sociological description. This is the case because the specification of roles and institutions includes artifacts, natural objects, physical settings, and other natural phenomena.

A third problem is the identification of a society. Sociological science is partly distinguished from psychology and biology in terms of its focus on repetitive patterns of behavior of all members of a society. Several important issues must be resolved before the usefulness of the concept of a society can be established. Fundamental is the specification of the population included. It has both contemporary and historical aspects. Particularly today, it is extremely rare for members of any regularly interacting population in an area not to interact also with members of neighboring groups. This raises the question of how to distinguish among groups. Moreover, given geographical locations, the range of interactions across groups tends to extend indefinitely. The problem is complicated by the phenomena of military conquest, revolution, secession, emigration, and immigration. Historically, there is the question of how to define the population as older members die and new generations are born, often producing significantly different demographic distributions. This raises the issue of whether or not it is meaningful to identify a society in terms of a population of persons. This problem will be addressed below.

A fourth problem for sociology is its distinction from and relationship to psychology. As pointed out in Chapter 1, socioanthropology never has been defined clearly enough to distinguish it from psychology. Three related problems reveal this confusion. One is the largely neglected problem of identifying the functional prerequisites of a society.[6] It involves the assumption that for societies to exist they must serve certain functions based on human nature. This view builds sociology on a psychological foundation, and properly so. However, it makes sociology fundamentally dependent on an adequate psychology.[7] A second source of the confounding of the two sciences has been the disposition to define the term "role" in psychological fashion, that is, as normative expectations of members of the group. As a result, role analysis requires prior psychological analysis. The third difficulty has been the introduction, primarily by philosophers of human science supported by anthropological concern over what to record about an observed group, of the question of the meaningfulness of the idea of a behavior. It is essentially the problem of how the continuum of movements of the individual over time can be divided meaningfully into discrete behaviors. The last two problems are closely related because the primary solution has been to identify behavioral units as actions, based on the intentions of the behaver (Parsons and Shils 1961).

The problem of the definition of a society will be addressed first. Then the distinction between and the relationship of sociology and psychology is suggested. A new approach to the functional prerequisites of a society is presented. A conception of the idea of role is offered which avoids confounding with the psychological states of members of a society. As this concept of role is based on the identification of repetitive behaviors, it addresses the issue of the specification of a behavior and the consequent issue of the identification of repetitiveness in behavior.

SOCIETY AS THE UNIT OF STUDY

Sociological science divides the total range of observations of human behavior into units identified as societies. A society is identified by those persons who are subject to the same system of ultimate physical coercion plus those who control that system, if they are not themselves subject to it. The system of ultimate physical coercion is one of roles. The roles that define the system are those that include the killing, physical punishment, detention, banishment, or confiscation of possessions of others and that are related to other roles in such a way that those who perform them normatively are not subject to physical coercion for doing so.

The emphasis of this definition is on a role system for physical coercion. This role system is systematically related to other roles. The population that participates in this role system constitutes the members of a society. The definition includes many possible roles that include physical coercion, such as those of soldier, policeman, executioner, slavemaster, parent, husband, etc.[8] Some members of a population may be subject to more than one of these roles, others, to only one. What is critical is that members be subject to at least one, except for those special and very few members who may control the performance of these roles or some of them and yet may not be subject to any of them, for example, absolute monarchs and dictators of ruling cliques.

Socioanthropologists are not agreed that such systems of ultimate physical coercion occur in all groups of regularly interacting persons (P. S. Cohen 1968; R. Cohen 1973).[9] Much of this controversy is due to the implicit reification of polities. It often is part of a search for the political aspect of a society. If a polity is recognized as a reification and abandoned as theory, the issues become clearer. The concern no longer is with what the political structure of the society is or is not. The focus can then be on role analysis and its clustering into institutions. At issue here is only the matter of whether or not there are always some sets of roles that constitute a system of ultimate physical coercion. The position taken here sides with those who claim there are, even though the systems vary markedly in nature.

The basis of the assumption that systems of ultimate physical coercion will be found in all groups is a derivation from psychology. It is a complex derivation, but its elements are fairly obvious. One is the human capacity for learning strong emotional attachments. Another is the inevitability of planning for the attainment of goals through the combination of emotional conditioning and the learning of expectancies. These plans inevitably require the predictability of the behaviors of others incorporated into the plans. A third is the great likelihood that in any group of substantial numbers of people there will be significant differences in emotional conditioning that produce differences in attitudes and values that may lead to conflict. It needs only to be added that in the webs of interactions of members of a group over periods of time, there will be some serious conflicts and some persevering frustrations that will interfere substantially with the goals and plans of various members. Although the great majority of these conflicts and frustrations will be managed without violence, there inevitably will be a significant and recurring proportion that require physical coercion of members. The nature of the general webs of interaction will ensure that across groups there will be considerable variation of the occurrence of such events. It also will determine that there will be variation in the forms of ultimate physical coercion. Nevertheless, it is reasonable to assume that all human groups will develop forms of interaction which constitute systems of ultimate physical coercion.[10]

Obviously, it is not possible in most cases to identify a society without considerable time and effort. During this time some members may die, new members be born, others leave or be banished, and still others immigrate into the group. This complicates identification of the population subject to the same ultimate system of physical coercion. Even the role structure may be changing. Clearly, human science is faced once more with the validity of the assumption that there is order in human phenomena. If change is constant and unsystematic, then there can be no human science. There may be narrative history, but not human science. Human science must rest on the basic assumption of order. It is not necessary to assume that order is synonymous with the absence of change. As many have recognized, there can be orderly change. It would be more useful to assume that there is more and less orderly change and that the degree of order in change is highly correlated with the rate of change. If there can be some way of assessing the rate of change, then there is a way of assessing order in human interactions. Although in the world today, high rates of change, and therefore of disorder, seem to be the rule in most human groups, there is sufficient observation of other times and places to warrant the assumption that it is not inevitable that high rates of change characterize human interactions at all times. There is reason to believe that there are periods of much slower rates of change in every society, giving them a quality of continuity that can be identified. The fundamental assumption of relativistic naturalism is that there is substantial order in the experience of human groups that can endure over a number of generations, with the result that the members share a worldview and a mode of thought that give meaning to their interactions. Breakdown of this order under processes of social change produces periods in the history of a group that are transitional to a new order. On the issues of periodicity in history and the existence of role structures, human science can justify assuming human history to be a series of periods of relative stability with identifiable structure interspaced with transitional periods of relatively high rates of change with identifiable processes of change.

The idea of the role structure of a society in no way reifies society or structure. As far as the science of sociology is concerned, society and structure are abstractions from the behaviors of individual members. If the behaviors change, the structure changes. However, at the same time, it is possible to understand patterns of interaction that occur across several generations in terms of a single role structure. This is not the same thing as is implied by terms such as the society allocating people to roles or of roles existing although no one fulfills them. The latter are reifying accounts. They erroneously assume the structure or role exists independently of behaving persons.

Once identified, a society is defined historically in terms of a particular role structure. Given that there is always some rate of change in a society, the role structure is changing over time. However, in stable periods the rate is slow enough to identify a role structure undergoing small changes over a number of generations of the population. As the rate of change increases, the specification of the role structure becomes very complex. This identifies, sociologically, a transitional period toward a new role structure and, therefore, a new society. As both the role structure and the population change during this transitional period, it is not meaningful to refer to the old and new role structures as a change in a society. It makes more sociological sense to refer to a change from society X to society Y. There still is a historical dimension, because the nature of society Y is the resultant of the nature of society X and the processes that produced change in it. The sequence of role structures and their processes of change over time can be called the history of a civilization or some such term. The combining of societies due to conquest, expansion, or diffusion can be called the fusion of civilizations. The breakup of civilizations by revolutions, emigrations, or secessions can be called the branching of civilizations. The fusions and branchings are properly related to civilizations because they always involve an evolutionary process determined by previous forms.

RELATIONSHIP OF SOCIOLOGY TO PSYCHOLOGY

The great diversity of patterns of interaction within and among known human groups both in the present and historically reflects the great flexibility of the capacities of human nature. At the same time, it tends to mask the biological unity of that nature. Behind the variety of patterns there lies a set of common functions that all of them must serve in some form if they are to have any stability at all. This has long been recognized in anthropology in terms of the functional prerequisites of a society. However, as its formulation depends upon the view of human nature assumed, it is a psychological concept and therefore subject to the state of the science of psychology at the time. To date, no psychological theory has been proposed that is adequate to the task of providing a conceptualization of these functional prerequisites.[11]

In this fundamental way sociology inevitably is related to psychology.[12] Psychological science must provide the conceptualization of the functional prerequisites of a society. Only armed with these can the explanation of particular role structures and processes of change to new role structures be essayed. In essence, *explanation* in sociology occurs in terms of the form and extent of fulfillment and nonfulfillment of the functional prerequisites that exist for the various members in the pattern of interactions that constitutes the group life. This does not necessitate psychological analysis of members of a group before explanation is possible. What is required is the application of the functional prerequisites to the role structure. That is to say, both the form and the adequacy or inadequacy of any given role structure can be determined by relating the structure to the functional prerequisites in the context of the ecological system in which the group participates.

Basic to sociological explanation is the recognition that the role structure always provides the system of social stratification of the group. This is because it reveals which members perform the various sets of roles and the characteristics of members that qualify for these sets. As discussed in Chapter 7, social stratification is based on shared age-grading systems. In this way sociological description of role structure provides the basis for collective psychological explanation. Those individual members of the group who perform in similar sets of roles will share very substantially the content of the universal components of personality. There will, of course, be variation around these shared characteristics, but what is shared within a stratum will account for the vast majority of the variance in the behavior of members of the different strata. In this way psychological analysis is dependent on sociological analysis.

Yet, explanation of role structure and changes in the role structure requires of psychology mainly the specification of the functional prerequisites of a society. It is possible, by application of the functional prerequisites to the various strata as identified by role analysis, to determine the degree of fulfillment for each stratum at any time and therefore the areas of conflict or strain among the various strata and the avenues for change. The dynamics of group life are explained in terms of properties of role structure as they are related to fulfillment of the functional prerequisites.

That is, the role structure reveals the forms in which the functional prerequisites are being served, the forms in which some members are attempting to manage with or increase the fulfillment of them, and the resistance to change by other members. In this limited fashion sociology overlaps psychology. As indicated earlier and explicated below, no further overlap is entailed in the concepts of either roles or repetitive behaviors. Sociological science supplemented only by the provision of the functional prerequisites of a society by psychological science is the source of description and explanation of the broadest ranges of social patterns of interaction and their changes over time.

Throughout the following discussion of functions, it is important to bear in mind that these are the functions of a society in the sense of the functions that patterns of human interaction serve. These will be referred to as functions of a society but imply no reification of society. In sociological science the focus is on the functions of the pattern of interactions among the members of a society because these patterns can occur even though, for some members of the society, some of the functions are insufficiently served or not served at all. Hence, they are the functions that must be served to some extent if there is to continue to be *some* pattern of interaction, even though the pattern does not serve to fulfill all of the functions for every member. Illustrations of this distinction are suggested in the following discussion. The functional prerequisites are dichotomized into survival functions and integrative functions.

It is important here to emphasize that there is rarely, if ever, a one-to-one correspondence of the fulfillment of a function and a particular role or institution. Virtually any role can serve to fulfill any of several functions and more than one function at the same time.[13] This does not make the stipulation of the functions of a society a useless exercise. It does mean that analysis of interactions of members of a society cannot be done piecemeal. At least a very substantial proportion of the behaviors of members of a group must be known before it is possible to begin to understand how they are serving the functions of a society.

FUNCTIONAL PREREQUISITES OF A SOCIETY

The prerequisites are generated by the development of the flexible capacities of human nature. These capacities permit an enormous range of patterns of group life. Societies vary on a dimension of stability-instability. The patterns reflect varying degrees of efforts to manage the dynamics produced by the stresses which come from failure to serve adequately some of these functions for some segments and individuals in the group. Central to the pattern that characterizes the life of any group is the nature of the ecological system of which it is a part. This system consists of the neighboring groups with which the group interacts and the nonhuman environment in which it exists.[14] As discussed in the previous chapter, these three components of the ecosystem are interdependent. Neighboring groups and the nonhuman environment always are used in the group pattern of life for problem solving and stress management. Inevitably, these efforts create stress or the potential for stress either immediately or in the future, contributing to the dynamics of the society in complex ways. It follows that the functional prerequisites of a society constitute only limits within a broad range on the patterns of life that can provide sufficient stability for continuity of the group. The nature of neighboring groups and of the nonhuman environment constitute additional limits. The group can only be understood in the context of its place in its ecological system.

Survival Functions

Survival functions of a society encompass what is necessary for a substantial portion of members of a society to survive long enough to reproduce a new generation and to socialize them until they, in turn, reproduce. This requires a minimum of thirty to thirty-five years. Survival functions include at least the following:

1. *Sustenance*. Production and distribution of food and drink sufficient for at least a substantial segment of the population to survive the minimal period of time. This refers only to a subsistence level of existence.

2. *Protection*. Provision of materials and services for protection from the elements, and from threats to life from flora or fauna or members of other societies sufficient for survival of a substantial segment of the population for the minimal period.

3. *Health*. Provision of materials and services for the preservation of health threatened by illness and injury, including human wastes and decaying human bodies, of at least a substantial segment of the population for the minimal period.

4. *Reproduction*. Arrangements and services for the reproduction of new members, including conception, pregnancy management, and birth, sufficient to ensure at least enough minimally functioning new members to continue a web of interactions.

5. *Child-care*. Arrangements and services for the care and guidance of the newborn sufficient to allow at least enough of them to survive long enough to reproduce and provide child-care for the next generation.

The preservation of the society may not be seriously threatened even though whole segments of its members may not be provided for in one or more of these ways. Some segments of a society might receive less than minimal health services or levels of sustenance, producing very high rates of illness and mortality, but also have a very high reproductive rate, while others may have a slow reproductive rate but very extensive health services and levels of sustenance. Variations of social stratification allow for many possibilities. However, the role structure of the society always will reflect the arrangements which become necessary because of the failures of fulfillment of these functions for some members. These functions constitute constraints upon the forms which societies may take.

This does not constitute a strain toward stability or equilibrium in societies. At any period in the history of a group, some portion may be striving to maintain the current pattern and other portions striving to change it in various ways. In some cases, portions of the group for whom these functions are not being adequately met will resist efforts to change it, either because these do not appear to be the changes they desire or because they are uncertain of the longer-range changes that may be entailed. However, if the functions are not served for a substantial proportion, the society will disintegrate. When a society starts such a disintegration, there may be efforts to reverse the process, or there may be a breakup of the society into two or more new societies, or the society may enter into a transitional period, marking the end of the old web of interactions and the beginnings of a new web constituting a new society even though there is a substantial continuation of membership through descent. In any case, during this process of disintegration and its management, the behaviors of the members of the society can be described and explained as attempts to fulfill these functions and the integrative functions described in the following section.

Integrative Functions

The integrative functions of a society are those which impose constraints on its form because members of a society must integrate, each within his own person, the learning that occurs sequentially through his life span. Each must integrate as much as possible in order to maintain smooth, orderly functioning with his environment or else suffer discordant emotions or sensory unpleasures. As human motivation is based on experiencing pleasures and avoiding unpleasures, any experiences of discordant interaction with the environment become the potential basis for learning how to avoid them in the future. This learning must then be integrated with previous learning. To maintain orderly interaction, the anticipating, goal-seeking, planning human being must integrate his learning. Moreover, his learning begins at birth (if not during the prenatal period) when his capacities to deal with his environment are extremely limited and when, therefore, he is quite dependent on others. It continues throughout his life. Any problems he has with this integrative process will produce behavior designed to resolve them in some fashion. This behavior potentially creates problems for the integrative efforts of others. The stability of group life is a function of integration of learning of all members of the group.

Belonging/Community

The individual must develop a deep sense that he is an accepted and important part of his group, who contributes to it in ways that are recognized by others and who is included in the group's rituals and activities. The sense of importance as a member is provided by recognition, inclusion, and support by other members. It is based on the long period of dependency of children who are inevitably born into a social group. The forms in which this dependency is treated can vary immensely, but they all inevitably engender the sense of belonging or community in its basic form. Although it can be wounded at any time, including very early in childhood, there seems no basis on which it could be destroyed entirely. The resulting sense of isolation, rejection, and alienation will produce either efforts to restore the sense of belonging or a defensive retaliation against the rejection. It is the foundation of human social life. The sense of belonging or community is expressed in group life by rituals of solidarity such as group dances, chants, anthems, even orgies of a legitimate type, and by self-adornment and other symbols, including gestures, artifacts, natural formations, etc. These rituals and activities can involve direct or vicarious participation. They preserve the sense of community in the face of threat, the symbolic overcoming of threat, the joyful expression of the passing of threat, or other bases of group well-being. Many recreational activities or other forms of diversion express this sense. Even the group forms of the control of physical violence partially serve this function because the experience of being physically attacked, or the threat of it, carry the sense of rejection. Thus the existence, recognition, and celebration of the group's forms of justice provide part of the sense of belonging and community.

Preservation of Specific Emotional Attachments

The conditioning of strong pleasurable emotions to persons, objects, activities, or settings makes the individual anticipate interactions with them with enthusiasm. Loss of any of them is the psychological basis of the emotion of sadness, varying from wistfulness to grief. Thus, the individual will resist or resent any such losses, except when the loss is part of other changes in his life that he anticipates will produce even greater pleasures. The strongest emotional attachments of humans are those that occur early in childhood when the ability to dampen emotional reactions has not developed and those that are displacements from these early attachments. The need for this function is manifested in such phenomena as natal, engagement, and marriage ceremonies, altruistic sacrifices, mourning and burial services, preservation of mementoes, artifacts, or settings, and in a negative form by resistance to loss, deprivation, or change of loved or sentimental arrangements, and by expressions of envy, jealousy, or depression.

A special case of the provision for the maintenance of strong emotional attachments is that of self-esteem. To the extent that the individual learns early that his self as a distinct entity plays a key role in his understanding of what determines the conditions of his life, as is highly developed, for example, in our individualistic society, self-esteem will constitute a central basis of stability and smooth functioning with the environment. Difficulties with self-esteem will generate strong efforts to establish it with many potentials for disturbance of the stability of others.

Shared Meaningfulness of All Experience

This refers to the individual's ability to understand whatever happens to him directly or vicariously. The understanding is necessary to planning in an integrated fashion for interaction with his environment, particularly given the human capacity to plan over very long ranges of time. Lack of understanding of experience produces fear because of the inability to respond to the situation, at present or in anticipation. Inability to understand experience carries the threat of disruption of plans and interference with goals. Inevitably, the most basic experiences of humans require meaning. This includes birth, death, sexual experiences such as orgasm, menstruation in women, erections and ejaculations in males, natural phenomena such as the appearance and disappearance of the sun, moon, and stars, earthquakes, volcanoes, hurricanes, tornadoes, floods, blights of crops, dreams, illusions, encounters with strange peoples, bizarre behaviors of others, accidents, and chance phenomena, etc. It is the explanation of such experience which permits the continuation of orderly interaction with the environment. Explanation is a manipulation of learning that has already taken place, although in this case it is likely to be based on unconscious forms of learning. That is to say, the meanings placed on experience cannot come from whole cloth. Rather, they often are projections or other defensive operations that give the understanding an apparently irrational quality. As explained earlier in the discussion of worldview, they usually are metaphors for the unconscious learning.

As a function of a society, the provision of meaning is particularly significant because of its shared nature. Meaning is not much use for planning in a complex social world if it is idiosyncratic. The human capacity for speech plays a central role in the creation of shared meaning. The presence of speech in the older generations of the group directs the attention of the young in the same ways, produces very similar concepts, and therefore also produces similar systems of classification. The resulting support for the meanings applied to experience serves to confirm them, while providing for similarity of reactions and, therefore, effective planning.

Examples of shared meaningfulness of experience include not only religious beliefs concerning life and death, but attribution of special abilities to the insane, magical medical practices, concealment of body products from others, practices for isolating or purifying women during menstruation, phallic cults, the couvade, cargo cults, cosmologies, symbols and gestures of good and bad luck, etc.

Shared System of Values

The values that members hold provide the directions for life. They constitute what is important, what counts, what can most deeply affect the person. It follows that the value system must be widely shared among members of the group. Different values are the most powerful sources of human friction. As the individual pursues value realizations, he becomes aware that most others recognize the legitimacy of these pursuits and behave similarly. This not only confirms the importance of the values but makes them seem inevitable. They become part of the worldview in the form of key aspects of human nature. In this way, what feels important also is given profound meaning. Shared values contribute importantly to the basic cohesion of group life. If values vary across the strata of a society, there is the foundation of caste or class conflict.

Predictability of the Future

It follows from the nature of humans as anticipating, planning beings that sufficient stability must be present in group life if long-range goals are to be attainable. Predictability, however, does not mean the absence of change. There can be predictable change. Members of the group need only be able to anticipate the changes, or more importantly, the types or forms of changes to be expected, in order to plan for them. Change cannot be arbitrary or fundamental. It must be meaningful and gradual enough to allow for adjustments. Uncertainty about the outcome of planned behavior, most of which is based on value realization and therefore of great importance to the individual, produces anxiety. Uncertainty can only be overcome or avoided by the attainment of sufficient understanding or information to be able to plan effectively. Without predictability the many forms of alliances, agreements, and mutual undertakings that always characterize group life would be impossible. This is reflected in the many phenomena observable in all human groups concerning loyalty, betrayal, commitment, laws, equity, record keeping, vows, etc. The need for predictability also is manifested in divinative practices, searches for omens, the emergence of members regarded as having insight or foresight into events, ritual observances designed to ensure the occurrence of future events—such as rain dances, etc. Many forms of behavior reflect the effort to manage anxiety in the absence of predictability, including nervous gestures, drug use, compulsive behaviors, etc.

Opportunity for Goal Attainments

Predictability and meaningfulness are not sufficient to maintain stable group life. Members also must have a firm belief that means are open to them for the achievement of their goals, the realization of their values. To have goals and values but find no pathways to their attainment is one of the most disruptive conditions for group life. The frustration engendered inevitably produces the disposition to overcome the obstacles to goals, and this usually means disruptions of the plans of other segments of the group. At least, it means that the other segments must devote resources to prevent these disruptions, which usually involve the employment of power to control the frustrated segments.

Opportunity is the foundation of hope. Humans can endure profound hardships if they have hope. One of the bases of hero worship in human groups is the affirmation in the life of the hero of the possibilities of overcoming obstacles either to individuals or to the whole group. A not uncommon expression of this prerequisite for a society is the development, in groups without opportunity, of religious beliefs representing hope in some form of life after death, for example, a better life in another realm of being, the power one's spirit after death can exercise over the lives of others, vicarious achievement through offspring, etc. Another form is the occurrence of compensatory activities in which a secondary type of goal attainment is possible. Many recreational and social service practices serve this function, for example, in the United States today, fraternal organizations in which office can be achieved, sports in which success partially substitutes for lack of economic status or masculinity, and charities in which moral value realization can compensate for guilts generated in occupational striving.

Summary

It is emphasized that these functional prerequisites of a society are to be understood as constraints on the forms that group life can take. It must make provision for these things or it will develop institutions that reflect the inadequacy of their provision for at least some segment of the group and the reactions of other segments. These latter constitute stress-management developments of the society. They can vary in their effectiveness from highly stabilizing to manifestations of the disintegration of the group, such as riots, rebellion, civil war, emigration of a substantial segment, exploding criminal activity, and widespread resort to escape activities such as drugs and physical or mental illness.

It is crucial to recognize that the degree of stability in a human group is a function of its relationship to the total ecological system of which it is a part. The relationships to neighboring groups and to the nonhuman environment are as important as are the internal dynamics. It is common, for example, for groups to attempt to maintain stability by redirecting discontent outside the group, with the resultant deterioration of relationships to neighboring groups. Social problems may engender efforts to acquire slaves or land or goods from neighbors in ways creating group conflict. It is similar with the nonhuman environment. Group life may be temporarily maintained at the cost of exhaustion of game or other food supplies, deterioration of the soil for crops, erosion, pollution of air or water, creation of conditions for disease, etc. These conditions then interact with the internal life of the group to produce many forms of stress. It is most useful to recognize the interactions among the three components of the internal dynamics of the group, its neighboring groups, and the nonhuman environment. It follows that the forms in which the functional prerequisites of a society are provided must encompass the whole system. Or, rather, the more the whole system is taken into account in these forms, the greater the cohesion and the less the stress or instability in group life. The history of humankind can be understood in these terms.

In all of these integrative functions of a society, the forms of behavior expressed often are symbolic. There are at least two reasons for this. One reason is that significant proportions of early learning, which form the more general structure of mind, are never the direct focus of attention. The most important example of this is the learning of primary worldview, which always is expressed later in life in symbolic, usually religious, forms. The second reason is that normative conflicts produce defensive forms of resolution. Much expression is in a form which displaces meaning in time or place or figures to disguise the immediate content. A great deal of the group's artistic expression will be of this nature.

It must be reemphasized that the foregoing are functions of group interaction. They are functions only in the sense that the web of interactions that constitutes a society will inevitably contain behaviors to serve them, or to restore or increase them, at least for some substantial proportion of the members. Humans will inevitably express themselves in ways that serve these functions. The web of interactions that sociologists study can be approached in a search for the particular forms in which these functions are being served for at least some segment of the membership of the society, and for the forms which reflect the failure of one or more of these functions to be served for other segments. They constrain the forms which a society may take. These are not severe limits. They permit great but not unlimited diversity. The human being is not infinitely malleable. Although human nature is a constant in the equation of determinants of total environmental matrices, it constrains those forms in a dynamic way by restricting *the kinds of sequences of experience across the life span of a generation* that can occur without producing disruption in the societal form. Once particular content is introduced into the learning of a generation, there are limits to what can happen later without introducing stress and resistance. The constraints on the web of interactions of members of a society are summarized in Figure 10.1.

Figure 10.1
Constraints on the Pattern of Group Life

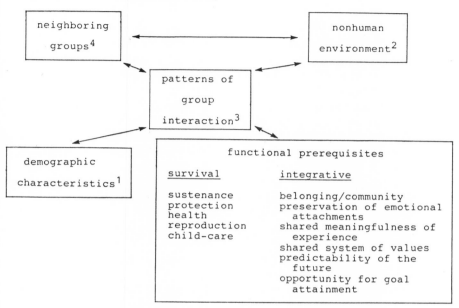

[1]Demographic characteristics of the group do not affect other aspects of the ecological system except as they are mediated by the pattern of group life.

[2]The nonhuman environment affects the functional prerequisites via its role in evolutionary processes.

[3]The pattern of group life also can affect the functional prerequisites via its role in evolutionary processes.

[4]Neighboring groups are unlikely to affect significantly either demographic characteristics or functional prerequisites except through their effects on the nonhuman environment or the pattern of group life.

ROLES AND ROLE DESCRIPTION

Historically, the members of a society have developed a pattern of interactions among themselves and with artifacts, members of other groups, and the nonhuman environment that fulfills the functions of society to various degrees for various segments and individuals. It is a dynamic pattern in that, at any point in time, it is changing. In stable periods the rate of change is slow. In transitional periods it becomes very rapid. Each new generation is born into this pattern. Each member of the new generation develops a round of life during each age-grade which constitutes the maximal value realization he can arrange, given the state of development of his flexible capacities, that is, his learning. Each round of life is a variant of the types of rounds of life extant in his group or stratum, normative or abnormative. Every round of life is lived primarily through the performance of common scripts. These scripts are organized sequentially and systematically in time and space. They constitute the main bases for role analysis.

A role is defined as a set of behaviors repeatedly performed by one or more individuals that is systematically correlated with a set of behaviors repeatedly performed by the individual and/or others with artifacts in particular settings and in particular time frames.

The first characteristic of roles is that they are behaviors. Behavior here refers to movements and speech. Consequently, role description requires no use of psychology. The intentions, goals, or meanings of behavior for the actors are irrelevant.[15] The second characteristic is that the set of behaviors in a role is repeatedly performed. One member of the society alone may repeatedly perform them or many members may. This aspect of roles has long been one that has plagued socioanthropology because of the problems of specifying what constitutes a behavior and what constitutes a repetition of behavior. These problems are greatly magnified by the prominence of speech in role behaviors. These difficulties must be faced and resolved before sociological science can be established as an integral part of human science.

The primary reason why the problems of defining a behavior and identifying repetitions of behavior have been so formidable can be traced to the realist view of science and its grounding in the Individualistic mode of thought. The realist view always has been largely oblivious of order and pattern in human affairs. There has been no sense in this approach that the behaviors of any member of a group have developed from birth in a context of a combination of a nonhuman environment and a human environment consisting of three or four older generations that constitutes an ecological system.[16]

There is order and pattern in the environment of every human being. Those members of his group who constitute significant parts of his particular environment have already learned ways of representing that order. The behaviors of those older generations, which are based on this representation of order, are part of the order in the new member's environment. The new member has the inherent capacities, with rare exceptions, to represent this order. Since there is extensive overlap in the particular environmental influences of at least members of the same stratum of a group, there will be extensive shared representation of order. This shared representation is the basis on which the behavior of the new member becomes part of the order in the environment of others and later members. His round of life is a recognizable variant of the rounds of life, normative or abnormative, of other members of his group. His script performances are recognizable variants of the script performances of other members of his group.

This is the basis, in psychological terms, for the justification of sociological science. Role description develops from the observation of the repeated script performances in the relatively stable rounds of life of members of a society. It follows that sociological science does not proceed by the methods of realist science, which entail observing behavior in momentary and discrete fragments. Those methods are what have plagued anthropologists from the beginning in their efforts to decide what to record of their observations.[17]

Role analysis starts with a search for order—the patterning in the interactions among group members, artifacts, settings, and time frames. The key lies in script performances that are revealed by the repetitions of behaviors with artifacts, in settings and time frames. Extended observation of the daily life of the group must precede any attempt to specify roles. The task is the description of group life. All the key sociological questions can then be asked of this description. They include: What is the role and institutional structure of the group? What is the system of social stratification in the group? What rate of change is occurring in group life? How well is this ecological system fulfilling the functions of a society for the various strata of the group? What are the primary sources of discontent and conflict? What are likely to be the consequences of the introduction of a new technology in fashion X, Y, or Z?

The search for the order in group life is regulated by theory of sociology. The sociologist is looking for the common scripts. He is identifying which members of the group perform in its various roles and what are their demographic characteristics. He is noting the ways in which space is used in terms of identifiable settings for particular role performances. He is listing artifacts and specifying which ones are included in which roles. He is noting variations in role performances that are correlated with different subgroups and various demographic characteristics. He identifies the basic time frames in terms of intervals between, sequences of, and duration of role performances. He is recognizing the reciprocality in role performances that reveal the institutions of the society.

These aspects of sociological science have been stated as if the ecological system under study were that of a relatively small society without extensive interaction with other groups. The larger the system, the more complex is the sociological task. Work with larger groups requires teams of sociologists, translation of observations into statistical form, and correlation of data from the various teams with the aid of computers. This is not a human science that can be conducted in the fashion of current social science. It is a new institution or set of institutions that must be part of a society significantly different from that in which traditional social science operates. The institution will be addressed in the concluding chapter.

It is important in sociological science to recognize that the behaviors of all members of the society must be included in role description. The disposition of some social scientists to regard children and deviants as secondary or irrelevant, because children are merely in training for full participation in the society and deviants do not contribute constructively to the society, cannot be accepted (Parsons 1951, 27–32). The behaviors of these members are as much a part of the role structure as those of any other segments of the population. The roles they play are very important in understanding perpetuation and change of social stratification, how the various functions of a society are being served, the nature of emotional attachments, the age-grading system, distribution of demographic characteristics, etc.

To many social scientists, no doubt, this description of the work of sociological science will appear woefully unscientific. Observing common script performances, for example, appears to ignore the measurement necessary for specifying what behaviors are included and excluded. In addition, the role of speech in script performances introduces difficult problems of interpretation and of definition of equivalence necessary for postulating repetition. These concerns are important for sociological science but not in the way realist science dictates. This is because the basic process of science is reversed in relativist science. The general picture is formed first, then refined by more detailed and precise observation. This approach places all the later, more refined work in a perspective and in a context that regulates determination of what is required. This reverses realist science which, lacking any perspective or context except implicit worldview, results in the use of precise measurements and observations lacking any regulation at all, often producing unrelated and unrelatable research findings.

The key to the problem of what constitutes a behavior lies in the idea of scripts. Realist social scientists have been perplexed in their determination of behaviors by the great variety of movements and speech utterances they can observe. Obsessed with individual differences and with very brief behaviors taken, one or a few at a time, the only solutions they can find are either the specification of stimulus-response habits understood mainly as aggregations rather than extensive patterns or in terms of actions defined by the intentions of the performers. Once the script performance approach is appreciated, the human scientists can look for scripts and analyze them, not by specific behaviors or intentions, but by interactions with particular persons, objects, and settings in particular time frames. Such an approach will not be overwhelmed by, for example, the many variations one could observe in watching American mothers bathe their children. The script approach emphasizes repetitive interaction patterns at an abstract level. If some mothers bathe the child in a bassinette, and others in the kitchen sink, and others in a tub on the floor, and some sing to the child while doing so, and some use talcum powder, and some a washcloth while others use a scrub brush, there always are common elements such as a receptacle into which the child is placed, water applied to the body, a particular setting, a particular time frame, etc. Moreover, sufficient observation will reveal that the variations are not infinite but actually correlated with particular life conditions which will be recognized readily as aspects of social stratification. Such patterning cannot be found using the realist approach. There certainly will be some problems of the scientist identifying the relevant abstract classes of elements. However, this problem is generic to the relativist approach; it constitutes an inescapable restraint on cross-cultural understanding.

The problem of speech is particularly important and complex because repetitiveness of role performance often lies in the equivalence of meaning in speech rather than in similarity of sounds. This introduces the issue of the necessity of knowing the language of the group before role description can occur. This, in turn, raises the key issue of realism versus relativism in knowledge and science. The key to the solution of this problem lies in the monolinguistic approach to linguistic analysis long known to anthropologists (Pike 1967). In this approach speech is treated as behavior, and its meaning is determined from its correlation with the other dimensions of behavior, that is, with the use of artifacts, nonspeech behaviors, settings, and time frames. The fact that in all languages it appears that very similar meaning can be conveyed in a variety of forms is not an insuperable barrier to role analysis. To begin with, the variety of forms is quite limited. More importantly, the meaning lies in the correlational pattern. For example, the pilot of a plane in the cockpit can convey to the copilot in several ways that the latter should take over the controls. The copilot can convey in several ways that he will do so. A sociologist observing behavior in the setting of the cockpit of a flying plane can fairly readily identify the set of speech sounds and/or gestures systematically correlated with the taking over of controls by the copilot. Admittedly, this is a very simple example, but it points the direction. It is reasonable to assume that the overwhelming majority of human behavior is correlated with very limited speech. There are, of course, special problems with certain roles in which extensive speech occurs, such as teacher, diplomat, lawyer, politician, and psychotherapist roles in current American society. Still, the general nature of these roles can be discerned and distinguished on the bases of the other parameters, such as setting and reciprocal role performances, and then refined by additional methods, including the use of informants as sources of hypotheses.

Another major problem for sociological science lies in the time dimensions of role performances. In understanding some roles, behavior occurring at considerable intervals of time must be correlated. This is another reason why in relativist human science very extensive observation of behaviors is required before analysis or description can occur. Many role performances in most groups probably do not entail more than brief time intervals. As the general picture of role structure begins to emerge, these parts of role performances occurring at considerable time intervals are revealed by their intrusions. These intrusions can then be analyzed for their relationship to role structure in terms of their correlations with individuals performing reciprocal roles, settings, artifacts, and time frames.

Role analysis of a society during transitional periods of its history presents some special problems. The term "transitional period" refers to a period of time during which the role structure is changing rapidly. This means that there will be a great deal less order and pattern in the behaviors of members than during stable periods. However, it does not mean that there is no order at all. The functions of a society will constrain the process of change. One key to these constraints lies in the three- or four-generational composition of the membership. The rate of change will be reflected in the variations of roles by generations. As change occurs, younger generations will introduce variations of role performances reflecting the determinants of change. For example, in this society today one can observe a variety of forms of family structure reflecting how technological change is affecting sexual roles. Two-career families and one-female-parent-families with and without working mothers and supplemented by child-rearing roles of babysitters, nursery schools, and day-care centers are increasing. In other times or societies, change may be reflected dramatically in the increase of forms of physically coercive roles as manifested by insurgent groups and protest activities and reciprocally by increases in the proportion of the population recruited to conventional coercive roles (the police). The phases in the transitional process from one relatively stable role structure to another will be reflected in the ratio of the various role variants as they are distributed across living generations. Some of the oldest roles will be manifested mainly by the oldest generation, and the newest by the youngest. The ratio of old and new in the middle generations will reveal the trend. The reports of the oldest generation plus written and other artifacts in conjunction with analysis of the changing age-grades for children can be used to gain a longer perspective on the change process.

SOCIOLOGICAL EXPLANATION

The neglect of systematic development of role and institutional analysis of societies leaves a huge gap in sociology. Principles of sociology can confidently start with the limits on institutional structure and its dynamics placed by the nature of the nonhuman environment, the sharing of it with other societies, the demographic characteristics of the population, and the functional prerequisites of a society. However, these constitute very broad limits. Within them there is room for considerable variation of form. In addition, the dynamics of interaction among these factors produce a historical dimension of great complexity. The basic task of identification of types of societies, types of institutions, and principles of change of form of societies remain largely unachieved. There is a substantial literature in socioanthropology and history on which sociologists can draw in the attempt to formulate a theory of sociology. The bulk of it will need to be reworked toward role and institutional structure, or at least approached in this fashion, to make it useful for the task.

Fundamental to the development of sociological theory will be identification of the relationship of systems of social stratification and forms of demographic distribution of the population to types of societies and types of changes in societal form. The ways in which the members of a society are distributed in the role structure and the demographic bases of that distribution will be central to the understanding of how the functional prerequisites are being met for each stratum and therefore for understanding the strains toward change in the institutional structure. In addition, it will be important to gain as clear a picture as possible of the age-grading system or systems in the society in order to understand the dynamic process by which change is generated from generation to generation.

It may appear that explanation in sociology on the basis of how the role structure is related to the fulfillment of the integrative functions requires a great deal of psychological interpretation. This is illusory because a life-span dimension inheres in the role structure. That is, age will be a central aspect of demography, and ages will be grouped in accordance with the age-grading system of the group. Moreover, this will be correlated with the system of social stratification. As a result, sociological explanation with respect to the fulfillment of integrative prerequisites can be provided in terms of the nature of the roles and the number of members performing in each role of the role structure considered on the age dimension.[18] The sequence of changes in the role structure, with age and the numbers performing each role, will reflect the presence of problems and the ways in which they are being managed, for example, the roles of striker, strikebreaker, drug pusher, divorce lawyer, prison guards, soldiers, rebels, executioners, psychotherapists, etc. What will be found in cross-societal analysis will be that certain types of roles or forms of role structure for younger age groups will be correlated with certain types of roles or role structures for later age groups. This will provide an explanation at the sociological level that can, but need not, be reduced to the psychological.

The crowning contribution of sociological science will be in the light it shines on the underlying dynamics of human history, in the changing patterns of societal forms, the forms of intersocietal relationships, and the ecological systems of regions. Such light will be of enormous importance to this society in its efforts to understand itself and the many other increasingly interdependent societies together with which the shape of the future of life on this planet will be determined.

11

Human Science and Society

The primary task of human science is to provide for the total society a sociological and a collective psychological understanding of the behaviors of all humans across space and time. Across space because all persons on this planet today are interdependent and becoming more so. Across time because the nature of any group's life today is a period in the ongoing process of change, a perspective on which can be provided only by the understanding of that process. The organization for this task follows from the views presented in the previous chapters. The total population of humans to be understood is divided, in sociological science, into societies, or groups of currently closely interrelated societies, or sequences of historically related societies. The basic disciplines of human science are given by this division. Within these disciplines every human scientist specializes in sociology, psychology, or biology. Within these specializations each specializes in current or historical study. The contributions of these three sciences permits the understanding of the behaviors of members of every society from the most specific physiological level of biology to the most general institutional and historical levels of sociology, within the limits of the theories applied.[1]

In the task of understanding the behaviors of members of each society, sociological science has the primary role. Not only does it identify the groups to which each individual belongs, it establishes the role structure of that group and, in doing so, identifies its system of social stratification. From this analysis the social stratum of every member and the general nature of the age-grading system of each stratum can be specified. These provide the context for psychological and biological science. Thus, human science has a hierarchical form of organization. Sociology provides the understanding of the type of society and its current status with respect to the process of historical change, the type of institutions and roles that characterize it, and the relationships of each individual to the role structure. With the benefit of this background, the psychologist then can identify the shared personality characteristics of each stratum in terms of worldview, mode of thought, type of identity, ideology, expressive style, practical knowledge, perceptual-motor skills, and unconscious dynamics. He also can specify the common variants of these among the members of a stratum. These two levels of analysis provide the general understanding of the members of the society.

Individual psychological and biological levels of analysis are primarily for selective problem solving as required by segments of the society served by human science. There is no reason to have a psychological or biological understanding of every individual member of any society. The individual personalities of members of special significance to the society of the human scientists can be studied if that information is necessary for personal interactions with them or because they currently exercise special influences in their group.[2] Biological analysis generally is limited to the understanding of genetic variations and matters of health or illness regarded as requiring attention. Figure 11.1 summarizes this organization of human science.

Three additional disciplines would comprise the theoretical levels of analysis for each science. Some, in each science, could be concerned with comparing and contrasting the results developed for particular societies. This would result in the identification of types of societies and institutions in sociology, types of components of personality (including abnormative forms in psychology), types of ranges of functioning, and evolutionary forms in biology. After sufficient analysis of individual societies has been accomplished, these theoretical analyses would serve to elaborate and, perhaps, to modify the theories being employed in each science.

It should be recognized that such traditional academic areas of interest as those in the economic and political aspects of a society, as well as those concerned with specific aspects across societies, such as technologies, music, or art forms, etc., are not meaningful units or areas of analysis. A scholar could not begin to understand the selective and arbitrary set of observations each entails without a knowledge of their relationships to the overall nature of the life of the group at the sociological or collective psychological levels. Such fragmentation of human fields of behavior is a product of the individualistic mode of thought in the service of individualistic concerns.[3]

CONTRIBUTIONS OF HUMAN SCIENCE TO SOCIETY

There are four basic ways in which human science serves society. The primary way is through its provision of the three theories of biology, psychology, and sociology. These constitute the forms in which experience of

Figure 11.1
Organization of Human Science

Disciplines

Sciences	Single Society	All Societies

Sociology:
  Modern
	role and institutional structure
	social stratification
	demography
	rate and direction of change
		comparative typologies '
		  and processes of
		  evolution

Historical	evolutionary sequence of the
	  above through specified periods of
	  stability and/or transition	

Psychology;
  Collective:
    Modern
	universal components of personality
	  by social strata
	relative fulfillment of functional
	  prerequisites by strata
	major variations of the above
		typologies of person-
		  alities
		evolution of types of
		  personalities

Historical	evolutionary sequence of the above
	  by strata for specified periods
	  of stability and/or transition	

Individual:
    Modern
	identification of nonnormative
	  members and bases of
	  nonnormative behavior
	referral to biologists of members
	  whose nonnormative behavior
	  is not psychogenically based
		typologies of
		  nonnormative
		  personalities
		  and conditions
		  producing them
		evolution of types

Historical	identification of forms of
	  nonnormative personalities
	  during specified periods of
	  stability or transition
		of nonnormative
		  personalities

Biology:
  Modern
	identification of normative range
	  of physiological functioning
	  and of bases of nonnormative
	  behaviors by strata
	
	development of methods to restore
	  normative functioning
		typologies of range
		  of normative and
		  nonnormative
		  functioning
		evolution of the **ranges**
		  of normative and

Historical	identification of past ranges of
	  normative functioning and bases
	  of nonnormative functioning by
	  strata
		nonnormative
		  functioning

all human phenomena is interpreted. They can be taught to new generations through the public school system and to older generations through the system of higher education or in adult education programs via the secondary school system. Such teaching could parallel current practice for the natural sciences. It would provide a uniform, explicit framework of thought while establishing human science with the authority now enjoyed by the natural sciences.

The second contribution of human science is an understanding of their own society for all citizens. This would consist of the sociological analysis of the role and institutional structure, the collective psychological analysis of all its strata, and the historical sociological and collective psychological analyses of the society since its inception. It, too, could be disseminated through the public school system. For each science there might be a three- (or more) course sequence, for example, the science of sociology, sociology of American society, and historical sociology of American society.

Human science also would provide the understanding of all other societies, both those currently existing and those of the past. Such information would be made available not only to the public school system but to public libraries and to governmental agencies, businesses, and other organizations on the bases of their interests.[4] This knowledge would provide the general background information for the understanding of current events around the world.

The fourth contribution of human science would be the provision of expert advice to agencies of government, businesses, and other organizations with respect to decisions contemplated on public policy, legislation, foreign policy, etc. Just as natural scientists currently are consulted on space programs, military problems, discovery of resources, manufacture of synthetic materials, etc., human scientists would be consulted on the short- and long-range effects of current and long-range programs sociologically as well as psychologically on the various strata of the society. The authority of human science would be similar to that of the natural sciences. Public officials would not be subject to the current choices among opposing authorities and contradictory evidence. They would not have to decide on some bases of their own what the effects of particular programs or legislation might be, but only which consequences of the alternative programs and legislation were in the best interests of the society.

These contributions of human science to society could become available in the near future, perhaps a period of twenty to thirty years, if a concentrated collaborative effort with governmental support were instituted promptly. The efforts of all interested scholars who grasp the significance of the relativism of knowledge would be reoriented toward the realization of these contributions. The effort will have to be programmatic. This means that far-reaching changes in the roles of institutions of higher education will be required, as well as fundamental changes in the relationships be-

tween these institutions and the governments of the communities in which
they are located. Such changes raise many profound ideological issues.
These must be made explicit and squarely faced by human scientists. There
is no ideologically neutral ground with respect to these issues. To fail to
face them is to take a stand for the status quo. The sooner the issues are
joined, the faster will be the process of their resolution and the more open
and clear the implications for all members of the society.

Before the issues can become well defined, it is necessary to outline the
general nature of the methodologies of the new human sciences. Once
these are understood, the requirements to achieve the goals of human
science will become clear. There can be no doubt that serious controversies will be generated, because the possibility of change in any major institution of a society entails changes in every other. However, it is already
clear that our society is in a period of rapid change. What is to be proposed is not a revolution because the revolution already is occurring. Rather,
it is a scenario of one form in which the change process could be guided.
It is a vision of the future of this society from the perspective of the
scholar devoted to the understanding of human affairs and the use of such
understanding for the solutions of human problems.

METHODOLOGY IN HUMAN SCIENCE

The greatest contribution which human science can make to the society,
beyond the provision of theories, is the comprehensive understanding of
its current nature. There can be no meaningful problem solving without
the knowledge of the total system. The current piecemeal, bridge-cross-
ing, squeaky wheel approach to human problems is a product of the individualistic worldview and mode of thought. It permits no understanding
of the ramifications of solutions employed across institutions, strata, and
time. It is inevitably ideological in nature because it ministers implicitly to
a constituency and does so in a manner that minimizes or biases the impact
on selective other constituencies most influential in the process of problem solving. Only a thorough understanding of the total system, of which
what are regarded as social problems are particular manifestations, permits
anticipation of the effects of a solution as they resonate through the system. Americans have never had anything like the understanding which can
be provided by human science. To have this, human scientists must be
provided with the conditions necessary for their methodology.

Sociological Method

As emphasized in the previous chapter, sociological science constructs
the role and institutional structure of a society from the repetitive patterns
of behavior of all of its members. For small preliterate groups, one scholar

or team of scholars may be able to achieve this goal within a short period of time. For a very large society such as our own, the task is much more complex. On the other hand, sociologists can draw on a great deal of material from many disciplines for the organization of their task. Moreover, a programmatic effort will be able to enlist far greater numbers of scholars and trainees than any project possible in realist science.

The first step must be the establishment of the research program in terms of a detailed division of labor. Direction of the program could rest with those doctoral-level sociologists willing to participate in colleges and universities across the nation. This distribution dictates the division of labor. It will have to be coordinated through a central location which has or can be provided with the equipment required to gather the data in a computerized form. This form of data would be the resultant of prior computerized forms at, at least, regional if not local centers. Such direction at all levels would be located at institutions of higher learning for reasons to be discussed later in this chapter. Under the direction of local professors of sociology, the program could be carried out mainly by graduate and/or undergraduate students majoring in sociology, perhaps supplemented by others especially trained for the project.[5]

The best methodology would be worked out by the members of the profession, guided at every step by the previously formulated theory of sociology. No attempt will be made here to spell out that methodology. However, a few suggestions will be offered to indicate the possibilities. Certain to be considered will be area sampling. This can be either or both sampling of persons or settings. In the case of persons, the initial form of data collection would be greatly facilitated by what can be called the behavioral interview. This could take the form of a daily diary of the individual's behaviors. Clearly, this method would have to be supplemented by others. However, it should be kept in mind that sociological analysis is of patterns of repetitive behaviors across individuals or by the individual across time. It requires nothing in the way of psychological information concerning the individual's feelings, intentions, beliefs, etc. The diary is a record of behaviors in time and setting. This eliminates some of the concern about invasions of privacy.

There can be no doubt that a viable human science will require a public attitude of trust. Sociological analysis can ensure anonymity of individuals that is guaranteed both by the professional integrity of scholars and by law, perhaps something along the lines currently used by the Bureau of the Census or the Internal Revenue Service. The public must be well aware of the services provided by human science to the public welfare. Even these measures, however, will not suffice to make the behavioral interview alone adequate for the task. It can be supplemented by specific behavioral interviews, or a sampling of them, for those with whom the individual indicates interaction in his behavioral interview. In addition, samplings of local settings within samplings of time could be used to reveal unreported behaviors.

Relativist human science guided by theory already recognizes that life in any group is patterned in time and settings. For example, American life generally is organized around the time period of a week, divided into workdays and nonworkdays. It also is organized into settings in terms of homes, businesses, stores, schools, parks, etc. The patterns of organization of the life of an individual will not be difficult to establish. Repetitiveness will be regulated by these time and setting patterns.

If data collection uses sampling of types of settings, the behavioral record could be based on direct observation rather than on interviews. Through the local colleges and universities the population of settings can be readily established. They would then be sampled within the context of time sampling. All behaviors in these settings, interactions with specific others, and the duration of interactions or behaviors would be recorded. Samplings of types of settings can be systematically varied to substantiate the patterns being discovered. The goal is to establish role structure by demographic characteristics and locations, not to understand individuals.

There should be little doubt that the vast bulk of the role structure of the society in its general form and with its major variants can be readily established. The difficulties will lie in two areas. One is the fleshing out of roles into more specific forms. The problems here are those of deception by individuals, conscious or unconscious, and of interpretations of the speech aspects of behavior, particularly in those roles which require extensive speech. Again, it must be emphasized that the data collection occurs over considerable periods of time and therefore represents multiple instances of behaviors either of one individual or multiple individuals in the same roles. This is nothing like the kind of data collection in sampling in realist research. It provides a wealth of material within which the patterns can be discerned under the guidance of theory. There also will be special problems of noncompliance by individuals and of those in sensitive roles, either in terms of public attitudes or of national security, internal and international. There is no reason to assume that, inherently, these problems cannot be solved methodologically if there is a public commitment to the goals of human science and a pervasive public trust in human scientists.

Psychological Method

Psychologists are oriented to their work by the results of the sociological analysis which reveals the system of social stratification in terms of sets of roles or types of variations of sets of roles and the demographic distribution of individuals among the roles. That analysis also reveals the age-grading system of the society and its variations, because age periods for role distribution are central to the system of social stratification. With this orientation to the population, the collective psychologist can sample individuals by strata to determine the universal components of personality and the common variations of them within each stratum.

The starting point for collective psychology must be the results of the data collected by the sociologists through the behavioral interview and whatever supplementary measures are used. If sampling of types of settings has been used, then the results must be analyzed to construct the behavioral picture for individuals. Personality is better assessed by discerning the patterns in a broad range of behaviors and settings under the guidance of psychological theory than by self-reports of beliefs and attitudes. Additional behavioral data on individuals in the psychological sample can be gathered from a further sampling of those with whom they interact. The sociological analysis of role structures, for example, of the family, the school, local peer groups, etc., also is very useful to psychologists in attaining a developmental perspective on the individual. Care must be taken at this step to first gain from the sociological analysis an understanding of the rate of change that the society is undergoing. The more rapid the rate, the less reliable is current role structure for assessing developmental influences in the past, although there may well be variations of role structure helpful in revealing older and newer aspects. Sociological science reveals the rate of change in terms of the development of new roles, the ratio of old and new role forms, the extent of deviant roles and of coercive roles not integrated with traditional coercive roles, etc.

The next step in collective psychological analysis is to compare individuals first within each stratum to discern the shared aspects of personality and the common variants. Then these results are compared across strata to reveal the differences among them. The whole analysis can then be used in conjunction with the functional prerequisites of a society to assess stratum differences in fulfillment of the prerequisites and in conjunction with the overall role analysis to *explain* the existence of the roles and institutions that reflect problems of fulfillment for each stratum and their effects on the other strata—for example, growth of labor unions, strikes, sabotage, lockouts, relocations, incidence of crime, infrastructures of power, riots, drug use, etc.

Individual psychological analysis, as emphasized earlier, is not part of the description and explanation of the group. It plays its part in group problem solving by analyzing the personalities of those individuals who are deviants in the proper sense of behaving so differently from the normative patterns of their stratum that they generate specific roles designed either to isolate them from their community (examples in our society include criminals, the mentally ill, the mentally retarded, etc.) or to facilitate their special contributions to the community (geniuses, the creative, etc.). Individual psychology also can be used to discover those personalities particularly suited to roles of special usefulness to the group, for example, diplomats, policemen, military generals, preschool teachers, etc. Obviously, the extent of such service will depend on the nature of the group at the time in terms of values and ethical views of the appropriate use of human science. Any efforts to change the personalities of deviant individuals would not be part of human science but an application of it, requiring extensive training in it, supplemented by specialized training in treatment practices. Such efforts are not part of human science because they go beyond the descriptive and explanatory functions of science to implement ideological decisions. Issues of the ideological nature of human science itself are addressed in an upcoming section.

Biological Method

Biological science also plays primarily a problem-solving role. It attempts to help those individuals who are not functioning, temporarily or chronically, within the normal range in the society and for whom there is reason to believe that external environmental influences (psychological treatment) will not suffice. This population includes those with hereditary differences, illnesses, and injuries. However, in order to be able to understand how these individuals differ in their functioning from those within the normative range, it will be necessary for biologists to understand normative functioning. This is not the same thing as understanding how the human body functions, although it includes the latter at a very general level of conceptualization. It differs because the functioning of all individuals in any society or stratum constitutes a particular variant of the potential for functioning of the human organism. Biologically, people are not functioning either healthily or unhealthily or normally or abnormally. They are functioning according to a pattern determined by the interaction of a number of influences with a history over their course of development since conception.

The normative range of functioning of members of a society is determined by such factors as diet, inherent potentials for particular variants in specific organ systems, such as those traditionally recognized in the field of allergies and psychosomatic illnesses; aspects of the environment, such as the quality of air and water; climate; and the types of stresses generated in their rounds of life, including the ways in which they attempt to manage stress. All of these variables must be considered from the standpoint of the developmental history of the individual.[6] Among the members of any group there will be a normative range of functioning based on a pattern of shared values of these variables. Those who are temporarily functioning outside this range are doing so because some condition or set of conditions *in interaction with their particular variant of normative functioning* has occurred. The same condition or set of conditions interacting with another variant may not result in functioning outside the normative range or may result in a different form of abnormative functioning. Biologists, therefore, must become familiar with the properties of the normative range and its major variants if they are to help the individual restore normative functioning. No attempt will be made here to suggest biological method for this beyond noting that it requires assessment of samples of normatively functioning members of the society using the longitudinal method.

The problem-solving efforts of biologists must be considered in the larger collective psychological and sociological contexts of their impact on the life of the group. There is much precedent for this, such as in the long-standing issues of eugenics, sterilization, and, more recently, genetic engineering. However, they have not occurred within the context of a relativistic human science with explicit theories to develop the sociological and collective psychological understanding of the society, and the employment of those theories, that permit a systemic understanding of short- and long-range consequences.[7]

HUMAN SCIENCE IN SOCIETY

Relativistic human science will play a radically different role in society than has realist social science. Its focus is on constructing understanding of, first, its own society and then others, sociologically and psychologically. The rationale of this goal is that no meaningful solutions to social problems and no meaningful guidance to public policy can occur without it. One must understand what one is dealing with before attempting to alter it. Societies are systems in the sense that altering some aspect of them inevitably ramifies through the other aspects.

It follows that human science is fundamental and essential to the functioning of its society. Its function is value-neutral in the sense that its goal is to understand as fully as possible and in that the application of this understanding is not one of its functions. One source of limits of the possibility of such understanding is the clarity, consistency, and comprehensiveness of the theories formulated in each of the three sciences. This source of limits can be minimized by an intense collaborative effort of as many scholars of human behavior as can be recruited. It must and can be a programmatic effort. The range of human phenomena that must ultimately be understood is given in the subject matter of current human biology and all the disciplines of the social sciences and humanities. The various contributions and limitations of extant theories in all disciplines already have received extensive attention. Many problems of value biases, conscious and unconscious, in current social science have been made patent. Most of the significant issues have been developed. What is needed now is a refocusing of effort from realist research to theoretical formulation.

The endeavor can start within every college and university by the development of a program by interested faculty. A division of labor can be introduced in terms of specialization in the three human sciences with important safeguards for interfacing by some overlap from scholars from each of the other two sciences. Regional coordination and interchange of ideas can be channeled through the conventional meetings of scholarly associations with a hierarchy of broader groupings up to the national level. Traditional house organs or new publications can be utilized to disseminate tentative formulations and air key issues which arise. Great effort and constant vigil will be necessary to maintain focus on the overall goal and to minimize factionalism and the intrusions of attitudes in the process. Dedication to the public spirit inherent in the function of human science in society and to the spirit of academic freedom must constantly guide the participants. A keen sense of the subtle influence of carrying on the enterprise in a period of rapid change in our society must prevail. Behind it all will be the realization that the understanding of human phenomena is always and inevitably regulated by implicit worldview unless by explicit theory. There is no neutral ground. The children in our homes and schools will learn *some* way in which to think about and interpret themselves and those around them. Public policy will be based on *some* framework of thought about human affairs. Human problems will be approached on *some* basis. Human scientists should be imbued with the faith that the product of their efforts is by far the most useful to their society.

Formulation of theories cannot be understood as an exercise in metaanalysis. The guidelines to the scope of the task are not set by the empirical research so far published. These must be understood as highly circumscribed and selective forms of observation of human behavior, many in the atypical situation of the experimental laboratory. At best, they can suggest some considerations for subareas of theoretical formulation. The scope of the enterprise is set by an appreciation of the subject matter encompassed by all the disciplines of the social sciences, humanities, and human biology. Within that context, some very general model or models for each science, such as those suggested in Chapters 6–9 for psychology and Chapter 10 for sociology, can be considered as a tentative approach to the organization of the task. The issues of philosophy of science raised by these models need to be clarified and resolved before addressing the subjects of basic terminology and principles of their relationships.

It should not take long, perhaps a year or two, when regular workshops are taking place and arrangements have been made for dissemination of ideas and issues, for the full range of considerations to become evident. As this is occurring, the second phase of the process will be generated. This is the exchange of perspectives among scholars from different disciplines that allows each scholar to appreciate the limits of his thinking established by the specialization that has characterized scholarly work to date. The resulting new general perspective will permit each scholar to consider and to offer his contributions within a shared framework and, at the same time, to appreciate the contributions of those from other disciplines. General dissemination of the results of the programmatic workshops should serve to entice additional participants, particularly as the appreciation grows of the revolutionary impact of the relativistic view of knowledge and science.

Crucial to the development of the new human science and its function in society will be the attitude of the general public to it. At present, it appears that the public view of social science is an unstable mixture of respect for the scientific enterprise based overwhelmingly on the contributions of the natural sciences, readiness to accept the authority of expertise, a profound hope for help, a puzzled but tolerant doubt about the contributions thus far, and a largely unconscious resistance from the still powerful residues of the individualistic worldview. Human scientists cannot expect to capitalize for very long on this still generally positive attitude. The absence of consensus, the divisiveness and schisms across and within the disciplines of social science, accompanied by increasing public familiarity with what they have to offer via courses in secondary schools and the contents of bookstore shelves, augurs poorly for the immediate future. However, public awareness of the commitment and potential functions of the new human science can turn this process around. The establishment of the new human science will provide the foundation for an authority approaching that of the natural sciences. No longer will the public be treated to the contradictory testimony of various social science experts before congressional committees, the courts, and the mass media. No longer will they be dependent on untrained or semitrained journalists and television commentators for interpretations of the behavior of their fellow citizens and citizens of other countries. No longer will they find their search for help in the vague and faddish "how to" literature or the impenetrable and unintegrated jargon of professional publications.

The new human science is imbued with the value to be able to serve its society and, within its relativistic limits, all humankind. This is not a value that in any way encroaches on the proper exercise of its endeavors. It is the same value for intellectual integrity which has existed in the individualistic natural and social science search for knowledge per se. The gravest issues of the effects of values on human science arise, not from within it, but from its relationship to the larger society.

Formal knowledge, at least in large modern societies, is always a social construction. However, the manner in which it is constructed and the consequences for the society certainly can vary markedly. The social and natural sciences in the United States and Europe emerged hand in hand with the capitalistic way of life. Thus, they were essentially competitive in nature. Careers have rested on publication, and there has been a status hierarchy of institutions of higher learning. A great deal of the social constructionism of these sciences is due to this competition. The new human science can only be part of a different social system, one based on centralization and collectivism. Much of the work of gathering observations can be decentralized, but the programmatic character of human science will require centralization in the construction of interpretation of them which will constitute substantive sociological and collective psychological knowledge. Social constructivism is most likely to occur at this stage of the process. Interpreting the full range of observations, even with an agreed upon theory for each science, will be very complex. The adequacy of sociological and collective psychological theory will determine the limits of alternative interpretations. However, even with highly developed theories, influences from both within and without the institutions of human science will play roles in determining the dominance of one form of understanding to be treated as official and to be disseminated throughout public education. Commitment on the part of human scientists to public service and to the highest degree of professionalism will be required to preserve the maximal degree of integrity of the enterprise.

VALUES AND HUMAN SCIENCE

It follows from the discussion earlier on methodology of the three sciences that its usefulness depends fundamentally on public support and participation. For sociological science to provide a comprehensive understanding of its own society, the public must be willing to provide the information required and to support government policies designed to prevent subversion of the process by those who regard it either as interfering with, or to be used for, their personal interests. There is much evidence that Americans, once convinced that certain information to be provided by citizens is in the public interest, will support legislation necessary to obtain it, as, for example, that required by the Bureau of the Census and the Internal Revenue Service. There also is ample evidence that Americans are very concerned about preventing the abuse of such information and of the power to obtain it.

Human scientists, then, must work toward two primary goals. The first is the establishment of very high standards of professional ethics. There already is much machinery in place for this, but it must be upgraded and be far more vigilant, public-spirited, and cognizant of the potentials for abuse inherent in the new methodology. The second is a program of public education to inform citizens of its commitment to public service through the most complete and useful understanding of our way of life. The public must regard the human scientist as a kind of public servant who makes reliable knowledge available to all. The aspiration is to the authority and respect currently enjoyed by natural scientists. However, the task of achieving it is far more difficult and fraught with danger. It is more difficult because it deals with information about people, not nonhuman objects and processes. It is relatively unthreatening for the individual to admit that he knows little about the natural world and to think that, if the natural sciences can provide the knowledge that leads to its mastery, it is all to the good. He is keenly aware, and growing more so, that the power of such knowledge might be used in ways of which he would not approve. But how this might be done is not nearly so immediate and clear to him as knowledge about himself and his fellows. Most of such thinking occurs in the individualistic form today and can be expected to change markedly over the ensuing generations. But it must be understood and dealt with now in the establishment of human science.

Gaining the authority and respect now accorded natural scientists is fraught with danger because science is an institution or set of institutions within a system of institutions in which values are an integral and inescapable part. The aspiration of human science to provide comprehensive knowledge of this total system inevitably encounters the attitudes, not only of selected persons and groups who regard such knowledge as not in their own interests or to be co-opted by them, but of the human scientist himself as a citizen with other interests besides those involved in his professional identity. As long as realist science prevails, with its fragmented, selective, and very limited forms of knowledge, the social scientist engaged primarily in pursuing career ambitions has little fear that this knowledge can be used against his interests. However, once the kind of knowledge sought by the new human science is developed, it will be obvious to all that it will be used to make the most important and far-reaching decisions affecting all members of the society.[8] This gives human scientists the gravest responsibilities.

They must make clear to the public that any interference with the application of their methodologies seriously distorts, to the public detriment, the knowledge they produce. They must be prepared to oppose with the utmost dedication any such interference. Their ethics must countenance legislation designed to discourage abuses of the power invested in them in order to ensure the trust of the public. Beyond this, they must anticipate and be prepared to deal with the forms of interference presented by individuals or groups who do not wish to cooperate or who would attempt to conceal or distort the information necessary. There should be no underestimation of the magnitude of this problem. Incorporating information about deviant individuals may well be the least of it. Far more important will be the efforts of those who wish to co-opt human science for their goals and who have great influence in the form of political clout and mass media persuasion of the public. This is the central problem of value-neutrality in human science with which the Marxists and scholars of the sociology of knowledge have long been concerned.

To deal with this problem, the institutions of higher education must become the impregnable bastions of human science. In many ways they have long served to preserve the integrity of knowledge. However, particularly in recent decades via the influence of government and business research funds combined with the process of rapid change in society, many weaknesses have developed. It will be necessary for these institutions to become deeply involved in the passage of legislation necessary for the integrity of human science. They can draw parallels to the contributions of the natural sciences. They can draw on the capital already accumulated to strengthen the view that knowledge is a tool and that the solutions to human problems can be no better than the tools used to arrive at them. They can appeal to the American ideal that power should reside in the citizenry and be used democratically with traditional safeguards for those with minority views. Perhaps especially significant will be the argument that the understanding of other societies in the world today will be seriously flawed if human scientists are prevented from developing the complete understanding of our society necessary to discern how we influence and are influenced by them.

CONCLUSION

The choice is clear. Scholarly understanding of human behavior can continue on its present paths without either self-understanding or clear direction, or it can reexamine itself, resolve explicitly the profound issues generated by the breakdown of the individualistic worldview and mode of thought, and redefine its relationship to the larger society. Fundamental to this reappraisal must be the recognition of the relativism of knowledge and of science. Only with this recognition can the current fragmented drift in direction, with consequences beyond hope of anticipation, be halted and replaced by a new human science explicitly directed by theories of sociology, psychology, and biology and designed to serve society by provision of the best possible understanding of its own and other peoples in the present rather than in some indefinite and inevitably illusory future.

The recognition of the relativism of knowledge and science carries with it another, even more fundamental, understanding. It is that human science must function under the guidance of a system of values that can transcend its limitations. Relativism of knowledge entails that the understanding of other societies is a function of their similarity to our own. The less similar, the less valid, in unknown ways, is our knowledge of them. Yet, if human science plays its proper role, public policy will be based on this knowledge. Therefore, appreciation must grow for the potentials for future relationships in this increasingly interdependent world to be complicated and to increase stresses, with the most profound dangers for humankind. The only way in which these dangers can be minimized is through the regulation of public policy by values that make paramount the importance and dignity of all human beings and all ways of group life. Only then can the misunderstandings of relative knowledge be open to an increasingly better understanding generated by continued interaction in the fundamental process of historical dialogue among equally human ways of life. Only if we understand our integral relationship to the history and nature of this ecological system we call planet Earth, and therefore of our kinship in sharing it with all other groups, can we ensure the future of humankind, minimize the inhumanity of humans to other humans, and pass on to our children and all future generations the promise of the full realization of their human potentials.

Notes

Chapter 1. REVOLUTION IN SOCIAL SCIENCE

1. Criticisms come from too many sources to cite, including practitioners in each discipline, those in closely related disciplines, philosophers of science, farewell speeches of outgoing presidents of disciplinary associations, those attempting to use the products of social science in applied fields, and graduate students. For a brief perspective on the range of criticisms, see the initial chapters of Fiske and Shweder (1986) and Secord (1982).

2. This line has roots in the long-standing controversy over whether or not language structures thought. See Crick (1976).

3. A major development arising from Kuhn's impetus is the social constructivist movement in the sociology of knowledge combining the relativist view of knowledge with the role of values and ideology in science (Bloor 1976; Knorr-Cetina 1981; Latour and Woolgar 1979).

4. For these developments in linguistics, see Greenberg (1977, 8–9). A study of historians (Landes and Tilly 1971) revealed that about 50 percent of them held the identity of social scientist. See also Kauffman (1977).

5. See, for example, Inkeles (1963).

6. The idea that worldviews exist and then break down and are eventually replaced by a new worldview constitutes a psychological account of periodicity in history. See Homans (1979, 386–87).

7. A general statement of it can be found in Wayland (1842). Wayland has been identified as the key figure in this school of thought, and his book has been the most popular college text in the United States for most of the nineteenth century (Meyer 1972). It is important to distinguish between the highly reflective expositions of theologians and the widely shared worldviews of typical members of a society which tend to be more simple and implicit. Hereinafter, all references to individualism, the individualist, and individualistic worldview refer to this formulation or to those holding it.

8. Here "mind" is synonymous with "soul." In the individualistic worldview

the mind/soul outlives the physical body and goes before God for a final judgment based on the morality or immorality of the free choices made during mortal life.

9. Note that the only accepted criterion of progress in social science in the quote given earlier is "doing even better what he or she is now doing."

10. Lipset asserts, "the sociologist has to treat politics as an independent variable precisely because of the separation among society, economy, and polity" (1969, xx). See also Smelser (1967). Both Lipset and Smelser give a more modern account of the disciplines of the social sciences but reveal the continuing force of the original division. Debates over the application of Kuhn's views to sociology appear to fail to identify the normal paradigm of social science in which this conceptualization of disciplines and the use of the scientific method are the central elements. Consequently, the existence of many alternative paradigms is mistaken for the absence of a normal paradigm (Gutting 1980).

11. An example of an anomaly for the individualistic mode of thought can be found in the controversy in physics over the nature of subatomic particles. See Capra (1988, 80–85).

12. The implicit assumption of free will may help to explain the development of the ideas of economies and polities. They are a sort of emergent phenomena from the myriad interactions of free wills. Thus, perhaps, the distinction between macro- and microeconomics. This may also explain why so much of economic theory is based on trends and rates rather than on causal explanations.

13. See also Ember (1973, 700).

Chapter 2. WORLDVIEW AND MODE OF THOUGHT

1. Kearney's (1984) comprehensive effort with respect to worldview is an impressive exception. Unfortunately, I did not discover it until my conceptualization was completed, although I had read two of his earlier works (Kearney 1975, 1972). There are areas of considerable overlap between his and my views. However, there are also important differences. In general, Kearney takes the approach of a historical materialist which leads him to (a) reject relativism of knowledge in favor of the progressiveness of human consciousness, (b) confound ideology and worldview, and (c) reject most of the developmental approach to worldview in favor of a class-based etiology. Important aspects of the differences between Kearney's and my views will become apparent in Chapters 6, 7, 8, and 9. In this chapter I will address others as they arise.

2. See also Erikson (1968) on ideology.

3. Here the concept of belief is different from that of Kearney (1984) and Needham (1972). I see no reason to restrict the term "beliefs" to aspects of learning that the individual can articulate. They may be conscious or unconscious in their influence on behavior.

4. Erikson's (1963) view that major developments in the earliest psychosocial crises produce basic orientations to the key dimensions of life, such as the religious and the political, attributes a similar importance to very early experience.

5. This approach to initial classifications differs from Kearney's (1984, 68) basic distinction between self and other where "other" initially appears to include everything but self. Here the figures are the significant others in the child's life, and he is learning his relationships to them simultaneously as he learns about self.

6. This view of self also differs from Kearney's (1984, 42) in not postulating self or any other category in the classification system of a worldview as a category "universal within the species" or as "fundamental categories of human thought." The fundamental capacities of humans are discussed in Chapter 6.

7. In a number of sections I will attempt to illustrate theoretical points with examples from the psychology of recent generations of the American middle class. I refer to those over age sixty living today and several previous generations. The illustrations are from conclusions I have drawn from my own observations and from various historical sources (which do not lend themselves to citation) as I have attempted to understand this society and the experiences of younger generations.

8. This view of the etiology of religious beliefs does reflect projective and reifying processes as Kearney suggests. However, no additional explanatory power emerges from his value judgment that they result from "intellectual immaturity" defined ethnocentrically as the inability to distinguish "what is properly an aspect of the Self from what is external" (Kearney 1984, 88–9, 117–19).

9. Douglas (1973) points out that among the Mbuti pygmies the moods of the deity and the rain forest can be humored by the same means. One wonders how distinct is the forest from the deity.

10. The maleness of the Christian god, for these generations, may be traced to later differentiation of the primary figure in experience in the male-dominated family reinforced by the verbal references to the god in various settings. The quality of the Christian Heaven as a state of undifferentiated blissful love of God accompanied by no striving and no goals suggests the very small child's experience of loving comfort before conditional love was experienced.

11. The question of inconsistencies in worldview is a knotty one. First, it is necessary to distinguish between the beliefs of a worldview and those included in what may be called the institutional freight added to them. The translation of worldview beliefs into formal religion can introduce all manner of complications, often in the attempt to relate the beliefs to the past, as in the resort to the Bible in individualistic Christianity. A contradiction within the Old and New Testaments is not a contradiction in the individualistic worldview (Kearney 1984, 58–59). What has been called "the problem of evil" in Christianity, given a loving and omnipotent God, is also not such an inconsistency. Evil exists in the temptations of the needs and passions of the human body. God created humans with this nature. Another complication arises when questions are asked such as "Why did the god(s) do X?" The Christian answer, and probably that of many other religions, is that it is not given to mortals to understand God. This is not a compromise or a fudge, but easily can be understood in terms of the small child's inability to understand the reasons behind the behaviors of his caretakers. I see no reason to postulate a strain in worldviews or a tendency toward consistency. However, among individualists, a good case can be made for a disposition toward consistency of beliefs based on their self-system, not on their worldview. Such a disposition may not be part of self-systems of other kinds.

12. Worldview is related to logical reasoning in the sense of the syllogism in which conclusions follow from the definitions of terms in the premises. This view corresponds to the "logico" part of Kearney's logico-structural integration of worldview. However, that part of it that he calls "structural" and attributes to psychological, sociological, or biological causes appears to correspond to my con-

cept of "mode of thought," which I exclude from worldview. See his example of hierarchy in the analysis of cultural themes (1984, 62).

13. There may be special problems of constructing the classification systems of groups that use verbifying rather than nominalizing languages.

14. In not postulating causality as a universal component of worldview, I disagree with Kearney (1984, 84–88). Kearney claims that causality is found in the assumptions of all cultures, but it is not clear that it is not imposed in translation. He recognizes that causality has been abandoned by modern physicists but rather cavalierly attributes it to the processes physicists postulate. See my discussion of causality in Chapter 5.

15. See, for example, Sarason (1981, 120).

16. However, worldviews do include the values shared in the human group in the sense that their beliefs are abstracted from the behaviors of members as they pursue their values. For a definition and discussion of values, see Chapter 9. Worldviews can also include prejudices that result from widely shared defenses against widely shared conflicts. For example, the individualistic worldview includes beliefs about racial and female nature that incorporate common scapegoating.

17. It follows from this approach that the Marxist notion of false consciousness is based on a difference between its and the individualistic worldviews. If the blue-collar worker's self-blame for lack of achievement in life and the discriminated against minority member's self-hatred are examples of false consciousness, they are only false if the premises of free will and racial characteristics in the individualistic worldview are false.

18. For an overview of positions and issues on this topic, see Horton and Finnegan (1973).

19. See Chapter 6 for an explanation of this view.

20. Pike (1967) emphasizes the importance of nonlinguistic behavior in the study of speech. His concept of the "behavioreme" may prove useful in the study of modes of thought.

21. A possible example of what happens when the linguistic order does not match well the nonlinguistic order is the situation of women throughout the individualistic period. The language they heard represents very well the order in the male experience but not in the homemaking female. This is why some research revealed that women had a contextual mode of thought, but males an analytic mode. However, the contextual order of female life did not start until after age three. By then they were using the analytic language, which poorly served to express their experience.

22. This is why, with the changing society, there is an increasing recognition that the approach to social problems is always symptom treatment rather than a matter of understanding the complex field of forces underlying them.

23. Linguists have identified at least three major orders and other minor ones in which subject, predicate, and object occur in the linguistic spectrum (Greenberg 1977, 128). An effort to correlate these orders with key aspects of social patterns might prove illuminating.

24. The significance of this for the current issues of the conception of causality is obvious. Among individualists causality has its roots in the child's experience of how to interpret his own and others' behavior, that is, as freely chosen and therefore responsible for the consequences. When applied to the nonhuman realm, this

leads to the assumption that regular conjunctions of events have a cause-effect explanation.

25. The same problem occurs in the sports field. Individualists tend to attribute the outcomes of team sports to individual efforts, such as long runs in football, but this requires ignoring the roles of offensive linemen for whom there are no individual statistics.

26. Although historians have been major contributors to the idea of different modes of thought, the bulk of modern historiography is the explanation of other human groups by use of the individualistic mode. This tends to support the individualistic illusions that human beings think and experience similarly in all times and places and that there is progress in human history.

Chapter 3. RELATIVISM OF KNOWLEDGE

1. For a rare and revealing exception, see Fletcher (1984). However, his analysis appears to fail to recognize that scientists, too, inevitably but implicitly share the fundamental assumptions and way of thinking.

2. There are several important problems recognized by realists in this approach. They include concerns about whether experimentation can verify or only falsify, whether all facts or only most facts need be accounted for, how much testing of theory is sufficient to establish it, and whether ultimate proof and general theory are possible. They have, so far, not led to significant alteration of the approach.

Realists often present their method as hypothetico-deductive in nature. However, only a segment of the research genuinely is. The inconsistency is produced by the use of the term "theory" to refer to anything from a simple hypothesis to the most general theory (Rozeboom 1965).

3. These disproved commonsense ideas usually are beliefs of the individualistic worldview for which experience in our rapidly changing society no longer provides consistent support but which still exist in the individualistic rhetoric, such as racial, sexual, and age characteristics. Thus, the research, at best, reflects changes in behavior, not the truth about human reality.

4. An exception to this disposition is the questioning of causality (Bhaskar 1979; Harre 1975; Harre and Secord 1972).

5. One manifestation of this is the assumption commonly made by realist experimental psychologists that their research is revealing human nature—for example, of perception, memory, emotion, intelligence—when their sampling is overwhelmingly biased toward members of limited segments of their own society. Growing recognition of the importance of cross-cultural research is salutary but highly selective and naive about variables to control to manage cultural differences in subjects' approaches to the testing situation.

6. For the ideas of "rational bridgehead" and "technological mastery," see Hollis (1982). See also Sperber (1982).

7. The definition of rationality has long plagued clinical psychology and psychiatry. The mentally ill are said to distort reality by the use or overuse of defense mechanisms. The problem lies in identifying what constitutes realistic perception.

8. The recent rapid demise of behaviorism, particularly in its radical form, has led to a rebirth of cognitive psychology. Yet the enchantment with computer sim-

ulation of cognition continues the disposition to assume universal reason through the idea of simulating *the* human mind. See Gardner (1985).

9. Some have attempted to use indeterminism in physics to preserve the idea of free will, arguing that events in the brain, as physiological phenomena subject to unpredictable events, are inconsistent with the idea of determinism of behavior. The implication is that the unpredictability reflects the operation of free will.

10. For example, anthropologists have suggested that human groups can be distinguished on the basis of whether they have a guilt- or shame-based form of morality. This can only mean that the emotion of guilt or of shame gets conditioned to *types* of behaviors deemed unacceptable in the group. Another example may be the distinctions among romantic, chivalric, and platonic love.

11. Consider, for example, the recent emergence of process theology within Christian theology (Surin 1989).

12. The behavioristic orientation in psychology parallels that in physics and chemistry. It, too, is interested in control and manipulation rather than in explanation. Its view of habit learning does not explain the behaviors of any actual person. It only claims they are due to the particular history of contingencies of reinforcement. Neither does it explain how or why any such histories occur. This ahistoricity is a legacy of the individualistic view that past behaviors are unimportant compared to how the individual will behave in the future.

13. The terms "appearances" and "actualities" refer generally to phenomenal experiences. They vary, therefore, with the worldview and mode of thought by which experience is processed. For the relativist scientist, however, they refer to observations by human scientists on which there is intersubjective agreement.

14. Some of the more theoretical realists appear to recognize this relationship in terms of theory and its application. However, they do not address the key epistimological issues involved in proposing theories inconsistent with the individualistic worldview and so continue to use the realist paradigm of science. Some forms of this recognition are: philosophy of science of behavior–science of behavior (Skinner 1974); etic analysis–emic analysis (Pike 1967); generic hypotheses–sociological orientations (Merton 1957); conceptual scheme–empirical generalizations (Parsons 1951).

15. This is exactly what occurs today when government officials or businessmen consult social scientists on some matter of their expertise. The officials and businessmen try to assimilate the expert knowledge to their own worldview or substantive knowledge before using it. It is also why Lindblom and Cohen (1979) point out that practitioners in applied fields often are regarded as having more usable knowledge than social scientists. The practitioners do the integrating which social scientists regard as premature.

16. Greenberg claims "there exists a range of everyday situations which can be expressed in all languages of the world" (1977, 126). Whether they are expressed in all languages or whether every language can find a way to express them that appears commensurable is the issue.

Chapter 4. NATURALISM OF SUBJECT MATTER

1. Powell's (1979) discussion of the Russian approach to neuropsychology strongly indicates the operation of a different worldview. Mandler challenges, "If

we are, as we were, afraid to postulate complex mental mechanisms, we will never find the corresponding complex physiological mechanisms" (1969, 14).

2. All standard introductory textbooks in psychology have at least one early chapter on the biological bases of behavior. The reductionism is most clearly illustrated in Krech et al. (1982), in which each part presents first chapters on the psychology of some aspect of human nature and then a chapter on the physiological bases of it.

3. Take, for example, the attempts of neuropsychologists to explain consciousness in terms of "slow-wave micropotentials" (Pribram 1971, 105), "hyperneurons" (John 1976, 43), and "reentrance" (Edelman and Mountcastle 1978).

4. The approach to consciousness via attentional processes has been suggested by a number of neuropsychologists (Pribram 1976, 88; Powell 1979, 80; Gazzaniga and Ledoux 1978, 145–46; Pope and Ringer 1978, 106). Biofeedback has been explained in terms of attention deployment (Lazarus 1977).

5. See Jaynes (1976, 11). However, Jaynes is not making the important distinction here between consciousness per se and self-consciousness. His simile translates readily into the distinction between consciousness and the "constantly observing 'I'," with the flashlight representing the "I."

6. It is possible that classification of basic emotions among human groups will be found to have a similar pattern to that found for colors by Berlin and Kay (1969). See also Osgood, May, and Miron (1975).

7. The likelihood that there are only two levels of reflection in human thought stems from the improbability of a need for understanding beyond that of meaning. In any religious belief system, for example, there is no reason to go beyond the existence and attributes of the gods. In transitional periods, questions about the existence of gods are reflections at the second level.

8. Raising the question of changing worldview in my course on youth and middle age, I have found that many students now place mind in the body but preserve the idea of a soul as well. They are unable, however, to ascribe any clear properties to soul.

9. Evidence for the breakdown of the rigid individualistic distinction between humans and other species today is the great interest in the linguistic and intellectual capacities of chimpanzees and dolphins, the tendency to attribute complex feeling states to other species, even plants, and the possible existence of superior alien beings.

10. For another approach to a deterministic explanation of the belief in free will, see Mandler and Kessen (1974).

11. Given the relativism of knowledge, the objective environmental situation cannot be known even though it is assumed to exist.

12. This view appears similar to the idea of the human being as a generative mechanism as advanced by both Bhaskar (1979) and Harre (1975). However, it emphasizes that the person is always behaving, not fluctuating between behavior and generation of behavior.

Chapter 5. SUMMARY OF THE PHILOSOPHICAL ASSUMPTIONS OF RELATIVISTIC NATURALISM

1. This approach appears to correspond to what Shweder and Bourne (1984, 173) call "the sociocentric/organic frame." It also is the approach to reality of quantum theory in physics (Capra 1988, 80–86).

Chapter 6. HUMAN NATURE

1. It has been suggested that it is meaningful to formulate a psychology limited to one society or human group. This is valid only in the sense that the general conceptual model for all groups is applied to one group by using the systematic order of environmental influences observed for that group. It is not meaningful in the sense that there are different conceptual models for each group.

2. The recognition of rigidity in the assumption of behavioral dispositions serving survival or reproduction among some sociobiologists is manifested in their introduction of the idea of something like switching points during development. For example, particular conditions may serve to switch development into the homosexual or heterosexual course. The switches are genetically determined. The problem with this approach is that the more forms of sexual practices one observes, the more switches one needs. The more switches postulated, the closer does the model approach that of flexible capacities shaped by environmental influences. See, for example, Laughlin and D'Aquili (1974).

3. See, for example, Gardner (1985, 6) and Krech et al. (1982, 452).

4. Generalization and discrimination work together to account for the idea of a capacity for abstraction.

5. The capacity for anticipation includes most of what is intended by the term vicarious learning. The child can learn what follows what by observing the sequences in the experiences of others. The capacity for imitation includes another aspect of vicarious learning.

6. Postication most obviously entails a process or processes usually included in the notion of memory. However, the distinction between learning and memory has long been unclear. A capacity for memory or several types of memory has not been included because it is not clear that it is not encompassed by one or more of the capacities listed.

7. It is difficult not to be impressed by the richness of probability terms in the English language, for example, seldom, occasionally, never, rarely, often, usually, always, possibly, probably, maybe, etc.

8. Sexual experience has both peripheral and central forms of significance, of which only the central is conditionable; yet it is not generated from learning, and so must be included in the survival type.

9. This account of emotions has many similarities to that of Sylvan Tomkins (1962) but also significant differences.

10. The Schachter and Singer (1962) theory of emotion suffers seriously from the confusion of the biological and psychological levels of conceptualization and from neglect of the possibility that situational conditions have complex emotional conditioning.

11. What is attended to and what is recognized must be understood in terms of

the apperceptive effects of the total organization of the person at the time his attention is captured by the occurrence of the emotion. This helps to explain the difficulty in understanding what becomes conditioned to the emotion.

12. Complex emotions are combinations of the primaries in either their innate or conditioned forms or both. Although the possible combinations are legion, the pattern of group life inevitably will select a limited number.

13. This was one reason cited by Sigmund Freud for his postulation of the sexual and aggressive instincts. The hedonic theory of motivation based on the emotions, which is presented later in the chapter, provides an avenue for the incorporation into the model of a great deal of Freud's and his followers' contributions to psychology.

14. This position rejects the view that those who speak fluently more than one language employ more than one mode of thought. It is a matter of the commensurability of environmental matrices. However, it may be possible that very different languages learned simultaneously in childhood via frequent travel may reflect compartmentalized modes of thought.

15. The survival type of significance experience occurs through either exteroception, as with pain, taste, etc., or interoception, as with hunger, thirst, etc. Those based on interoception cannot be conceived as representations of the order in the environment. They are representations of the order in the human body. However, they appear to be alike in involving sensory receptors in the peripheral nervous system and different from the emotions which occur in the central nervous system.

16. Why there are pleasurable tastes and smells is unclear from an evolutionary standpoint. They may be conditioned in infancy on the basis of the sweetness or sourness of maternal milk. It may be that the ratio of natural foods for humans that taste sweet to those that are bitter is very lopsided. There seems little reason to believe that sunsets, flowers, and other "beauties of nature" have either innately or universally hedonic effects. However, some of them may well have a basis in curiosity or in contentment via their symmetry or rhythmicity, which is innately, if very primitively, organizing in the sense that being rocked in a cradle is.

17. The research on pain and pleasure centers in the brain suggests a central source of hedonics (Heath 1972). The survival sources of significance may be tied innately to these. If a central source of hedonics is assumed, how types of disorganization and organization in planning are related to it will have to be worked out.

18. There is good reason to doubt the conditioning of survival forms of significance. While it is clear, for example, that a child will eagerly accept an offered cookie, it seems possible that any hedonic accompaniment of this action is mediated by gestures, facial expressions, or words of the offerer or in the child's own subvocal speech.

19. This principle relates the hedonic theory to the work in learning theory on the relationship of the CR to the UCR, extinction, and schedules of reinforcement and to the psychoanalytic theory of partial gratification and instinctual derivatives.

20. There are very rare and special cases in which the conditions for significance do not produce significance at the time they occur but are delayed. Some elaboration of the relationships between significance and attentional processes is necessary.

21. The hedonic experience which occurs when the goal is attained can be related to positive reinforcement of expectancies. Primary reinforcement would be

hedonic experience from either survival significance or primary emotions. Secondary reinforcement would come from conditioned hedonic experience.

22. Reflective attention on one's thoughts is equally functional because it selects information from the self-system of worldview or ideology to enter into ongoing organization.

23. However, it also can be noted that this work script conflicted with the scripts of the housewife mother in individualistic girls, setting up difficult choices of means of value realization.

24. The basic work on plans and the feedback principle is Miller, Galanter, and Pribram (1960).

25. There also must be room in the psychology of human nature for the inheritance of different overt physical characteristics such as height, weight, physiognomy, handicaps, etc. These, too, interact differentially with various environmental influences to determine personality development.

Chapter 7. ENVIRONMENTAL INFLUENCES THROUGH THE LIFE SPAN

1. The geographical limits of the interactions of members of a group with other groups and with the nonhuman environment define the matrix. Obviously, neighboring groups may have interactions with still other groups, and the nonhuman environment of the group is influenced by nonhuman things and processes beyond those with which the group interacts. They are the bases of overlapping matrices of human groups and reveal that the planet is the ultimate matrix.

2. For an overview of theory of culture, see Shweder and Levine (1984).

3. For example, Geertz (1973, 10), while specifically rejecting the reification of culture, claims, "though ideational, it does not exist in someone's head; though unphysical, it is not an occult entity."

4. The concept of webs of meaning leaves unclear the role of unconscious dynamics. The interpretations individuals in any group give to experience almost always include unconscious meanings. The question arises of whether or not culture as a web of meaning includes these unconscious meanings. On the other hand, the environmental influences on the individual do include those which produce the conflicts and defensive processes which constitute these unconscious meanings.

5. The classic work on age-grading is Eisenstadt (1956). Neugarten et al. (1968) have applied age-grading to adult development in the United States, using the term "age-stage."

6. They are one of Murdock's "universal cultural categories" used in the Human Relations Files at Yale University.

7. Erikson's (1963) psychosocial crises constitute a stage system covering the life span. However, his final three crises, lacking grounding in instinctual development, unlike the first five, are vague, and he is highly selective in his consideration of environmental influences during them.

8. A stereotype of people in an age-grade is related to the social anthropological view of the expectations marking age-grades. However, it differs in being more in the nature of a caricature of the emotion-laden aspects of the age-grade than an expression of group norms.

9. Freud's psychosexual stages correspond very closely to the first five of these

age-grades. Erikson's last three psychosocial crises appear to correspond to the last three age-grades, although there is some doubt about the crisis of generativity versus stagnation.

10. It is hard to jibe, for example, with the evidence that among seventeenth-century noble French families the infant was contracted out to a peasant mother surrogate for the first two years of life. See Hunt (1970).

11. Bronfenbrenner (1979, 11) suggests activities, roles, and relations as the elements of the macrosystem. However, roles would seem to include both activities and relations and belong to sociological conceptualization. He confounds the approach further by defining roles in terms of expectations that are in the person, not the environment.

12. In some preliterate groups, for example, one can invoke the powers of the immanent spirits of deceased persons.

13. This points up one problem of the idea of "developmental tasks" as an approach to stages of development. It is that they have a teleological quality. This reveals that the tasks identified are those normatively accomplished or partially accomplished during the age-grade. However, this approach often confounds the ideal with the normative.

14. This approach essentially agrees with that in socioanthropology called "positionalist." See Bock (1980, 189–90).

15. Abnormative variations often are accounted for by clinical psychologists and psychiatrists in such terms as "too much," "too little," "over," and "under," when they are assessing the experiences to which they attribute mental illness.

16. They are also misleading. One major consequence of the reifications of the social sciences has been the generation of a host of which came first, the chicken or the egg issues. Among them are whether social systems precede cultures or vice versa; mind or culture; language or culture. Another consequence has been the development of the dialectical view of the conflict between the individual and his society.

17. See also Greer (1969, 55), Bernstein (1978, xxi), and Lipset (1969, xx).

18. The idea that ideas exist independently of people, for example, in books, is also a reification. See Popper (1972). Ideas spoken or printed are sounds or a set of marks on a surface. They are meaningless to anyone who does not speak the language of the person expressing them. See Bloch (1953, 53–54).

19. Research on identical twins, even those raised apart, on which much of the argument for genetic determination of psychological characteristics rests, is flawed by the use of operationally defined, atheoretical, and culturally relative traits and by superficial consideration of the relationship of specific environments to the characteristics studied.

20. Lesbians and homosexuals also have had to play the central role in gaining limited recognition that their sexual behavior is not necessarily genetically determined or conflict-based.

Chapter 8. UNIVERSAL COMPONENTS OF PERSONALITY

1. For a list of forms of belief in immortality, see Lifton (1977).

2. Shweder and Bourne (1984) suggest the possibility of types of worldviews, citing the sociocentric/organic and the egocentric/reductionist. Pepper's (1972) "world

hypotheses" suggest an approach to such a typology. Kluckhohn and Strodtbeck's (1961, 12) value orientation scheme is relevant but seems more appropriate to a typology of groups at the sociological level of conceptualization.

3. The significance of Freud's work on compulsive personality and its relationship to ritualistic behavior seems obvious here. It should be noted that compulsive personality is established in Freud's view in the anal stage, which is placed with the first three years of life.

4. In relativistic naturalism this understanding of appearances is substantive knowledge.

5. As used in political science and sociology, ideology appears to be always of the highly articulated type. See Shils (1968).

6. In many—perhaps all—groups there will be a few designated spokesmen for the normative (conservative) ideology to whom the average member can refer or defer when necessary. Clergy often fulfill this function.

7. The author's individualistic mode of thought creates difficulty in conveying these non-individualistic ideas. Here the word "he" refers, not to the "constantly observing I" or the "mind," but to the total physical organism which is the person.

8. It seems probable that a contextual/situational/concrete view of the individual expressed in terms of role performance rather than characteristics of the person, as appears to be the case in Bali, is one form which compartmentalized identity may take (Shweder and Bourne 1984). The earliest relationships may be prototypes of later role performances.

9. Failure to develop a discrete body image despite the capacity to have the experiences on which it is developed reveals that it is a failure at the reflective level. The child's attention is not systematically drawn to what he has developed in the way of a body image.

10. Identity has a core of attributes based on the worldview beliefs about human nature and the nature of classes of humans (or of members of the group) to which the individual or subgroup belongs.

11. This is not to say that the mode of thought is the only fashion in which experience is processed by the individual. Registration of experience probably always is much more complex than is the mode of thought. However, it is likely that such processes quickly give way to the mode of thought during the waking state. They probably are responsible for much symbolic content and creative ideas, but significant for the organization of behavior mainly when they evoke already established and defended conflicts.

12. Individual variations of human nature in terms of specific physical capacities such as visual and auditory acuity, perfect pitch, pain thresholds, attention span, etc., are capacities important in the development of perceptual-motor skills.

13. These conflicts constitute a reconceptualization of the idea of Oedipal conflict in terms of the development of sexual identity and changing parent-child relationships.

14. This type of conflict is directly related to Freud's concept of anal character. However, there seems no sound reason to attribute it even largely to toilet training, although there is little reason to doubt that toilet training is one area in which caretakers would manifest such rigid expectations.

Chapter 9. DEVELOPMENT OF PERSONALITY THROUGH UNIVERSAL AGE-GRADES

1. Actually, the initial one-word sentence can be understood to include much more, such as "There is a big red ball in the box under the table." The language and activities of the group will determine what elements there are to be ordered.

2. Recent work on the child's learning of concepts suggests the processes of generalization and discriminative elimination rather than of induction (Moskowitz 1978).

3. The first universal age-grade was divided into two age-grades for middle-class individualists. The first age-grade was roughly the first year of life and was commonly called infancy. The second included the next two years and was called the toddler stage.

4. Other children, including siblings, can be understood as variations of the self because the child could only consider them at first in these terms and was prone to think about them in terms of their relationships to parent figures. Primarily, they were thought about in terms of "the good me" and "the bad me" and then differentiated in terms of attributes of the self.

5. The belief that Christ died for the sins of the individual can be understood as a metaphor for the child's sense of the termination of his unacceptable desires as he learns to behave in those ways which ensure parental love. For a poignant example of experience in a child with an atypically harsh parent, see McLoughlin (1975).

6. For a very similar approach to the conceptualization of values, see Rokeach (1973). However, Rokeach defines values in terms of beliefs, not concepts, regards values as universal, varying only in relative strength for different groups, and includes a behavioral component.

7. Motivation usually is conceived in terms of such abstractions as satisfaction, happiness, self-esteem, or self-actualization, which fails to identify what experiences produce such states. Conceived in terms of specific conditions, such as a Cadillac, a mansion, blonde hair, a swimming pool, it becomes unmanageable due to length, individual variation, and frequent changes. Values identify the level of conceptualization that specifies ends, not means, and motivation that is widely shared among members of a society.

8. When I have asked my students, among whom many are middle-aged, to identify the kinds of experiences that are important in life or that can affect them strongly, they have consistently been able to specify no more than four or five. However, when I suggest others, most readily agree.

9. This does not explain, of course, why various human groups have different value systems. The answer to this question must be sought in the ecological niche of each group and in its historical development.

10. This view of values as basic social motivation appears related to Becker's (1976) idea of "universal desires" and to Skinner's (1974) general reinforcers. It owes much to the idea of motives proposed by Henry Murray (1938) and his followers.

11. This is most obvious in the thought of those who attempt to set up utopian societies and countercultures, but these people have abandoned trying to change their group and have attempted to establish a new one.

12. For individualists, the second universal age-grade also was divided into two age-grades. One was from about ages three to six. It often was identified as "pre-schooler." The second began with the markedly new set of conditions that the child faced in school, which became compulsory by law at age six.

13. For examples of research on differences in expressive styles between recent American middle- and working-class children, see Miller and Swanson (1966).

14. For an example of expressive style based on moral values see Levine (1984) on the "serious-comic drama."

15. Normative conflicts, not being experienced as conflicts after early childhood, are never the subject of treatment in the group. Abnormative conflicts, if established during primary personality organization, will be impossible to resolve. Those occurring later will most often be exacerbations of normative conflicts produced by later atypical conditions. Treatment of these will not resolve the basic conflicts but, if successful, produce more effective defenses, that is, socially legitimated forms. Those acute abnormative conflicts produced by temporary atypical conditions and not building on basic conflicts can be resolved by treatment or spontaneously.

16. These continuities in personality apply only during stable periods of the history of a group.

17. Midlife and terminal reorganizations of personality produce personality changes that, in stable periods of a group's history, are generally recognized as wisdom, but in transitional periods as obsolete or as old-fashioned ideas.

18. Parental generations try to instill their values in their children but are thwarted by the lack of support in other experiences of the younger generation. For many of the younger generation in America today, the rhetoric of the older generation predominates, often making the young think they learned the parental values and later freely chose to abandon them. It is more likely that they did not learn the values at all.

Chapter 10. THE SCIENCE OF SOCIOLOGY

1. This science is called sociology rather than anthropology for two reasons. Anthropology is equivalent to the term "human science" and therefore covers all three sciences. In addition, its literal translation as the science of man tends to offend those who wish to overcome sexist language.

2. A good deal of socioanthropological analysis and of the issues in the discipline reflect the hopeless movement back and forth across the sociological and psychological levels of conceptualization. The same behavior is used to derive both sociological and psychological concepts. Then the two are juxtaposed or correlated with implied causality (Kobben 1973, 592; Greenstein 1969, 170–71).

3. It is the case that the more specific the science, the more complete the account of what is observed because abstraction neglects variation around the shared. In this sense only, the reductive sciences complement or add to the knowledge provided by the abstract sciences.

4. Geertz (1973) is representative of the emic view. For the etic view, see Levine (1973). The terms "emic" and "etic" are from Pike (1967).

5. Eventually the most promising approach to knowledge seems most likely to be one that combines in a new and integrated form the earth sciences and human

science to explain ecological systems that can be combined in a hierarchical form into increasingly inclusive ecological systems, culminating in that for the entire planet.

6. The classic and only extensive effort is that of Aberle, Cohen, Davis, Levy, and Sutton (1950). For a more recent but less thorough effort, see Harris (1980).

7. For a similar view, see Homans (1964, 968).

8. There also can be special temporary coercive roles, including those in which a substantial proportion of the community participate, as in stonings, lynchings, etc.

9. Naroll (1973) opts for a definition in terms of "the culture-bearing unit," but this requires a prior psychological analysis.

10. There may be a special problem of defining a society for populations of very loosely knit groups of small numbers living in general proximity to one another.

11. One of the major limitations of psychoanalytic theory is lack of an explicit theory of learning that could be used to specify prerequisites. Maslow's (1970) hierarchy of deficiency and growth needs or motives has much similarity to the present view but suffers from problems of assuming hierarchy and of vagueness of formulation.

12. In societies in which identity is highly compartmentalized according to roles performed, it may well be the case that the sociological level is prior. However, sociological units might then be psychologized.

13. This view of functions of a society sharply distinguishes it from structural-functionalist theory, which is based on the reification of society.

14. The demographic characteristics of the group constitute another important source of limits.

15. Like many with Marxist orientations, Bernstein (1978, 106) objects to the study of behaviors rather than meanings on the grounds that behavior does not distinguish between acceptance of norms and alienated conformity to norms. This distinction is proper to psychological analysis only. In sociological analysis, alienated conformity would appear in repetitive behaviors that express it, such as drug use, political actions, deviancy, psychopathology, etc.

16. To say that there is order in human affairs and that the human scientist can construct this order does not reify it. It has no existence beyond the behaviors and processes of humans and things. The order changes when these change.

17. For the recognition of this, see Whiting and Whiting (1973).

18. Specifying the number of members of a group performing in particular roles and the number of performances of roles in given periods of time incorporates into sociology much of the research on rates of events in various disciplines of the social sciences.

Chapter 11. HUMAN SCIENCE AND SOCIETY

1. Parsons's (1977, 106) addition of a biological system to the personality, culture, and social systems he and Shils (1961) proposed made his a four-science theory. His cultural system was difficult to integrate and had to be posited as on a different plane. It corresponds fairly well to the idea of collective psychology explained in this chapter. However, Parsons regards his systems as interacting envi-

ronments for one another in a horizontal, rather than hierarchic, structure. See also Gardner (1985, 79).

2. The individualistic approach to group and historical life in terms of the "great man theory" will be replaced by the view that the great bulk of behavior of any person reflects what he shares with others of his stratum and that much of what his uniqueness would generate is closely monitored by others.

3. This is not to imply that the accumulated work of scholars in the social sciences and humanities is not of great use in human science. The great bulk of it can be useful in developing substantive knowledge of particular groups. However, it will have to be translated into forms that are meaningful in terms of the theories of the three sciences.

4. However, the fundamental nature of any society as an integrated system entails that there must be centralization of decision making with respect to policies and programs if there is to be predictability. It already is obvious that the primary trend in this society is toward centralization of this sort. What remains to be determined is the nature of the centralization.

5. The idea here of "data collection" by such methods in no way implies a positivistic approach to knowledge in the conventional sense. Methodology at every step is dictated by theory and mode of thought.

6. The key idea here is that there is developmental conditioning of all organ systems. The current interest in reconditioning via biofeedback is one form of recognition of it.

7. Historical work in all three sciences has special problems concerning the reconstruction of the patterns of behavior of group life. There is a great deal to be drawn on in solving these problems in the methodologies historians have developed. It will have to be reworked using the theories of the new human sciences. For a useful suggestion with respect to historical psychological methodology, see Demos (1976).

8. Rapid change in our society has tended to focus most concern about values in social science on particular beliefs of the individualistic worldview such as those about the nature of women, minority groups, the aged, the insane, homosexuals, and children rather than on the larger issue of interference with or corruption of research by powerful interest groups.

References

Aberle, D. F.; Cohen, A. K.; Davis, A. K.; Levy, M. J., Jr.; and Sutton, F. X. 1950. The functional prerequisites of a society. *Ethics* 60:100–111.

Ackerman, J. S. 1969. The future of the humanities. *Daedalus* (Summer): 605–14.

Allport, G. W. 1961. *Pattern and growth in personality.* New York: Holt, Rinehart and Winston.

Bandura, A. 1989. Human agency in social cognitive theory. *American Psychologist* 44:1175–84.

———. 1991. Human agency: the rhetoric and the reality. *American Psychologist* 46:157–62.

Becker, G. S. 1976. *The economic approach to human behavior.* Chicago: University of Chicago Press.

Benedict, R. 1934. *Patterns of culture.* New York: Houghton Mifflin.

———. 1938. Continuities and discontinuities in cultural conditioning. *Psychiatry* 1:161–67.

Berlin, B.; and Kay, P. 1969. *Basic color terms.* Berkeley: University of California Press.

Bernstein, R. J. 1978. *The restructuring of social and political theory.* Philadelphia: University of Pennsylvania Press.

Bhaskar, R. 1979. *The possibility of naturalism.* Brighton, Great Britain: Harvester Press.

Bloch, M. 1953. *The historian's craft.* New York: Knopf.

Bloor, D. 1976. *Knowledge and social imagery.* London: Routledge and Kegan Paul.

Bock, P. K. 1980. *Continuities in psychological anthropology.* San Francisco: Freeman.

Brewer, C. L. 1981. The future of undergraduate psychology. *APA Monitor* 12 (September): S5.

Bronfenbrenner, U. 1979. *The ecology of human development.* Cambridge, Mass.: Harvard University Press.

Capra, F. 1988. *The turning point.* New York: Bantam Books.

Chomsky, N. 1972. *Language and mind.* New York: Harcourt, Brace and Jovanovich.

Cohen, P. S. 1968. *Modern social theories.* London: Heineman Educational.

Cohen, R. 1973. The political system. In *A handbook of method in cultural anthropology,* eds. R. Naroll and R. Cohen, pp. 484–99. New York: Columbia University Press.

Crick, M. 1976. *Explorations in language and meaning.* New York: Wiley.

Dalton, G. 1973. The economic system. In *A handbook of method in cultural anthropology,* eds. R. Naroll and R. Cohen, pp. 454–83. New York: Columbia University Press.

Demos, J. P. 1976. Perspectives on the history of childhood. In *Varieties of psychohistory,* eds. G. M. Kren and L. H. Rappoport, pp. 180–92. New York: Springer.

Douglas, M. T. 1973. *Natural symbols.* 2d ed. London: Penguin.

Easton, D. 1965. *A framework for political analysis.* Englewood Cliffs, N.J.: Prentice Hall.

Edelman, G. M.; and Mountcastle, V. B. 1978. *The mindful brain.* Cambridge, Mass.: MIT Press.

Eisenstadt, S. N. 1956. *From generation to generation.* Glencoe, Ill.: Free Press.

Ember, M. 1973. Taxonomy in comparative studies. In *A handbook of method in cultural anthropology,* eds. R. Naroll and R. Cohen, pp. 697–706. New York: Columbia University Press.

Erikson, E. H. 1959. The problem of ego identity. In *Psychological issues,* ed. G. S. Klein, pp. 101–64. New York: International Universities Press.

———. 1963. *Childhood and society.* 2d ed. New York: Norton.

———. 1968. Identity, psycho-social. In *International encyclopedia of the social sciences.* Vol. 7, ed. D. L. Sills, pp. 61–65. New York: Macmillan.

———. 1975. *Life history and the historical moment.* New York: Norton.

Fiske, E. W., and Shweder, R. S. 1986. *Metatheory in social science.* Chicago: University of Chicago Press.

Fletcher, G. J. O. 1984. Psychology and common sense. *American Psychologist* 39:203–13.

Frank, L. K. 1970. Organized complexities. In *Toward unification in psychology,* ed. J. R. Royce, pp. 227–33. Toronto: University of Toronto Press.

Freud, S. [1927] 1961. *The future of an illusion,* trans. and ed. J. Strachey. New York: Norton.

Gardner, H. 1985. *The mind's new science.* New York: Basic Books.

Gazzaniga, M. S., and Ledoux, J. E. 1978. *The integrated mind.* New York: Plenum.

Geertz, C. 1973. *The interpretation of cultures.* New York: Basic Books.

Globus, G. G.; Maxwell, G.; Savodnik, I. 1976. *Consciousness and the brain.* New York: Plenum.

Graham, S. 1990. We must deal with the problem of the seriously mentally ill. *APA Monitor* 21 (11): 2.

Greenberg, J. H. 1977. *A new invitation to linguistics.* Garden City, N.Y.: Anchor Press/Doubleday.

Greenstein, F. I. 1969. Personality and politics: problems of evidence, inference, and conceptualization. In *Politics and the social sciences,* ed. S. M. Lipset, pp. 163–208. New York: Oxford.

Greer, S. 1969. Sociology and political science. In *Politics and the social sciences,* ed. S. M. Lipset, pp. 53–65. New York: Oxford.

Gutting, G., ed. 1980. *Paradigms and revolutions.* Notre Dame, Ill.: University of Notre Dame Press.

Harré, R. 1975. *Causal Powers.* Totowa, N.J.: Rowman and Littlefield.

Harré, R.; and Secord, P. F. 1972. *The explanation of social behavior.* Oxford, England: Blackwell.

Harris, M. 1980. *Cultural materialism.* New York: Vintage.

Heath, R. G. 1972. Pleasure and brain activity in man. *Journal of Nervous and Mental Disease* 154:3–18.

Hollis, M. 1982. The social destruction of reality. In *Rationality and relativism,* eds. M. Hollis and S. Lukes, pp. 67–86. Cambridge, Mass.: MIT Press.

Homans, G. C. 1964. Contemporary theory in sociology. In *Handbook of modern sociology,* ed. R. E. L. Faris, pp. 951–77. Chicago: Rand McNally.

Homans, P. 1979. The case of Freud and Carl Rogers. In *Psychology in social context,* ed. A. R. Buss, pp. 367–93. New York: Irvington.

Horton, R.; and Finnegan, R., eds. 1973. *Modes of thought.* London: Faber.

Hunt, D. 1970. *Parents and children in history.* New York: Basic Books.

Hymes, D. 1979. *Foundations in sociolinguistics.* Philadelphia: University of Pennsylvania Press.

Inkeles, A. 1963. Sociology and psychology. In *Psychology the study of a science,* Vol. 6, ed. S. Koch, pp. 317–87. New York: McGraw-Hill.

Jaynes, J. 1976. *The origin of consciousness in the breakdown of the bicameral mind.* Boston: Houghton Mifflin.

John, E. R. 1976. A model of consciousness. In *Consciousness and self-regulation,* Vol. 1, eds. G. E. Schwartz and D. Shapiro, pp. 1–50. New York: Plenum.

Kauffman, W. A. 1977. *The future of the humanities.* New York: Reader's Digest Press.

Kearney, M. 1972. *The Winds of Ixtepeji.* New York: Holt, Rinehart and Winston.

———. 1975. World view: theory and study. In *Annual Review of Anthropology,* Vol. 4, eds. A. R. Beals and S. A. Taylor, pp. 247–70. Palo Alto, Calif.: Annual Reviews.

———. 1984. *Worldview.* Novalo, Calif.: Chandler and Sharp.

Kluckhohn, F., and Strodtbeck, F. L. 1961. *Variations in value orientations.* Evanston, Ill.: Row, Peterson.

Knorr-Cetina, K. D. 1981. *The manufacture of knowledge.* Oxford: Pergamon.

Kobben, A. J. F. 1973. Comparativists and non-comparativists in anthropology. In *A handbook of method in cultural anthropology,* eds. R. Naroll and R. Cohen, pp. 581–96. New York: Columbia University Press.

Koch, S. 1974. Psychology as science. In *Philosophy of psychology,* ed. S. C. Brown, pp. 30–49. New York: Barnes and Noble.

Krech, D.; Crutchfield, R. S.; Livson, N.; Wilson, W. A., Jr.; and Parducci, A. 1982. *Elements of psychology.* 4th ed. New York: Knopf.

Kuhn, T. S. 1962. *The structure of scientific revolutions* (2d ed. 1970). Chicago: University of Chicago Press.

Landes, D. S.; and Tilly, C., eds. 1971. *History as social science.* Englewood Cliffs, N.J.: Prentice Hall.

Latour, B.; and Woolgar, S. 1979. *Laboratory Life.* Beverly Hills, Calif.: Sage.

Laughlin, C. D.; and D'Aquili, E. G. 1974. *Biogenetic structuration.* New York: Columbia University Press.

Lazarus, R. S. 1977. A cognitive analysis of biofeedback control. In *Biofeedback,* eds. G. E. Schwartz and J. Beatty, pp. 67–87. New York: Academic Press.

Lefcourt, M. N. 1982. *Locus of control.* New York: Erlbaum.

Levine, R. A. 1973. Research design in anthropological fieldwork. In *A handbook of method in cultural anthropology,* eds. R. Naroll and R. Cohen, pp. 183–95. New York: Columbia University Press.

———. 1984. Properties of culture: an ethnographic view. In *Culture theory,* eds. R. A. Shweder and R. A. Levine, pp. 67–87. Cambridge: Cambridge University Press.

Lifton, R. J. 1971. Protean man. In *Family in transition,* compiled by A. S. Skolnik and J. H. Skolnik, pp. 376–86. New York: Little, Brown.

———. 1977. The sense of immortality: on death and the continuity of life. In *New meanings of death,* ed. H. Feifel, pp. 273–90. New York: McGraw-Hill.

Lindblom, C. E.; and Cohen, D. K. 1979. *Usable knowledge.* New Haven: Yale University Press.

Lipset, S. M. 1969. Politics and the social sciences: introduction. In *Politics and the social sciences,* ed. S. M. Lipset, pp. vii–xxii. New York: Oxford.

McLoughlin, W. G. 1965. Pietism and the American character. *American Quarterly* 17 (Summer): 163–86.

———. 1975. Evangelical childrearing in the age of Jackson: Francis Wayland's views on when and how to subdue the willfulness of children. *Journal of social history* 9 (Fall): 20–43.

Mandler, G. 1969. Acceptance of things past and present: a look at the mind and the brain. In *William James: unfinished business,* ed. R. B. McCleod. Washington, D.C.: American Psychological Association.

Mandler, G.; and Kessen, W. 1974. The appearance of free will. In *Philosophy of psychology,* ed. S. C. Brown pp. 305–24. New York: Barnes and Noble.

Maslow, A. M. 1970. *Motivation and personality.* 2d ed. New York: Harper and Row.

Masterman, M. 1970. The nature of a paradigm. In *Criticism and the growth of knowledge,* eds. I. Lakatos and A. Musgrave, pp. 59–90. Cambridge: Cambridge University Press.

Mendelsohn, E. M. 1968. World view. In *International encyclopedia of the social sciences.* Vol. 16, ed. D. L. Sills, pp. 576–79. New York: Macmillan.

Merton, R. K. 1957. *Social theory and social structure.* Revised. New York: Free Press.

Meyer, D. H. 1972. *The instructed conscience.* Philadelphia: University of Pennsylvania Press.

Miller, D. R.; and Swanson, G. E. 1966. *Inner conflict and defense.* New York: Holt.

Miller, G. A.; Galanter, E.; and Pribram, K. H. 1960. *Plans and the structure of behavior.* New York: Holt.

Moskowitz, B. A. 1978. The acquisition of language. *Scientific American* 239 (5):92–108.

Murray, H. A. 1938. *Explorations in personality.* New York: Oxford University Press.

Musgrave, A. 1971. Kuhn's second thoughts. *British Journal for the Philosophy of Science* 22:287–97.

Naroll, R. 1973. The culture-bearing unit. In *A handbook of method in cultural anthropology,* eds. R. Naroll and R. Cohen, pp. 721–65. New York: Columbia University Press.

Needham, R. 1972. *Belief, language and experience.* Chicago: University of Chicago Press.

Neugarten, B. L.; Moore, J. W.; and Lowe, J. C. 1968. Age norms, age constraints and adult socialization. In *Middle age and aging,* ed. B. L. Neugarten, pp. 5–28. Chicago: University of Chicago Press.

Newcomb, T. M.; Turner, R. H.; and Converse, P. E. 1965. *Social psychology.* New York: Holt, Rinehart and Winston.

Osgood, C. E.; May, W. H.; and Miron, M. S. 1975. *Cross-cultural universals of affective meaning.* Urbana, Ill.: University of Illinois Press.

Parsons, T. 1951. *The social system.* Glencoe, Ill.: Free Press.

———. 1977. *Social systems and the evolution of action theory.* New York: Free Press.

Parsons, T.; and Shils, E. A. 1961. *Toward a general theory of action.* Cambridge, Mass.: Harvard University Press.

Penfield, W. 1975. *The mystery of the mind.* Princeton, N.J.: Princeton University Press.

Pepper, S. C. 1972. *World hypotheses.* Berkeley: University of California Press.

Piaget, J.; and Inhelder, B. 1969. *The psychology of the child,* trans. H. Weaver, New York: Basic Books.

Pike, K. 1967. *Language in relation to a unified theory of the structure of behavior.* Revised. Hawthorne, N.Y.: Mouton.

Piper, W. [1930] 1990. *The little engine that could.* New York: Platte and Munk.

Pope, K. S.; and Ringer, J. L. 1978. Regulation of the stream of consciousness: toward a theory of ongoing thought. In *Consciousness and self-regulation,* Vol. 2, eds. G. E. Schwartz and D. Shapiro, pp. 101–37. New York: Plenum.

Popper, K. R. 1972. *Objective knowledge.* Oxford: Oxford University Press.

Popper, K. R.; and Eccles, J. C. 1978. Natural selection and emergence of mind. *Dialectica* 32:339–55.

Powell, G. 1979. *Brain and personality.* New York: Praeger.

Pribram, K. H. 1971. *Languages of the brain.* Englewood Cliffs, N.J.: Prentice Hall.

———. 1976. Self-consciousness and intentionality. In *Consciousness and self-regulation,* Vol. 1, eds. G. E. Schwartz and D. Shapiro, pp. 51–100. New York: Plenum.

Riesman, D.; Denney, R.; and Glazer, N. 1950. *The lonely crowd.* New Haven, Conn.: Yale University Press.

Rokeach, M. 1973. *The nature of human values.* New York: Free Press.

Rosenthal, R. 1964. Experimental outcome-orientation and the results of the psychological experiment. *Psychological Bulletin* 61:405–12.

Rozeboom, W. W. 1965. The art of metascience or what should a psychological theory be? In *Toward unification in psychology,* ed. J. R. Royce, pp. 64–153. Toronto: University of Toronto Press.

Samuelson, P. A. 1981. *Economics.* 5th ed. New York: McGraw-Hill.

Sarason, S. B. 1981. *Psychology misdirected.* New York: Free Press.

Schachter, W.; and Singer, J. E. 1962. Cognitive, social, and physiological determinants of emotional state. *Psychological Review* 69:379–99.

Secord, P. F., ed. 1982. *Explaining behavior.* Beverly Hills, Calif.: Sage.

Senders, V. L. 1978. Psychology and the future. *American psychologist* 33:642–44.

Shapere, D. 1964. The structure of scientific revolutions. *Philosophical Review* 73:383–94.

Shils, E. A. 1968. Ideology. In *International encyclopedia of the social sciences,* Vol. 7, ed. D. L. Sills, pp. 66–76. New York: Macmillan.

Shweder, R. A. 1986. Divergent realities. In *Metatheory in social science,* ed. E. W. Fiske and R. A. Shweder, pp. 163–96. Chicago: University of Chicago Press.

Shweder, R. A.; and Bourne, E. J. 1984. Does the concept of the person vary cross-culturally? In *Culture theory,* eds. R. A. Shweder and R. A. Levine, pp. 158–99. Cambridge: Cambridge University Press.

Shweder, R. A.; and Levine, R. A. 1984. *Culture theory.* Cambridge: Cambridge University Press.

Skinner, B. F. 1971. *Beyond freedom and dignity.* New York: Knopf.

———. 1974. *About behaviorism.* New York: Knopf.

Smedslund, J. 1980. Analyzing the primary code. In *The Social foundations of language and thought,* ed. D. R. Olson, pp. 47–73. New York: Norton.

Smelser, N. 1967. Sociology and the other social sciences. In *The uses of sociology,* eds. P. F. Lazarsfeld, W. H. Sewell, and H. L. Wilensky, pp. 3–44. New York: Basic Books.

Sperber, D. V. 1982. Apparently irrational beliefs. In *Rationality and relativism,* eds. M. Hollis and S. Lukes, pp. 149–80. Cambridge, Mass.: MIT Press.

Sperry, R. 1985. *Science and moral priority.* New York: Praeger.

Suppes, F., ed. 1977. *The structure of scientific theories.* 2d ed. Urbana, Ill.: University of Illinois Press.

Surin, K. 1989. Process theology. In *The modern theologians,* Vol. 2, ed. D. F. Ford, pp. 103–14. Oxford, England: Blackwell.

Tomkins, S. S. 1962. *Affect, imagery, and consciousness,* Vol. 1. New York: Springer.

Wann, T. W., ed. 1964. *Behaviorism and phenomenology.* Chicago: University of Chicago Press.

Wayland, F. 1842. *The elements of moral science.* Boston: Gould, Kendall, and Lincoln.

Weil, J. L. 1974. *A neurophysiological model of emotional and intentional behavior.* Illustrated by G. DeVry and E. A. Gampp. Springfield, Ill.: Thomas.

Whiting, J.; and Whiting, B. 1973. Methods for observing and recording behavior. In *A handbook of method in cultural anthropology,* eds. R. Naroll and R. Cohen, pp. 282–315. New York: Columbia University Press.

Author Index

Subject Index

abstraction, 23, 24, 25, 96, 234 n.4.
  See also discrimination; generalization
academic freedom, 220
actualities, 56, 57, 232 n.13. *See also*
  appearances
adult development, 182–84
age-grades: activities, 126–27; in anthropology, 122–23, 236 n.8; definition, 123; and deviance, 237 n.15;
  individualistic, 239 n.3, 240 n.12;
  not teleological, 237 n.13; period of
  life span, 129–31; and psychosexual
  stages, 236 n.9; and psychosocial
  crises, 236 nn.7, 9; and role structure, 128; sets of conditions, 124–
  29, 237 n.11; settings, 127–28; and
  social change, 133–34; and social
  stratification, 132–33, 210; and
  stages of development, 123; systems,
  28, 31, 37, 123–25; universal, 156–
  57, 164–66, 173–75, 182–83, 183–
  84
agency, 15. *See also* subjectivity
age-stage, 236 n.5
alienated conformity, 241 n.15
anal character, 238 n.14
anger, 98, 100
anomalies: for individualistic world-

view, 13–14, 233 n.9; in Kuhn's
  theory, 8; for mode of thought, 9,
  228 n.11; in naturalistic relativism,
  59–60; for worldview, 8–9, 10
anticipation, 97, 234 n.5. *See also* expectancy
anxiety, 98, 100
appearances, 56, 60, 232 n.13, 238
  n.4. *See also* actualities
area sampling, 216
attention, 96. *See also* attentional processes
attentional processes, 67–69, 233 n.4,
  236 n.22
attitudes, 99, 185; definition, 101; and
  values, 111, 168

behavioral interview, 215
behavioreme, 230 n.20
behaviorism, 13, 51–52, 232 n.12
beliefs, 23, 26–27, 228 n.3. *See also*
  anticipation
Beyond Freedom and Dignity (Skinner),
  16–18
biofeedback, 233 n.4, 242 n.6
biological science, 64–67, 210–12;
  conditioning of organ systems, 218,
  242 n.6; definition, 65, 212; meth-

ABOUT THE AUTHOR

QUIN McLOUGHLIN is Professor Emeritus of Psychology at Roosevelt University in Chicago. He is co-author (with P. E. Mott, F. C. Mann, and D. P. Warwick) of *Shift Work: The Social, Psychological, and Physical Consequences* (1965).